THE LESSONS OF MODERNISM

THE LESSONS OF MODERNISM

AND OTHER ESSAYS

Gabriel Josipovici

ROWMAN AND LITTLEFIELD
TOTOWA, NEW JERSEY

√© Gabriel Josipovici 1977

First published in the United States 1977
by Rowman and Littlefield, Totowa, N.J.

Library of Congress Cataloging in Publication Data
Josipovici, Gabriel, 1940–
The lessons of modernism, and other essays.

CONTENTS: Four writers: An art for the wilderness,
Franz Kafka, 1883–1924. Fernando Pessoa, 1888–1935.
Walter Benjamin, 1892–1940. Saul Bellow. – Modernism
and culture: English studies and European culture.
The lessons of modernism. Linearity and fragmentation. –
Voice and body: Words and music today. The rake's progress.
Maxwell Davies's Taverner. Two moments in modern music-theatre.
The importance of Stockhausen's Inori.

I. Title.
PR6060.064L4   809   76–58862

ISBN 0–87471–957–7

Printed in Great Britain

For Chickie and Albert
with love

Contents

Preface

The essays printed here were written between 1970 and 1976, often in response to specific requests. Thus the essay on Kafka formed part of a tribute to him on the fiftieth anniversary of his death; the essay on Saul Bellow was written as the Introduction to the Viking *Portable Bellow*; and the essay on Maxwell Davies's opera, *Taverner*, was written to coincide with the world première of that work at Covent Garden in 1972. The piece on Stockhausen's *Inori* was written immediately after seeing that amazing work, partly to try and make sense of it for myself and partly out of disappointment at the failure of the critics to say anything illuminating about it.

Nevertheless, this is not an entirely random collection, and that for two reasons. First of all I have carefully chosen the essays to form a volume, and as I worked at putting them together I grew more and more aware of the ways in which each threw light on the others, sometimes quite explicitly, as with the Kafka and Stockhausen pieces, sometimes indirectly, as with the essays on *The Rake's Progress* and 'Linearity and Fragmentation'. There was even, I discovered in the final stages of preparing the book for the press, one element that united all the essays, however diverse they might be in subject-matter and treatment. Just as my previous critical study, *The World and the Book*, was at heart an attempt to explain to myself the effects of Proust's *A la recherche du temps perdu*, so this, I now see, is the result of a long struggle to come to terms with a work I love and yet feel deeply uneasy about, Thomas Mann's *Dr. Faustus*. That novel, it will be recalled, deals not only with the tormented life of the composer Adrian Leverkühn, but also with the general problem of the possibility of culture in the modern world, and with the question of the limits of artistic expression, particularly as it relates to music and music-theatre. The present volume also falls into three interrelated sections: essays on writers; essays on culture and education; and essays on the limits of expression, the relation of words to music, and the entire problem of the viability of opera and music-theatre today.

A great deal is said in *Dr. Faustus* about 'the breakthrough', the modern artist's attempt to break out of the trap of Romantic forms and Romantic despair. It is at this point, it seems to me, that Mann's own affinity with the nineteenth century blinds him to one crucial aspect of modern art. Many of the essays that follow, I now see, are attempts to reformulate the problem so as to allow that aspect to emerge, so it may be useful here to sketch in the outline of what I am about.

There is an image of the self which has been taken for granted by the majority of people in the West since the seventeenth century. The self is seen as a stronghold, clearly bounded, well defended by powerful walls, buttressed by possessions. When the self thinks, it looks inwards, shutting out the confusions of the great world beyond the fortress in order to focus more clearly on what goes on within. If the self is an artist it signs what it makes and identifies it both as his possession and as his gift to the world.

In natural reaction to this image, which they saw as philistine, bourgeois, repressive and self-indulgent, the great modern artists like Joyce, Valéry and Eliot produced a notion of the artist as impersonal, shedding the self, refining it out of existence. They asked the critic to focus not on the biography or the background of the artist, but on the work itself which, they argued, rose phoenix-like from the ashes of the self. Such a reaction was understandable, but misleading. For the self cannot simply be shed like an old suit of clothes. The dispossession of ourselves is a painful, even a terrifying business, and all of us naturally shrink from it. For if we let go of ourselves what is there except chaos, destruction and death? Is such a letting-go even possible, or only another kind of romantic dream?

The crucial insight, which was partly obscured by the incisive formulation of a Joyce or a Valéry, is that the self, which had seemed so firmly rooted, so much a part of nature, to the men and women of the eighteenth and nineteenth centuries, was in fact a *construction*. It was built up by impulses within us in order to protect us from chaos and destruction. Of course in this it was helped by social institutions, but these too, it became clear, were anything but natural. The issue thus is not simply to shed the self and acquire impersonality; it is rather that it was felt to be destructive both to cling to the self and to shed the self.

It is when the matter is viewed in this light that a place is found for art. Art, the making of an artefact, becomes the means whereby the artist frees himself from the shackles of the self without disintegrating into chaos. In this view the artist is no longer either thinker or prophet, looking inwards or upwards for the truth and then conveying it to a grateful multitude; rather, he is a gymnast, developing his potential with each new exercise successfully mastered. The analogy, like all such, is inadequate, but it will do. It suggests an image of human personality not as a stronghold but as a coiled spring. The same spring is there in each of us, but most of us, for one reason or another, never give it the chance to uncoil, and it rusts and grows useless. A few manage to tap at least something of their potential. One feels that artists like Stravinsky and Picasso tapped their potential to the full. Yet the point to be made – and it is made *by* their work as well – is that there is no mystique about what they have done. It depends less on an entity like 'genius' and more on qualities we can all share, like courage, humility and dedication.

Such a formulation also finds a place for the work itself, for the space it inhabits and the time it requires to read or listen to it. Nevertheless, to look at only this side of the picture is as wrong as to see modern art only in terms of *angst*. The truth is that there is a constant dialectic between the pain and fear occasioned by the shedding of the self and the pleasure to be had in the making of what is other than the self. This is particularly evident in an art that uses language, and the lives and careers of Kafka and Pessoa are exemplary in this respect. The essay on 'The Lessons of Modernism', in an effort to simplify and clarify, ends by suggesting that the two lessons of modern art are those of silence and of game, and that we must see them as two poles, not two alternatives. One might then say that Thomas Mann concentrated a little too much on the silence aspect of the situation, while recent critics, particularly in France, where the influence of Valéry has never ceased to grow, have perhaps concentrated a little too much on the game aspect. In following through the often desperate lives of Kafka and Pessoa, as well as in the essays on music-theatre, I have tried to show how complex and fraught with ambiguity is the relation between silence and game, and between self and other.

To see things in this way is to recognise that there is not a 'system of aesthetics' that exists in a realm outside our daily lives. We too, as readers and critics, are faced with the same problems as the artist. Freedom from self is also felt by us as both a need and a terror. But that is not all. Since our very language and our institutions are designed to bolster up the stronghold of the self, the art about which I am talking is in a sense written *against the grain* of both language and institutions. Thus essays *on* such art become themselves essays directed against the bewitchment of our intelligence by means of language. That is why there can be no vantage point *above* the fray at which we can arrive, however tempting the myth of such a vantage point may be (and this preface is not one either). That is also why the writings of the later Wittgenstein are still, it seems to me, our best guide to the dangers inherent in any attempt at formulation of our problems. For, unlike so many recent theoreticians of literature, Wittgenstein was aware of the fact that the problems do not simply disappear once they have been identified. And they don't because we have too much at stake in reinstating them.

It is always a part of ourselves we are struggling against, and to define a way of reading as 'ideology' is to perpetuate another myth, the myth that there is an evil force outside ourselves, stopping us from understanding (or acting). The art I am concerned with in the following essays, however, tries to stop that struggle within us not by knocking out one or other of the participants, but by harnessing the energy of both. Think of judo, not boxing.

And this brings me to the second point of unity in this collection. There is, it seems to me, no such thing as disinterested criticism, and these essays are *interested* in that they were written at the same time as novels, stories, plays for radio and for the stage. Criticism, as I see it, is a form of conversation – with oneself, with ones friends, with unknown readers. I believe that it should be above all persuasive. Certainly I have got the most pleasure from those critics – Jarrell, Benjamin, Auden, one or two others – who were not so much concerned to judge as to communicate their enthusiasm for works of art. At the same time the fact that one is struggling to solve certain artistic problems for oneself often helps to sharpen ones awareness of what is going on in other works of art. The essays on music-theatre in the present volume in particular would never have got written if I had not suddenly grown interested in writing plays for radio and the stage and felt at the same time that existing Western non-musical theatrical traditions left me cold. However, as someone who is musically illiterate I present them with all too great an awareness of their shortcomings and only hope they will encourage others, better equipped than myself, to explore these themes. I do believe though that whatever I discern in the theatrical aspects of these works would be confirmed by detailed study of the music.

Ultimately, then, whatever unity this volume possesses depends on the unity of what I am. The danger is that one is only a bundle of ticks, for ever repeating the same narrow range of ideas, and that unity is only another name for obsessiveness. But that is a risk one has to take, and anyway not something one can in the end do anything about.

It is impossible to thank all those from whose conversation I have benefited, or all the dedicated editors whose care and erudition has saved me from many blunders. Gordon Crosse, John Mepham, Tony Inglis, Roger Moss, Sue Purdie, Maria Fitzgerald and my mother all commented, at one point or another, on the essays, and made valuable suggestions. The University of Sussex was generous with leave and I am grateful to it and especially to the School of European Studies for the sympathy and encouragement it has always shown me.

Lewes, August 1976   G. J.

Acknowledgements

All but two of the chapters in this book, or earlier versions of them, have already appeared in print, and I am grateful to the editors and publishers concerned for permission to reproduce them:

1 *European Judaism,* vol. 8 no. 2 (summer 1974).
3 *Times Higher Education Supplement,* 25 Jan 1974.
4 Introduction to *The Portable Saul Bellow* (New York: Viking Press, 1974).
5 Angus Ross (ed.), *English: An Outline for the Intending Student* (Routledge, 1971).
6 *English in Education,* vol. 6 no. 2 (summer 1972).
7 *Prospice* 1 (Nov 1973) and Gabriel Josipovici (ed.), *The Modern English Novel: The Reader, the Writer and the Work* (Open Books, 1976).
8 *Times Literary Supplement,* 27 Oct 1972.
9 *Tempo,* no. 113 (1975).
10 *Tempo,* no. 101 (1972).
12 *Radical Philosophy,* no. 11 (summer 1975).

The author and publishers wish to thank the following who have kindly given permission for the use of copyright material:

ATICA, S.A.R.L. for poems from *Obras Completas de Fernando Pessoa,* vol. 3, *Obras Completas,* vol. 5, and *Obras Completas,* vol. 1, by Fernando Pessoa.

Boosey & Hawkes Music Publishers Ltd for the extract from *The Rake's Progress* by W. H. Auden and Chester Kallman, from the libretto of Stravinsky's opera.

Edinburgh University Press for extracts from *Selected Poems of Fernando Pessoa,* edited and translated by Peter Rickard.

Faber & Faber Ltd and Alfred A. Knopf Inc. for 'Earthy Anecdote' from *Collected Poems of Wallace Stevens.*

Martin Secker & Warburg Ltd and Schocken Books Inc. for extracts from: 'The Diaries of Franz Kafka' edited by Max Brod (US edition 'The Diaries 1910–1913' by Franz Kafka. Copyright © 1948 by Schocken Books Inc. Copyright renewed © 1975 by Schocken Books Inc., and 'The Diaries 1914–1923' by Franz Kafka. Copyright © 1949 by Schocken Books Inc.). 'Letters to Felice' translated by James Stern and Elisabeth Duckworth (US edition 'Letters to Felice' by Franz Kafka. Copyright © 1967, 1973 by Schocken Books Inc.). 'In the Penal Settlement', translated by Ernst Kaiser and Eithne Wilkins (US edition 'The Penal Colony' by Franz Kafka. Copyright © 1948 by Schocken Books Inc. Copyright renewed © 1975 by Schocken Books Inc.). 'Wedding Preparations in the Country', translated by Eithne Wilkins and Ernst Kaiser (US edition 'Dearest Father' by Franz Kafka. Copyright © 1954 by Schocken Books Inc.).

PART I

FOUR WRITERS

1 An Art for the Wilderness: Franz Kafka, 1883-1924

It is indeed a kind of Wandering in the Wilderness in reverse that I am
undergoing: I think that I am continually skirting the wilderness and
am full of childish hopes (particularly as regards women) that
'perhaps I shall keep in Canaan after all' – when all the while I have
been decades in the wilderness and these hopes are merely mirages born
of despair.

THE EYES

Our relation to the books we come across in our lives is a mysterious
one. Some we fall in love with because they said the right things at the
right time; others are lost to us for ever because we were not ready
for them when they crossed our paths and chance does not bring us
into contact with them a second time. With the books which have
meant most to us there is nearly always the sense of an inexhaustible
richness, of something we have to grow up to and into, and which will
never reveal itself entirely. Nevertheless, with such books, there is
always the sense of an instinctive understanding, an awareness that
what is lacking is really only the ability to make such understanding
fully conscious. Kafka is the only author I know to whom this does not
apply. My own experience may be special in this respect, but I have
found that, from the moment I began to read him, I felt at once
infinitely close to him and infinitely distant. And ever since that time,
as I have read and reread his novels and stories and diaries and notebooks and more and more of the voluminous correspondence that is
slowly being made available, I have never had any sense of a gradual
growth in understanding. There has only been the repetition of that
initial sense of infinite closeness and infinite distance, of total familiarity
and absolute alienness. It is this, it seems to me, that is so haunting
about Kafka, that makes him, fifty years after his death, as enigmatic
to us as he was to his friends and first readers in the course of his brief
unhappy lifetime.

From his photographs he stares out at us with a face at once angelic and animal. It is a face completely gathered up into the eyes, which are so big there seems to be little room for any other features. He stares out at us so directly from the print that he appears to hide absolutely nothing, and yet for that very reason to allow us no words to express what it is that is revealed. That is why his photographs disturb us in the same way as do his writings. Walter Benjamin, in a beautiful paragraph which is very close to the spirit of Kafka in its combination of melancholy and precision, speaks of one such photograph. 'It was the time', he says in his essay, 'A Short History of Photography', published in 1931, seven years after Kafka's death –

> It was the time when those studios appeared with draperies and palm-trees, tapestries and easels, looking like a cross between an execution and a representation, between a torture-chamber and a throne room, and of which shattering testimony is provided by an early photograph of Kafka. A boy of about six, dressed in a tight-fitting, almost deliberately humiliating child's suit, overladen with lace, is seen standing in a kind of wintergarden landscape. The background teems with palm fronds. And as if to make these up-holstered tropics still stickier and sultrier, the subject holds in his left hand an immoderately large hat with a broad brim of the type worn by Spaniards. He would surely disappear into the setting, were it not for his immeasurably sad eyes, which dominate the landscape that was predestined for them.

We would do well to bear this passage in mind in the course of what follows, for it brings out clearly both the horror of being looked at which was such an important element in Kafka's character, and the radiance of his eyes, to which all who knew him bear repeated testimony.

THE FATHER

The double sense of infinite nearness and infinite distance, which Kafka's writings, like his photographs, engender, is one which precisely duplicates his own relations to himself. Writing to Brod in 1914 he says: 'What have I in common with the Jews? I have hardly anything in common with myself, and I ought to stand quietly in a corner, content that I can breathe.' And, more gnomically, in the *Diaries*: 'Far, far away from you, world history unfolds, the world history of your soul.' If we are to catch the movement of Kafka's writing and of his life (and movement is what the writing is all about, the weight is always on the verbs, never on the nouns or adjectives), then it is necessary to understand the role played in them by four characters: the Father, the Woman, Illness, and Writing itself. Each is deeply entangled with all the others, but it may be possible to separate them to the extent at least of seeing how they interconnect and with what results.

One must begin where Kafka himself began, with the father, Hermann Kafka. He was there before Franz and he is thus, in a sense, *the* world into which Franz was born and with which he tried all his life to come to terms. What emerges most clearly from the book-length letter Kafka wrote to his father late in life and never sent, is Hermann's size and his arbitrary exercise of authority in the eyes of his son.

> I was, after all, depressed even by your mere physical presence. I remember for instance how often we undressed together in the same bathing-hut. There was I, skinny, weakly, slight, you strong, tall, broad. Even inside the hut I felt myself a miserable specimen, and what's more not only in your eyes but in the eyes of the whole world, for you were for me the measure of all things. But then when we went out of the bathing-hut before the people, I with you holding my hand, a little skeleton, unsteady, barefoot on the boards, frightened of the water, incapable of copying your swimming strokes, which you, with the best of intentions, but actually to my profound humiliation, always kept on showing me, then I was frantic with desperation and all my bad experiences in all spheres at such moments fitted magnificently together.

Elias Canetti, in *Der Andere Prozess*, the gentle and understanding book he has devoted to an analysis of Kafka's letters to Felice, has drawn attention to the frequency with which Kafka returns to this motif of his own thinness. When Kafka lay dying in the Kierling sanatorium, unable to speak any more because of the tubercular laryngitis with which he was afflicted, and reduced to jotting down on pieces of paper whatever he wished to say to his devoted friend Robert Klopstock, who was with him to the end, he recalled one day a trip he might have taken with Felice and her friend Grete Bloch: 'Once I would have accompanied her to the Baltic with her friend, but I was ashamed of my thinness and my usual pusillanimity.' Even more revealing is the letter he wrote to Milena in which he noted:

> A few years ago I was in the habit of going out on the Moldau in my bathing-suit. I rowed up river and then let the current take me down and stretched out on my back as I passed under the bridges. From them I must have presented a rather comic spectacle, because of my thinness. An employee of the office, who had once seen me

from one of the bridges, after having suffiicently brought out the comedy of the situation, summed it up in these words: it reminded one a little of the Last Judgement at the precise moment when the lids of the coffins are lifted and the dead still lie there, motionless.

Canetti comments:

> The figure of the thin man and the dead man are seen as one and the same; linked to the image of the Last Judgement there emerges a picture of the physical person which is totally despairing and anguished. One could say that the Thin Man or the Dead Man, who here are one, has only just enough life left to let himself go with the current and present himself at the Last Judgement.

As we will see, however, everything in Kafka must be seen from two points of view, and the figure of the Thin Man is no exception.

To his physical domination the father added a mental one: 'From your chair you ruled the world. Your opinion was correct, every other was mad, wild, *meschugge*, not normal. . . . For me you took on the enigmatic quality that all tyrants have whose rights are based on their person and not on reason.' The mixture of arbitrariness and absolute authority exercised by the father seems to have left Kafka not only totally bewildered but also with an ineradicable sense that *whatever* he did was profoundly wrong. If he passed his exams at the end of the school year and went up a class, if the masters praised his work and he seemed all set for a successful career in the world, he knew deep down that this was only due to a temporary misunderstanding. Soon everybody would come to their senses and he would be sent back again to the lowest form, which he should never have left, or he would be punished for wrongs he had obviously committed, though what these might be he had no means of knowing.

FELICE

Kafka's relations to women must be seen first of all as an extension of his struggle with his father. 'The plans to marry', he writes in his letter, 'became the most large-scale and hopeful attempt to escape, and then the failure was on a correspondingly large scale too.' Marriage was the means of escape from the father, the way of showing him that he too could stand up and make his way like a normal person; but at the same time it was a way of appeasing the father, of turning into a father himself and thus returning to the fold and the parental blessing. Thus from the start Kafka's relations with women seemed likely to founder on the rock of this unresolved ambiguity.

Kafka's letters to Milena have long been known. Written between 1921 and 1922, they make up a book of roughly two hundred pages, and they have always been recognised as an integral part of his writings. But the six hundred pages of his correspondence with Felice Bauer, 'the girl from Berlin', to whom he was twice engaged, has only recently been made available, and only now been translated into English.[1] The volume not only helps to fill in what had always been a very mysterious episode in Kafka's life, it also makes abundantly clear the recurring pattern of his relations with the women with whom he fell in love.

Kafka was twenty-nine when he met Felice at the house of Brod's parents in 1912. He had not yet written any of the works we recognise as distinctively his, but, despite the traumas of his childhood, he felt himself to be on the threshold of a major literary career. The five years of his affair with Felice changed all that. By 1917 he had indeed written 'The Judgement', 'Metamorphosis', 'In the Penal Colony' and all we have of *America* and *The Trial*, as well as countless other stories and fragments. But his life had closed in upon him. He had only eight years to live and he sensed it. His attempts to lead a normal life had proved a failure; worse, his art was not only something he no longer believed in, it was, he felt, a blasphemy and a trap. The encounter with Felice was thus the most important event of his life, apart from his birth into the Kafka household, and we are fortunate that Canetti, who is hardly one to rush into print, has felt impelled to follow the five-year relationship with such profound understanding.[2]

As Canetti points out, the summer of 1912 was a high point of expectation in Kafka's life. Brod had prevailed upon him to publish a selection of his early writings, and it was to discuss the presentation of these that Kafka had gone round to his friend's house on the evening of 13 August 1912. He had also just returned from a trip to Weimar, in the early part of which Brod had been with him, and which had naturally been to some extent an act of homage to the greatest figure of German letters. That evening at Brod's Kafka handed round some of the photographs taken on the trip, and also discussed with Felice, who was a friend of the Brod family on her way from Berlin to Budapest to attend a wedding, the possibility of emigrating to Palestine, the Promised Land. It is this which he takes as his excuse to write to her, five weeks later:

My Dear Fraulein Bauer, In the likelihood that you no longer have even the remotest recollection of me, I am introducing myself once more: my name is Franz Kafka, and I am the person who greeted you for the first time that evening at Director Brod's in Prague, the one who subsequently handed you across the table, one by one, photographs of the Thalia trip, and who finally, with the very hand now striking the keys, held your hand, the one which confirmed a promise to accompany him next year to Palestine.

That was 20 September 1912, and by that date the following year Kafka had written to her more than half the letters which make up the large six-hundred-page volume just published. For although, like Proust, Kafka always talked of himself as weak and entirely lacking in will power, he was, like Proust, the most determined and tenacious of men where what mattered to him was at stake. And much was clearly at stake here. Within two months he had not only declared his love but had also managed to woo Felice into a reciprocation of it. On 23 March 1913 they met for the first time since that initial encounter. In June he proposed to her and she accepted him. In September he seems to have broken down completely and rushed away from everyone to a sanatorium in Riva, where he had a brief affair with a young Christian girl, G.W. It all seemed over between him and Felice, but with the help of the enigmatic Grete Bloch, a friend of Felice's who came to see Kafka in Prague, they renewed their engagement in January 1914.[3] In May Felice arrived in Prague and she and Kafka hunted for a flat into which to move after their marriage in September. In June Kafka travelled to Berlin with his father for the official engagement. On 12 July there took place in the Hotel Askanischer Hof in Berlin the episode Kafka refers to as the 'tribunal', attended by Felice, her sister, Grete Bloch, and Kafka's friend Ernst Weiss, following which the engagement was broken off. In August the war broke out (a real Last Judgement, particularly if one believes, as by now one surely must, that there were not two World Wars, but only one, with an uneasy truce in the middle, and if one remembers that practically all those mentioned in Kafka's letters and diaries were murdered by the Nazis). But by January 1915 Kafka and Felice had met again, in May he went on holiday with her and Grete Bloch, and in July 1916 he spent an extraordinarily happy fortnight with her in Marienbad. A year later they were once more officially engaged but in August he had his first haemorrhage and he wrote to her more or less saying he didn't ever want to see her again. The last letter is dated 16 October 1917 and it is written from Zürau, in the country, where Kafka had gone to stay with his favourite sister Ottla, to try and recover.

These simple facts give away enough to make the pattern of their relationship plain: Kafka would press for marriage but as soon as it looked like becoming a reality he would retreat wildly and instinctively. At the end he took even his illness as a sign that his body had at last rebelled against the plans he had tried to make for it. But what the facts don't show is that in the night of 22–3 September 1912, two days after the first letter to Felice, Kafka wrote, in one sitting, in ten hours, the story 'The Judgement', the first piece he fully acknowledged, and that he was to look back to that night as to a moment of absolute happiness, when the sense of his own destiny as a writer and of the value of his work was finally and incontrovertibly borne in upon him. Nor do they show that before the year 1912 was out he had written 'Metamorphosis' and most of *America*. Clearly the encounter with Felice had helped to release something within him. But it also began to work in the opposite direction. By early 1913, perhaps, as Canetti suggests, because she did not respond to his own work in the way he had hoped – she remains oddly silent when he sends her a copy of his first book and of 'The Judgement' with its dedication: 'A story for F.' – by early 1913 the familiar anguish and despair begin to creep into his letters to her. Then follows the second encounter, the offer of marriage and the mysterious flight to Riva, the reconciliation and the public engagement. Of that episode Kafka wrote in his *Diaries*: 'Back from Berlin. Was tied hand and foot like a criminal. Had they sat me down in a corner bound in real chains, placed policemen in front of me, and let me look on simply like that, it could not have been worse.' For if the encounter with Felice, with its promise of marriage, set him free to write, the looming actuality of marriage froze him. Already on the eve of the New Year, 1913, he had written prophetically to her:

> In your last letter there is a sentence you have written once before and so have I: 'We belong together unconditionally'. That, dearest, is true a thousand-fold; now, for instance, in these first hours of the New Year I could have no greater and crazier wish than that we should be bound together inseparably by the wrists of your left and my right hand. I don't quite know why this should occur to me; perhaps because a book on the French Revolution, with contemporary accounts, is lying in front of me, and it may be possible after all – not that I have read or heard of it anywhere – that a couple thus bound together were once led to the scaffold.

And Canetti drily comments: 'Marriage seen under the aegis of the scaffold – that is the image with which the year 1913 began for him.'

THE INNER WORLD

What was it that drew Kafka to marriage with such force and with such force turned him away from it? At first sight the answer seems simple: we are dealing here with a conflict between Kafka's desire for normality and his desire to write. But, as we will see, the conflicts in Kafka are never that clear-cut.

In a diary entry for 3 January 1912 Kafka had noted:

It is easy to recognise a concentration in me of all my forces on writing. When it became clear in my organism that writing was the most productive direction for my being to take, everything rushed in that direction and left empty all those abilities which were directed towards the joys of sex, eating, drinking, philosophical reflection, and above all music. I atrophied in all these directions. This was necessary because the totality of my strengths was so slight that only collectively could they even half-way serve the purpose of my writing. Naturally I did not find this purpose independently and consciously, it found itself, and is now interfered with only by the office, but that interferes with it completely.... I need only throw my work in the office out of this complex in order to begin my real life in which, with the progress of my work, my face will finally be able to age in a natural way.

This opposition between his writing and the sum of bourgeois values is clear and unambiguous and could be duplicated in the statements of any budding writer since the time of the Romantics. It is true that this is written before he met Felice, but his letters to her only bear out what he had written in his diary. He repeats to her again and again that writing is the only thing in his life, that in order to write he has to be completely alone, that if she marries him she will be marrying a monk who is chained to his work, can write only at night and cannot tolerate the slightest noise. When she says something about his 'literary interests' he corrects her sharply: 'I have no literary interests, but am made of literature. I am nothing else and cannot be anything else.' Ten days later he repeats: 'Not a bent for writing, my dearest Felice, not a bent, but my entire self.' To Milena eight years later, he makes the position even clearer: 'I cannot listen at the same time to your voice and to the terrible voices of my inner world.' And again: 'You were tied to your husband by an indissoluble marriage, a truly sacramental one (...), and I, by a precisely similar marriage to ... I don't know to whom, but the gaze of that terrifying spouse often lights upon me, I can feel it.' By this time Kafka seems to be seized with a positive terror at what is in store for him if he responds to either of the two voices, that of Milena calling him to her, or that of his writing calling him to itself. We are no longer in a personal world; we have entered a mythic world, where the individual, with his likes and dislikes, hopes and fears, no longer has a place. On 6 April 1922, the year of *The Waste Land*, he jots down in his diary: 'The three Erinyes. Flight into the sacred wood. M.'

The terror that is so evident in the letters to Milena and in the diary entries of those last years suggests that all had not gone according to the plans for 'ageing in a natural way' that Kafka had put down with such confidence in January 1912. What, exactly, had gone wrong? One can put it very schematically and say this: just as marriage, which had at first seemed to offer an escape from the father, had revealed itself, as it came closer to him, to be a kind of sacrifice of the self *to* the father; so writing, which had at first seemed the royal road to freedom and self-fulfilment, was found to stand, when he neared its centre, no less under the domination of the father than marriage had been. In order to understand how the father, always so implacable in his opposition to his son's artistic ambitions, could be discovered at the very source of writing itself, it will be necessary to pursue a little further the relation of Kafka to the women he loved.

NIGHT

There is a letter to Milena – they are all undated – in which Kafka speaks out for the first time about a subject that had clearly long been haunting him:

> You asked me once how I could call that Saturday 'good' which I lived through with such anguish. Loving you (and I love you as the sea loves the tiniest pebble in its depths; my love engulphs you no less ...); loving you, I love the whole world; your left shoulder is a part of it ... and your face beneath mine in the forest ... that is my only joy, my only pride, and I do not limit it to the forest. But precisely between this world of daylight and that 'half-hour in bed' of which you once spoke in a letter ... there is for me an abyss that I cannot bridge because I do not want to. On the other side it is night business ... ; here, it is the world and I possess it; must I then leap in the night to the other side of the abyss if I want to regain possession of it? ... Here is the world I possess and I would pass to the other side for love of an enervating philtre, a game of catch, a philosopher's stone, alchemy, a magic ring? Not that, it terrifies me. To want to grasp by magic, in one night, hastily ... what each day gives to our open eyes! (Perhaps one cannot have children otherwise, perhaps children are also magic, let us leave the question for the moment.) That is why by your side I experience the greatest anxiety as well as the greatest peace.

To understand Kafka's fear of the night and of the games of the night when children are produced, it is necessary to go back to some of his earliest letters. In a letter to Oskar Pollack of 1903 Kafka remarks in an aside: 'Let us honour the mole and his habits, but without making him one's personal saint.' And the following year, to Brod:

> We dig about in ourselves like moles, and emerge from our subterranean chambers with our fur all blackened and filthy, holding out our poor little red paws in the air to beg for a gentle mercy. During a walk my dog surprised a mole which was trying to cross the road. Without pause he kept jumping on her then letting her go, for he's still young and hesitant. At first this amused me, I found the agitation of the mole agreeable as it desperately and in vain looked for a hole in the hard surface of the road. But as the dog once again laid its paws on her she began to scream. Ks, kss, she complained. And then it seemed to me ... No, nothing seemed to me. It was only an illusion, because that day my head fell so heavily that I noted in the evening with surprise that my chin had sunk right into my chest. But the next day a young girl put on a white dress and fell in love with me ...'

There can be no doubt that what is suggested is that Kafka and the mole are one. Kafka does not deny it. On the contrary, the image of the chin sinking into the breast is one we find recurring in his writing whenever a human being is turning into an animal. And to this passage one could link the extraordinary letter to Milena in which he tries to explain to her why their love had to end in failure:

> I was a forest animal who hardly ever lived in the forest. I dug myself in wherever I could find a dirty ditch (...), when I saw by the light of the sun the most wonderful thing I had ever seen. I thought of nothing else, I forgot myself totally. I got up, I approached, fearful, to the heart of this new liberty which nevertheless brought back memories of my native air. I approached in spite of my fear, and I came into your presence. How good you were! I lay down at your feet as though I had the right, and I put my face in your hands and I felt happy, proud, free, powerful, at home – so much at home! (...) But at bottom I was only the animal, I belonged to the forest, I only lived here, in the sunshine, through your grace ... It couldn't last ...'

What is extraordinary about all these accounts is how unsentimental they are. This is because animality is never seen as innocence, a blessing, but always as anguish, exclusion, a curse. Yet for Kafka at least it is clearly equally painful to be on the other side, to smile with the dog and hear the cry of the mole. In a letter to Felice, trying to explain to her the meaning of a dream she has had, he says: 'If you had not been lying on the ground among the animals, you would not have been able to see the sky and the stars, you would not have been saved. You would perhaps not have been able to survive the anguish of the vertical position. And it is the same with me . . .'

We can see how very ambiguous the image of the Thin Man is in Kafka's imagination. On the one hand he blames himself and feels acute shame and guilt for being the puny thing he is. But on the other this very thinness and weakness brings him into immediate sympathy with the weak and fearful. At times he is very positive about it:

> Humility provides everyone, even he who despairs of solitude, with the strongest relationship to his fellow-man, though of course only in the case of a complete and lasting humility. It can do this because it is the true language of prayer, at once adoration and the firmest of unions. The relationship to one's fellow-man is the relationship of prayer, the relationship to oneself is the relationship of striving.

From this point of view the vertical position is the position of the Father. It is the position of authority, of the rapacious carnivore, striving to succeed. Viewed in this light the powers of darkness associated with the act of love are basically inhuman and evil, a way of discovering the secrets of the universe in order to use them for our own purposes. The other way, the way of prayer, is a denial of the vertical self which allows us to forge links with the whole of creation in a positive and non-destructive way. A very revealing comment on Marcus Aurelius in an early letter to Oskar Pollack throws further light on this: 'The whole book', says Kafka, 'really only deals with a man who, with clever phrases, a powerful hammer and a limitless perspective, wishes to make himself a man full of mastery, a man of bronze, completely upright.' This man of bronze, the Stoic ideal, is a more sympathetic figure than Hermann Kafka, but they stand for the same thing: self-mastery, success in the world – at the expense, naturally, of all that is small and defenceless. The extraordinary interconnection in Kafka of masochism and sympathy for all things that are not himself, even the inanimate, comes out well in a remark he makes in a letter to Felice: 'To be a large piece of wood, and to be pressed against her body by the cook, who with both hands draws the knife towards her along the side of this stiff log (approximately in the region of my hip) and with all her might slices off shavings to light the fire.' Even stronger is this passage in one of the Octavo Notebooks:

> I lay on the ground by a wall, writhing in pain, trying to burrow into the damp earth. The huntsman stood beside me and lightly pressed one foot into the small of my back. 'A splendid beast', he said

to the beater, who was already cutting open my collar and coat in order to feel my flesh. Already tired of me and eager for fresh action, the hounds were running senselessly against the wall. The coach came and, bound hand and foot, I was flung in beside the gentleman, over the back seat, so that my head and arms hung down outside the carriage. The journey passed swiftly and smoothly; perishing of thirst, with open mouth, I breathed in the high-whirling dust, and now and then felt the gentleman's delighted touch on my calves.

As Canetti remarks: 'One must withdraw from violence, which is unjust, by disappearing as much as possible. One makes oneself very small or one transforms oneself into an insect ... But this is impossible in marriage. Always, whether one likes it or not, one must be present to the gaze of the other.' At the same time the act of love is itself the most acute manifestation of mastery and destruction, during the course of which the child will be conceived. But the child is the 'false-small', the small which will grow into the large and powerful, not the anti-father but the potential father, 'the Small which one pushes into growing and which wants to grow, thus standing in complete opposition to Kafka himself, whose most profound tendencies are to become smaller and smaller, more and more silent, lighter and lighter, till the final annihilation.'

'NO!'

I think we can go still further, though Canetti himself does not do so. In the letter to his father Kafka had written:

Marrying, founding a family, accepting all the children that come, supporting them in this insecure world and even guiding them a little as well is, I am convinced, the utmost a human being can succeed in doing at all. That seemingly so many succeed in this is no evidence to the contrary, for first, there are not many who do, in fact, succeed, and secondly these not-many usually don't 'do' it, it merely 'happens' to them.

And although he goes on to say that 'doing' and 'happening' cannot in fact be kept clearly apart, it is obvious that for him the difference is crucial. His horror of committing himself stems from his profound sense of the sacrilege involved in lending oneself to a mere 'happening', especially when that may result in the bringing of yet more human beings into the world. Yet the doubt always remains that this may be his own fault, that he may be personally excluded from a meaningful world precisely because of his doubts.

Marriage for him can only make sense if it is truly a sacrament, if, that is, it is felt to be sanctioned, and thus necessary. But for Kafka there is nowhere this vital sanction could come from. Men act and live as though all they did they did by natural birthright, but this, for Kafka at least, it not the case. Meaning is not automatically conferred by birth – hence the horror that images of birth have for Kafka:

> The sight of the double bed at home, the used sheets, the nightshirts carefully laid out, can exasperate me to the point of nausea, can turn me inside out; it is as if I had not been definitely born, were continually born anew into the world out of that stale life in that stale room, had constantly to seek confirmation of myself there, were indissolubly joined with all that loathsomeness, in part even if not entirely, at least it still clogs my feet which want to run, they are still stuck fast in the original shapeless pulp.

That is the peculiar horror of being a father: that you create life in the magic darkness without full awareness of what it is you are doing. Fatherhood is the attempt by human kind to make nature and meaning converge, but since they can never do so, is it not really an irresponsible attempt to impose a lie upon the world, to impose purpose and meaning on what is only the product of chance and individual will?

The sense of life as not being *inherently* meaningful is brought out clearly by one very noticeable characteristic of Kafka's writing, the predominance in it of *gestures*. These gestures testify to a kind of unease on the part of the gesticulator, as if by the jerkiness of his movements he would find a way back to his natural environment. One short piece in his first book, *Meditation*, brings this out extremely well:

> To lift yourself out of a miserable mood, even if you have to do it by strength of will, should be easy. I force myself out of my chair, stride round the table, exercise my head and neck, make my eyes sparkle, tighten the muscles round them. Defy my own feelings, welcome A enthusiastically ... swallow all that C says, whatever pain and trouble it may cost me, in long draughts. Yet even if I manage that, one single slip ... will stop the whole process ... So perhaps the best resource is to meet everything passively, to make yourself an inert mass ... to stare at others with the eyes of an animal, to feel no compunction; in short, with your own hand to throttle down whatever ghostly life remains in you, that is, to enlarge the final peace of the graveyard and let nothing survive that. A characteristic movement in such a condition is to run your little finger along your eyebrows.

The alternatives here seem to be either wild and arbitrary movements, or total inertia, with only the eyes left alive. It is as though the protagonist were embarrassed by the number of possibilities open to him, that the recognition of these forced him to see how little necessity there was in *any* movement, and consequently made *all* human activities seem suspect. Kafka's characters never act because action is natural to them; they imitate human gestures in order to convince themselves that they are human. (Such imitation is of course the basis of early film comedy, and this helps to explain Kafka's affinity to it.) The story that best illustrates the nature of this imitation in Kafka is no doubt 'A Report to an Academy', in which an ape lectures to a gathering of scientists about his rise from the animal to the human kingdom. Until the day he was caught, he tells them, he had so many 'ways out', but all of a sudden he found himself in a cage and he had none. He didn't want freedom, that would have been too much to ask for, he only wanted 'a way out'. And, since he saw men walking about outside his cage, it suddenly came to him that the way out was simply *to imitate men*. So, laboriously, he learnt to ape their gestures, their actions, and, finally, even their speech.

This is why, even linguistically, Kafka never invents, he merely imitates the speech of those around him. He is reinforced in his feeling that language does not belong to him by the cultural situation in which he finds himself. But even in matters that seem less obviously social than speech, like marriage or falling in love, one has the sense that Kafka imitates in the hope that by doing so he will understand, that life will become meaningful for him as it clearly is for those who without hesitation do things like marrying and begetting children. In all his relationships with women there is the feeling that he is trying in some way to force an unequivocal 'Yes' or 'No' out of them, trying, as Maurice Blanchot has put it in one of the many brilliant essays he has devoted to Kafka, to transgress the limits in order to be told that he has transgressed. At least then he would *know* that it was his lot either to live out his life like other people or on the contrary to live it out in isolation. But each time his sense of the enormity of what he had started forced him to retreat before the unequivocal answer could come. (He once wrote: 'Not everyone can see the truth, but he can be it'. He himself could simply not *be* a lie.) By one of those ironies which do make of his life something exemplary, the 'No' did come in the end, but it was too late. As he lay dying he wrote to the father of Dora Dymant, the young woman who had looked after him with such devotion in the last year of his life, asking for her hand. The father showed the letter to a very holy rabbi who without hesitation shook his head emphatically. But whether this authoritative 'No' had to do with the fact that you do not marry your daughter to a man who will be dead inside the year, or with the fact that you don't marry your daughter to *this particular man*, whatever the circumstances remains a mystery.

WORDS

'I need only throw my work in the office out of this complex in order to begin my real life in which, with the progress of my work, my face will finally be able to age in a natural way.' Thus, as we have seen, Kafka wrote in 1912. Was he overoptimistic, or did he take a wrong turning? Was his faith in his writing so little justified that he could write in 1916 that he did not feel as though he had started to live? What precisely was the role Kafka felt himself able to assign to art in a life that seemed doomed to be lived always in the Wilderness?

Everything Kafka writes testifies to the *physical* reality words had for him. In 1911 he notes in his diary: 'I live only here and there in a small word in whose vowel ("thrust" in the above sentence, for instance) I lose my useless head for a moment. The first and last letters are the beginning and end of my fish-like emotion.' Ten years later, in a letter to Milena, he suddenly exclaims: 'Milena, what a rich, dense name! So rich, so full, that one can hardly lift it!' Words make such a profound and immediate impression that he merely has to write a sentence down to feel its perfection:

> The special nature of my inspiration in which I, the most fortunate and unfortunate of men, now go to sleep at 2 a.m. (...) is such that I can do everything, and not only what is directed to a definite piece of work. When I arbitrarily write a single sentence, for instance, 'He looked out of the window', it already has perfection.

However, it is not always like that: 'The tremendous world I have in my head. But how to free myself and free it without being torn in pieces? And a thousand times rather be torn to pieces than retain it in my head or bury it. That, indeed, is why I am here, that is quite clear to me.' The reason he cannot free the world he has in his head is that words cannot be thought of as purely sensuous objects for any length of time. On the other hand to accept words as counters in a system of signs is to feel their inadequacy to convey the unique. 'I can't write,' Kafka tells Brod in 1910, 'I haven't written a single line that I can accept, instead I have crossed out all I have written – there wasn't much – since my return from Paris. My whole body puts me on my guard against each word; each word, before even letting itself be put down, has to look round on every side; the phrases positively fall apart in my hands, I see what they are like inside and then I have to stop quickly.' And to Felice he says: 'How is it possible to write at all if one has so much to say and knows that the pen can only trace an uncertain and random trail through the mass of what has to be said?'

ABRAHAM

There is worse to come. The only justification for going against the father's wishes, for occupying himself with writing when he should be managing his brother-in-law's factory, marrying and begetting children, is that writing is in some ways a more exalted calling. Certainly that is what he feels in his moments of joy. But what if this is not the case? What if writing is not only weak and inadequate in its conveyance of the truth, but has nothing whatever to do with the truth? In a letter to Brod of 1921 Kafka sketches a little parable which perfectly expresses his feelings on the subject. He asks Brod to imagine an Abraham who presents himself dutifully with his son at the appointed time and place – but without ever having been called!

> As if, at the end of the year, when the best pupil in the class was about to receive the prize in all solemnity, and, in the silence before he does so, the worst pupil steps forward from the filthy bench at the back of the classroom while the whole class bursts into laughter. And perhaps he has not even misheard, his name was really called, it was the teacher's intention that the reward of the best pupil should be the punishment of the worst.

An undated fragment makes the same point in a different way:

> Anyone who has been in a state of suspended animation can tell terrible stories about it, but he cannot say what it is like after death, he has actually been no nearer to death than anyone else, funda- mentally he has only 'lived' through an extraordinary experience ... It is the same with everyone who has experienced something extra- ordinary. For instance, Moses ... From both, however, from those who have returned from a state of suspended animation and from Moses, who returned, one can learn a great deal, but the decisive thing cannot be discovered from them, for they themselves have not discovered it. If they had they would not have returned.

More clearly than anyone except perhaps the Wittgenstein of the *Tractatus*, Kafka sees the kind of falsification involved in talking about the world as though it possessed a meaning that we could discern. In order to do that we should have to be able to step *outside* the world, and once we had done that we would not return. That is the significance of the many aphorisms of the type: 'The crows maintain that a single crow could destroy the heavens. There is no doubt of that, but it proves nothing against the heavens, for heaven simply means: the impossibility of crows.'

Nevertheless, the urge to write cannot be denied. (And to read aloud what you have written – Canetti is surely right to point out that some of Kafka's happiest letters to Felice are those in which he recounts how he read this or that work of his to his friends.) Such an urge has a kind of primal quality which nothing can destroy:

> The strange, mysterious, perhaps dangerous, perhaps saving comfort that there is in writing: it is the leap out of murderers' row; it is a seeing of what is really taking place. This occurs by a higher type of observation, a higher, not a keener type, and the higher it is and the less within reach of the row, the more independent it becomes, the more obedient to its own laws of motion, the more incalculable, the more joyful, the more ascendent its course.

But, as this quotation makes plain, the very pleasure of writing seems tied to its lack of dependence on the world. But if it is not directly related to the world it is surely a nothing. Worse, since it gives the appearance of telling us about the world, it secretly poisons our own relation to it. For example:

> Have never understood how it is possible for almost everyone who writes to objectify his sufferings in the very midst of undergoing them; thus I for example, in the midst of my unhappiness, in all likelihood with my head still smarting from unhappiness, sit down and write to someone: I am unhappy. Yes, I can even go beyond that and with as many flourishes as I have the talent for, all of which seems to have nothing to do with my unhappiness, ring simple, or contrapuntal, or a whole orchestration of changes on my theme. And it is not a lie, and it does not still my pain; it is simply a merciful surplus of strength at a moment when suffering has raked me to the bottom of my being and plainly exhausted all my strength. But then what kind of surplus is it?

Once, God talked to Abraham; now He talks to no one, not even the writer. Words are thus reduced to being mere sensual objects, whose touch, as it were, is immediately gratifying, but which float free of any direct contact with the world or even with those who speak them. And if a man should want to write or speak in such a way that it will directly affect the world, that it will be felt upon the body of the world, then he will have to build a machine like that of the Penal Colony. And even that, in the end, proved incapable of tracing any words on the body of its master, only of butchering him in the most sickening fashion.

DEATH

The year 1922 was the time when Kafka perhaps came closest to grasping the world history of his soul. There is one huge letter to Brod which gets close to the articulation of the truth and manages to stay with it for more than a fleeting moment. We have traced the conflict between writing and the world, and then the conflict within writing itself; in this letter Kafka reveals that by this time the act of writing, no less than the act of love, was seen by him as a demonic temptation. The meditation is sparked off by an invitation to travel and Kafka's sudden terror at the thought:

> During last night's insomnia, as these thoughts came and went between my aching temples, I realised once again, what I had almost forgotten in this recent period of relative calm, that I tread a terribly tenuous, indeed almost non-existent soil spread over a pit full of shadows, whence the powers of darkness emerge at will to destroy my life ... Literature helps me to live, but wouldn't it be truer to say that it furthers this sort of life? Which of course doesn't imply that my life is any better when I don't write. On the contrary, then it's much worse, quite unbearable and with no possible remedy other than madness ... But what of the literary state as such? Creation is a splendid reward, but for what? Last night I saw very clearly, as clearly as in an object lesson for children, that these are wages earned in the devil's service. The descent towards the powers of darkness, the liberation of normally tethered forces, the ambiguous contacts, and all that takes place down there of which nothing is known while writing stories in the sunlight ... Maybe there exists a different kind of creation, I know no other. And the devilry of the whole thing is quite clear to me.

The extraordinary thing about this passage, which seems more at home in Mann's *Dr. Faustus* than in any real correspondence, is that Kafka clearly means exactly what he says. Writing is another form of night game, and it too serves the devil. But in what way?

The answer comes in two stages: 'It is vanity and a thirst for pleasure that keeps on buzzing round my face.' Vanity is the adoption of the upright position, the mighty hammer of the bronze man. To write is to control; more, it is to manipulate reality by a kind of magic; ultimately, it is to usurp the position of God himself. At this point vanity merges into something more difficult to understand, but which we have already touched upon in talking about Kafka's sense of not yet having been born. 'What simple souls sometimes wish: "I would like to die so as to see how I will be mourned", a writer of this kind achieves at all times.' Writing, in other words, is a way of having your death and staying alive. The imagination which is let loose in the act of writing can paint a thousand deaths as easily as a thousand lives, thus helping us to believe that we can avoid death. The supreme example of pride is the belief in our own immortality. That is the belief of the bronze man, but it is also the belief of the dominant, potent father. The bronze man and the father only come into existence as the result of the assertion of immortality by the self. But reality has a harsh way of dealing with those who wilfully distort it (for those, like his father, whose lives and actions were never in any way problematic, such considerations of course never apply; all Kafka is willing to say is that for those like himself, who perhaps come from a different world anyway, the above is true). He goes on, in the letter to Brod:

> There can be two main reasons for this fear of death. First a panic dread of death because one has not yet lived. I don't mean that to live one must have wife, children, fields and cattle. What is required in order to be alive is to give up seeking satisfaction in oneself, to go into the house instead of admiring it and wreathing it with flowers. . . The second reason – but in fact they are probably one and the same, at the moment I cannot tell them apart – is the following thought: 'The game I played is about to become reality. I have not redeemed myself with my writing. I have been dead all my life and now I am really going to die. My life was pleasanter than most, my death will be all the more terrible.'

To be alive in Kafka's sense does not mean to exist. It means understanding one's place in the world. But how is such understanding to be acquired, since we have no criteria for judging or measuring the world? The imagination, which had appeared to provide contact with some transcendental source, turns out to be only an instrument of the vanity of the self, avidly shielding the self from the reality of things, above all from the reality of death. And because we have not yet begun to live we cannot even die. Like the Hunter Gracchus, we are doomed to a perpetual wandering about the world, never laid to rest. This is indeed the Wilderness in which Kafka feels he has been wandering for close on forty years:

I think that I am continually skirting the wilderness and am full of childish hopes (particularly as regards women) that 'perhaps I shall keep in Canaan after all' – when all the while I have been decades in the wilderness and these hopes are merely mirages born of despair, especially at those times when I am the wretchedest of creatures in the desert too, and Canaan is perforce my only Promised Land, for no third place exists for mankind.

THE TRUTH

And yet the extraordinary letter to Brod does not end there. Kafka reverts to the cause of his meditations and goes on:

> My dread of the trip also stems from the thought that I shall have to leave my writing table for a few days at least. And this ridiculous thought is really the only one that is justified, for a writer's life truly depends on his writing-table, in fact he is never allowed to leave it if he wishes to avoid going mad, he has no alternative but to cling to it even with his teeth.

Despite everything Kafka can no more stop writing than he can stop breathing. And, if we look back over his work we can begin to see that there is a kind of cunning as well as helplessness in this. For all his work, from 'The Judgement' on is instinctively aware of the impossibility of art in the wilderness, and it evolves a strategy for overcoming this. (I say 'it' and not 'he' because Kafka was certainly not fully conscious of why his work evolved the way it did, certainly not before 1917.) In fact, in his hands, art becomes a weapon for the defeat of the bronze man, of the father, of the lies inherent in art itself.

'Truth is indivisible, hence it cannot recognise itself; anyone who wants to recognise it has to be a lie.' And it is possible to be a lie in such a way as gradually to bring all lies to the surface and so let the truth stand revealed. Marthe Robert, in her excellent short study of Kafka, has pointed out how often Kafka's writing consists of an initial affirmation ('The Great Wall of China has been completed at its most northerly point'), followed by a gathering torrent of qualification, which eventually robs the affirmation of all meaning. Kafka's strategy for making the truth gradually reveal itself relies on infinite patience: 'All human errors are impatience, the premature breaking off of what is methodical, the apparent fencing in of the apparent thing.' That is why the writing of 'The Judgement' was so important to him; in the course of that long night he felt that he had really been able to hold on to the thread until, inch by inch, without hurry but without dawdling, he had reached the very centre of his labyrinth, and found the minotaur, and returned alive.

But the writing of 'The Judgement' was important for another reason. If all error stems from the apparent fencing in of the apparent thing, then all stories, which begin and end, are the products and the disseminators of error. At the centre of the story usually stands the hero, with whom we as readers usually identify. This, we can say, is the innocence of the story. 'The Judgement' is about the end of innocence. It starts with the hero, George Bendemann, solidly rooted in the world. He is engaged to be married, he gazes dreamily up from a letter he is writing, his life spreads satisfyingly before him. His mother is dead, his father old and weak, the friend to whom he is writing a failure in distant Russia. It ends with the father standing over him, sentencing him to death, and with George carrying out the sentence, letting himself drop off the bridge into the river below, as 'the unending stream of traffic' rumbles over the bridge. It is as though Kafka had sat down to write with all the possibilities open in front of him, and was then led, *by his writing*, out of this meaningless world of an endlessly open future into the sudden necessary thrust of the inevitable end. Kafka's father had repeatedly told him to stop writing and live. But writing itself stands under the sign of the father – the sign of hardness, dogmatic assertion, the transformation of the arbitrary into the falsely natural. Writing *is* George Bendemann dreaming, at the start of the story, with all the rest of the world in the shadows. So Kafka writes in such a way that writing destroys itself and he is thus momentarily free of the father, of the anguish of the vertical position. Thus the story of the triumph of a father over his son becomes the story of the triumph of the son over the father.

'Josephine the Singer, or the Mouse Folk' is the last story Kafka wrote – he was correcting the proofs of it when he died. Kafka has come a long way in those twelve years since the writing of 'The Judgement', but the strategy has hardly changed. Once again the story is a *space* for a conflict of interests. As always, it is a conflict which runs so deep that no real clash can ever take place. This time there is not even a confrontation between the two forces; it is as though the story were about George and the traffic on the bridge not George and his father. Josephine stops singing because the people won't acknowledge her authority. She stops to spite them. They are a little sad, but shrug their shoulders and carry on. She is the loser – silent now, she will soon be forgotten. Writing here manages to express its own necessity and its uselessness. It never touches the world at any point, yet for him who is engaged upon it it is of vital importance. Neither side is right, the truth, which can only be shown, never stated, is that both have to be experienced simultaneously. In 'The Judgement' and 'Metamorphosis' death was a kind of finality (though Blanchot is surely right to point out that the horror of the latter story is compounded by the sister's final gesture of hope, which reminds us so forcibly of the absurd hope of the beetle-brother right up to the moment of his death). In 'Josephine', as in 'The Hunger-Artist' and 'The Burrow', the individual, with his desires, his sense of his own importance, his own immortality, is *decentralised:* we are made to live at the same time with his intolerable anguish, his inability to see beyond the bounds of what he can imagine, *and* with that which is not him, which it is beyond even the richest imagination to conceive. This is truly an art adapted to the peculiar condition of existence in the Wilderness, an art which *is* the truth because of the way in which it forces the lie of writing itself out into the open.

THE BLOOD

Though Kafka could never give up writing, and felt, in his paradoxical way, that if it was damnation it was also his only hope of salvation, he nevertheless longed for something else: 'Somewhere help is waiting and the beaters are driving me there.' And drive him there they did. In the letter he wrote to Felice breaking off their second engagement there lurks a strange sense of triumph, as if, after all the striving and uncertainty, he was about to enter the house at last:

> Here is the reason for my silence: two days after my last letter, precisely four weeks ago, at about 5 a.m. I had a haemorrhage of the lung. Fairly severe; for 10 minutes or more it gushed out of my throat; I thought it would never stop. The next day I went to see a doctor... Without going into all the medical details, the outcome is that I have tuberculosis of both lungs. That I should suddenly develop some disease does not surprise me; nor did the sight of blood; for years my insomnia and headaches have invited a serious illness, and ultimately my maltreated blood has to burst forth; but that it should be of all things tuberculosis, that at the age of 34 I should be struck down overnight, with not a single predecessor anywhere in the family – this does surprise me. Well, I have to accept it; actually my headaches seem to have been washed away with the flow of blood. Its course at present cannot be foreseen; its future development remains its secret; my age may possibly help to retard it. Next week I am going into the country for at least three months, to Ottla in Zürau...

As Walter Benjamin put it: 'Because the most forgotten alien land is one's own body one can understand why Kafka called the cough that erupted within him "the animal". It was the most advanced outpost of the great herd.'

A MACHINE FOR BREATHING

He died eight years later, of tubercular laryngitis. In his last days he was unable to speak and could only write down on bits of paper what he wanted to communicate. Then he was not able to do that either, and then he died. As we dwell on that painful death and on the tortured life that preceded it, we would do well to recall what he said in an early letter to Max Brod. Brod had published an article on contemporary German writers and had included Kafka's name among them. This was in 1907 and Kafka had not yet published anything. He wrote to Brod, suggesting that people would find it hard to see what his name was doing there in the midst of all these well-known people. The only reason he can think of, he says, is the following:

> A group of names which ends with Meyrink (obviously a hedgehog rolled up into a ball) is impossible at the start of a phrase if the other phrases are to breathe at all. It follows that a name with an open vowel at the end – inserted at this point – represents for the words in question the respiratory apparatus which saves them. My merit in the affair is slender.

In its modesty and wit, as well as in its quite physical relation to language, such a passage seems to catch the precise feel of Kafka's writing. It is also strangely accurate. His work, like his life, does not carve out a space for itself (which would mean elbowing someone else out of the way). What it does is to allow us – readers, writers – to breathe, even here in the Wilderness. That is why it is as new today as it was fifty years ago, why it lives for us and in us as do his eyes staring out from those cruel, cluttered photographs.

Notes

1. Franz Kafka, *Letters to Felice*, ed. Erich Heller and Jürgen Born, trs. James Stern and Elisabeth Duckworth (New York: Schocken Books; London: Secker & Warburg, 1973).
2. *Der Andere Prozess: Kafkas Briefe an Felice* (Munich: Carl Hanser Verlag, 1969).
3. Grete Bloch's role in Kafka's life is still a mystery. There is no doubt that when he had broken with Felice, and even after they had partly made it up, it was to her that he addressed his strange, reticent, yet clearly passionate letters (they are included in the volume with the letters to Felice). Years later she claimed to have had a child by Kafka which subsequently died, but the evidence does not seem to support this.

2 Fernando Pessoa, 1888-1935

Whatever you say, don't say it twice
If you find your ideas in anyone else, disown them.
The man who hasn't signed anything, who has left no picture,
Who was not there, who said nothing:
How can they catch him?
Cover your tracks.

> Brecht, from the first poem in
> *The Handbook for City Dwellers*

When I think of what is most radical in the literature of the past hundred years, of what embodies most clearly the essential spirit of modernism, I think of five grey-suited gentlemen: Constantin Cavafy, Franz Kafka, T. S. Eliot, Fernando Pessoa, Jorge Luis Borges.

Each belongs to a city and has made that city his own: Alexandria, Prague, London, Lisbon, Buenos Aires. All five, men of great courtesy and great reserve; solitary men, with few close friends though many acquaintances, without families though with their fair share of wives, mistresses and lovers; men profoundly aware of the traditions embodied in the stones of the cities through which they walk, though perhaps only because in their bones they feel themselves for ever removed from every tradition and even from history itself; men whose lives contain little that is dramatic or extraordinary, and who clearly chose such an existence consciously and deliberately, though some of them, like Kafka, may at times have longed for another, fuller, more active, more meaningful existence. They are the true revolutionaries of our era. Though they spoke quietly, made little or no effort to publish, were all, except for Eliot, unknown to the larger public till long after they had written their best work, they are the ones who have renewed the language and shown us a way forward.

Perhaps the strangest, the most inaccessible of them all is Fernando Pessoa, whose name, by a curious coincidence, is cognate with the Latin *persona*, or mask. 'Poets', Octavio Paz has said, 'have no biography. Their work is their biography ... Nothing in their lives is surprising – nothing, except for their poems.' This is true, but it is also true that to suppress one's life, wipe out one's biography, requires effort, patience, cunning. And the way that effort, that patience, that cunning, is deployed in the interests of anonymity, can reveal a great deal about the nature of the poetry that emerges. Unless we recognise that there is a dialectic at work here, that poem and writer are not two separate entities, though they are not one, that, as Eliot, has said, 'only those who have personality and emotions know what it means to want to escape from these things', we are likely to fall into the trap of reading literature as though it consisted merely of aesthetic objects created for our disinterested contemplation. Whereas what distinguishes the writers I have mentioned is the doggedness of their pursuit not of beauty but of truth.

Pessoa was born in 1888, the same year as Eliot. His father was a civil servant and music critic in Lisbon. One of his ancestors, Sancho Pessoa de Cunha, was a Jew, condemned by the Inquisition in 1706. His grandfather wrote light verse. Many of his ancestors were tuberculous, and his grandmother, who lived with them in the big house in the centre of the city, was slowly going mad, though she continued to dwell with the family till her death.

Five years after Pessoa's birth, his father died. Two years later his mother married again. Her new husband was the temporary Consul of Portugal in Durban, and in the following year, 1896, she and her son sailed for South Africa to join him. Pessoa was sent to English schools – as with Cavafy and Borges, English was to remain a living language for him all his life and its literature to play an important part in his development. He was a brilliant student, even winning, in 1903, the Queen Victoria Memorial Essay Prize, ahead of nearly nine hundred candidates for most of whom English was a native language. Two years later, however, he returned to Lisbon. He was seventeen. From South Africa he seems to have taken nothing: no memories, no friendships – only a thorough grasp of English. He was never in his life to refer to those ten years.

Back in Portugal he briefly attended University, but soon gave up; started a publishing venture which failed; and then became a commercial translator for Lisbon business firms. Despite a few offers later on of academic and literary posts, he kept to this job for the rest of his life: it was not arduous, and it provided him with a useful alibi.

Soon though he was publishing critical articles and poems in little reviews. He took to writing at his business addresses and even in cafés, and was well known in the avant-garde circles of pre-war Lisbon. His closest friend at that time was the brilliant but unstable poet, Mário de Sá-Carneiro, who was quick to recognise his genius. Soon Mário moved to Paris, and from there he kept Pessoa informed of the activities of the avant-garde: Picasso, Apollinaire, Max Jacob. But on 26 April 1916

Mário de Sá-Carneiro took his own life in a hotel bedroom in Montmartre, dressed in full evening dress, by swallowing down five doses of strychnine. Pessoa was twenty-eight, Mário twenty-five. For a few more years Pessoa stayed at the forefront of the Portuguese avant-garde, writing, talking, even editing one of the brashest of the little reviews of the time. He remained, however, a very private man, living first with his family, then alone; dressing with the utmost correctness; a man of few gestures in a peninsula of gesticulators; smoking up to eighty cigarettes a day; drinking more than was good for him, though no-one ever saw him drunk. At one time or another he ran an accountancy journal; wrote poetry under four different names; planned and perhaps even wrote a number of thrillers and a book on Shakespeare's life; decided to open an astrology parlour; dabbled in the Kabbalah; tried to decipher *Revelation*. Once, entering a café, he saw quite clearly a man's ribs through his clothes and skin; he had a premonition of Sá-Carneiro's death, and of an attack of apoplexy suffered by his mother when she was in Pretoria and he in Lisbon. At the end of his life he claimed to be a Rosicrucian, though the order was theoretically extinct.

In 1920 he had a brief affair with an employee of one of the firms he worked for. After a few months he broke it off, writing later to the girl: 'My destiny belongs under another Law, of which you don't even suspect the existence, Ophelia, and it is more and more subordinated to the obedience of Masters who neither allow nor pardon.' In 1934 his first and only book of poems was published. It was put together when the Secretariat for National Propaganda offered prizes for the two best poems on patriotic themes. The prize for the best long poem went to a Franciscan priest for a tedious diatribe against Communism; the other prize went to Pessoa. At this time though he had begun to make plans for the publication of what he considered his major writings, and he was still working on this project when he died, in November 1935, of acute hepatitis. Twelve volumes of his poems, essays, letters and philosophical reflections have been published, in Portugal and Brazil, where he is recognised as second only to Camões in the pantheon of Portuguese letters. There is probably as much again that still remains unpublished.

Such are the facts, and they do not help us much. Indeed, it would be foolish to expect them to. For what do even such intimate documents as letters really tell us when the letter-writer is so ironic and reticent a man as Pessoa? How can one tell what was going on in the mind and spirit of a man who once solemnly confided to a correspondent: 'Today I have decided to effect a major change in my life: I have decided to remove the circumflex accent from my name.'?

Perhaps though it is not his mind that we should try to examine, or his daily activities, but rather the relation between the various aspects of his life, and in particular the way he viewed his own relations to his art.

All his life Pessoa had been an enthusiastic and prolific creator of pseudonyms, personae, masks. On 8 March 1914, however, an event took place which was to change his life and the basis of his relations to his own inventions. This event is documented in a letter Pessoa wrote twenty years later to Casais Monteiro, and it is so strange an occurrence that it is worth quoting the letter in some detail.

After saying that since childhood he had created imaginary worlds and beings with the greatest of ease, he goes on:

Around 1912, I believe, I had the idea of writing a few poems in a pagan mode. I sketched in a few thoughts in irregular verse, then abandoned the project. However, in the semi-darkness of these gropings, the vague portrait of the person who had written such things had begun to take shape for me (without my knowing it, Ricardo Reis had just been born.) A year or two yater, I decided one day to play a practical joke on Sá-Carneiro – by inventing a bucolic poet of a rather complex kind, and introducing him to his works. I spent several days developing this fictive poet, but failed to give him life. One day, when I had finally given up all thought of the project – it was 8 March 1914 – I walked over to a high desk and, taking a sheet of paper, began to write standing up, as I always do when I can. And I wrote thirty-odd poems without interruption, in a sort of ecstasy whose nature I cannot define. It was the triumphal day of my life; I will never again know a day like it. I began with a title: 'The Guardian of the Flock'. And what followed the title was the appearance within me of someone to whom I there and then gave the name of Alberto Caeiro. Excuse the absurdity of the expression, but: In me had appeared my master. Such was the immediate sensation that flooded through me. So much so that as soon as those thirty-odd poems had been written I immediately seized another sheet of paper and wrote, also without a pause, the six poems which constitute the 'Oblique Rain' of Fernando Pessoa ... It was the return of Fernando Pessoa/Alberto Caeiro to Fernando Pessoa alone. Or rather, it was the reaction of Fernando Pessoa to his non-existence in the face of Alberto Caeiro.

This is strange enough, but more is to follow. He goes on:

After Alberto Caeiro had appeared – instinctively and unconsciously – I sought disciples for him. I wrenched the latent Ricardo Reis from his false paganism, discovered his name, and gave him to himself, as it were, for in that moment I already *saw* him. And, suddenly, a derivation directly opposed to Ricardo Reis, a new individual, surged within me. In one go, and at the typewriter, without interruption or correction, the *Triumphal Ode* of Álvaro de Campos surged forth – the triumphal ode with that name and the man with the name he carries.

I then invented a non-existent *coterie*. I gave the whole thing a realistic form. I graded influences, friendships, overheard discussions, divergencies of values, and in all this it seemed to me that it was I, the inventor of it all, who was the least real. It seemed as if everything took place independently of me. And this still seems to me to be the case. If one day I still decide to publish the aesthetic discussion that took place between Ricardo Reis and Álvaro de Campos, you will see how different they are, and how I am nothing in this matter . . .

A few further remarks on the subject . . . I see before me, in the colourless but real space of dreams, the face, the gestures, of Caeiro, of Ricardo Reis and Álvaro de Campos. I constructed their ages and their lives. Ricardo Reis was born in 1887 (I cannot recall the day or the month, but I noted them down somewhere), in Porto. He is a doctor and is at present in Brazil. Alberto Caeiro was born in 1889 and died in 1915; he was born in Lisbon but lived in the country for most of his life. He's never had a profession, and hardly any education. Álvaro de Campos was born in Tavira on 15 October 1890 (at 1.30 p.m., Ferreira Gomez informs me . . .). He is, as you know, a naval engineer, with a degree from Glasgow, but he now lives here, in Lisbon, without any occupation. Caeiro was of medium height, and though in reality frail (he died of tuberculosis), he looked sturdier than he was. Ricardo Reis is a little smaller, but hardy; sturdier, but dry. Álvaro de Compos is big (1m. 75 – 2 cms taller than me), thin, and with a tendency to stoop. All three are clean-shaven – Caeiro blond, blue-eyed; Reis dark with a lustreless skin; Campos neither dark nor fair, vaguely the Portuguese Jew type, but with smooth hair, combed back, and a monocle. Caeiro, as we know, received little education – primary schooling only; his father and mother died early, and he lived at home, off a small annuity. He lived with an old aunt – a great-aunt. Ricardo Reis, educated at a Jesuit college, is, as I have said, a doctor; he's lived in Brazil since 1919, in voluntary exile, since he's a monarchist; he's a Latinist by education, and a self-taught Hellenist. Álvaro de Campos received a common secondary education, after which he was sent to Scotland to study engineering, first mechanical, then naval. During one of his holidays he travelled in the East, as a consequence of which he wrote the 'Opiario'. His Latin was taught him by an uncle in Beira, a priest.

How do I write in the name of these three? ... Caeiro through simple and unexpected inspiration, without knowing how or what I am going to write. Ricardo Reis after abstract deliberation, which suddenly finds concreteness in an ode. Campos when I suddenly feel the need to write I know not what.

... Caeiro wrote Portuguese badly, Campos writes it quite well, though with errors ...; Reis writes better than I do, but with a purism which I consider excessive.

I have quoted so much of this letter not only because of the intrinsic interest of what it says, but also because it shows very clearly the way Pessoa coped with what was obviously a crucial event in his life and in his career as a poet. 'In me had appeared my master.' The echo of Dante may not be intentional, but that makes no difference. Dante had written, in the opening of the *Vita Nuova*, of his first sight of Beatrice, and of his sudden sense that the sight had altered his life for ever:

She appeared to me dressed in a very noble, modest and proper crimson colour, belted and bejewelled in a manner suited to her great youth. At this point I say truthfully that the spirit of life which dwells in the most secret chamber of the heart began to tremble so violently that it was dreadfully apparent in my slightest pulse; and trembling it spoke these words: *Ecce Deus fortior me, qui veniens dominabitur mihi.*

Dante is immediately overcome, and he goes on: 'From then on I say that Love ruled my soul, which was instantly subjected to him, and began to have such ascendancy and dominion over me through the power my imagination perceived in him, that I had no choice but to submit completely to his every whim.'

The intrusion of a 'Master' in Pessoa's life has exactly the same impact as it had for Dante: a power larger than him has taken him over. There is no doubting it or denying it, and the only question becomes: What does a human being do who has been called in this way?[1] The letter to Casais Monteiro outlines what Pessoa did: he submitted. Fernando Pessoa died and in his place not one but three poets were born. Yet in actual fact he did not die, and even as a poet he did not die. Throughout the rest of his life he wrote poetry not only in the name of the three heteronymns (he insisted on this appellation, since they were clearly far more than pseudonyms), but also in his own name. His own poetry, though, was bound to be affected. As he says in the letter, it became the poetry of Fernando Pessoa reacting to his own non-existence in the face of Caeiro, Reis and de Campos.

The night of 8 March 1914, then, was a watershed in Pessoa's life –

as the night of 22 September 1912 had been in that of Kafka. Before, he was a dilettante, writing verse in English and Portuguese with equal facility, living perhaps with an image of himself as poet, but essentially drifting. After that, everything was clear. The call had come, he would devote his life to responding to it. Let us see then if we can define a little more clearly the nature of that response by turning to the poetry of the three heteronyms.

As the letter makes clear, everything really started with the appearance of Caeiro. Caeiro was not only Pessoa's own master, but also that of the other two. What kind of person is he and what kind of poetry does he write?

In some notes written in English Pessoa says: 'To a world plunged in various kinds of subjectivisms, he brings Absolute Nature back again . . . Far from seeing sermons in stones, he never even lets himself conceive a stone as being a sermon. The only sermon a stone contains for him is that it exists . . . Out of this sentiment, or rather, absence of sentiment, he makes poetry.' Poem 14 of 'The Guardian of the Flock' contains the lines:

Olho e comovo-me,
Comovo-me como a água corre quando o chão é inclinado,
E a minha poesia é natural como o levantar-se o vento . . .

I look, and am moved,
Moved just as water flows where the ground slopes,
And my poetry comes as naturally as the wind rises . . .

[33][2]

Like Wallace Stevens, Caeiro not only feels no need to go beyond immediate reality, he sees the desire to do so as a form of dehumanisation:

Porque o único sentido oculto das coisas
É elas não terem sentido oculto nenhum.

. . . .

As coisas são o único sentido oculto das coisas.

For the only hidden meaning of things
Is that they have no hidden meaning at all.

. . . .

Things are the only hidden meaning of things. [41]

Caeiro is a natural. Jonathan Griffin[3] has likened him to a Zen master, and quotes a memoir of Caeiro 'written' by Campos, in which the latter is made to say: 'And I suddenly asked my master Caeiro, "are you content with yourself?" And he answered: "No: I am content." It was like the voice of the earth, which is all and nothing.' Here, however, we come up against a snag. It is not for nothing that the words of a Zen or Hassidic master are recorded by disciples. For if you are as much at one with the world as you claim to be, why should you feel the need to write at all? Poem 14 of 'The Guardian of the Flocks', from which I have already quoted, grows half-conscious of this contradiction, but quickly represses it:

Penso e escrevo como as flores têm cor
Mas com menos perfeição no meu modo de exprimir-me
Porque me falta a simplicidade divina
De ser todo só o meu exterior.

Olho e comovo-me . . .

I think and write, just as flowers have colour,
But with less perfection in the way I express myself,
For I lack the godlike simplicity
Of being nothing but my outward self.

I look, and am moved . . .   [33]

There is a basic contradiction between simply being, and writing a poem about simply being, because poems are not like flowers, they do not grow by themselves, but are made, and to try and suppress that fact can only lead to bad poetry and sentimentality, as in the following poem:

Quando a erva crescer em cima da minha sepultura,
Seja esse o sinal para me esquecerem de todo.
A Natureza nunca se recorda, e por isso é bela.
E se tiverem a necessidade doentia de 'interpretar'
A erva verde sobre a minha sepultura,
Digam que eu continuo a verdecer e a ser natural.

When the grass grows over my tomb,
Let this be the sign that I be totally forgotten.
Nature never remembers, that is why she is so beautiful.
And if you have the unhealthy need to 'interpret'
The green grass which will grow over my tomb,
Say that I continue to grow green and to be natural.

There is a story by Borges called 'Funes the Memorious'. It tells of a
man rather like Caeiro, a man who cut right through the abstractions
of thought and lived directly among the objects of the world:

> We, at one glance, can perceive three glasses on a table; Funes, all the
> leaves and tendrils and fruit that make up a grape vine. He knew by
> heart the forms of the southern clouds at dawn on the 30th. April,
> 1882, and could compare them in his memory with the mottled
> streaks on a book in Spanish binding he had only seen once and with
> the outlines of the foam raised by an oar in the Río Negro the night
> before the Quebracho uprising ... Not only was it difficult for him to
> comprehend that the generic symbol *dog* embraces so many unlike
> individuals of diverse size and form; it bothered him that the dog at
> three fourteen (seen from the side) should have the same name as the
> dog at three fifteen (seen from the front) ...'

What Borges presents us with, however, is a monster. It is not just that
Funes is paralysed. His physical disability is only an aspect of a mental
paralysis, for the very openness of his senses to impressions has made
him in effect incapable of action and of thought. What his story reveals
is the implication of the old Romantic dream: not a happy unity with
nature, but the utter breakdown of the self in the face of undifferenti-
ated impressions.

Funes is a fictional creation, just as Caeiro is, but where Borges can
put him back to bed when the story is over, the link of Caeiro with the
extraordinary experience of 8 March 1914 meant that Pessoa was
saddled with this unreal and unlikely figure for the rest of his life.
However, what in practice happened was that Pessoa allowed doubt to
creep into Caeiro's poetry, so that gradually it became not so much
Caeiro's as that of Pessoa-aware-of Caeiro:

> Acho tão natural que não se pense
> Que me ponho a rir às vezes, sòzinho,
> Não sei bem de quê, mas é de qualquer coisa
> Que tem que ver com haver gente que pensa ...
>
> Que pensará o meu muro da minha sombra?
> Pergunto-me às vezes isto até dar por mim
> A perguntar-me coisas ...
> E então desagrado-me, e incomodo-me
> Como se desse por mim com um pé dormente ...
>
> To me it seems so natural not to think
> That sometimes I start laughing to myself
> At what? I'm not quite sure, but something
> To do with the idea of people thinking ...

What will my wall think of my shadow?
That's what I sometimes wonder – till I notice
That I'm wondering,
And then I feel annoyed and ill at ease,
As if I found my foot had gone to sleep ...   [40]

This then is what seems to happen: the poems either suppress any hint of self-consciousness, and then grow false and sentimental; or they allow self-consciousness to creep in and turn it into drama, which makes for good poetry but does not really correspond to the *persona* of Alberto Caeiro created by Pessoa. In fact, despite all Pessoa's efforts to *create* Caeiro – the invention of a biography, of physical characteristics and the rest of it – the poems move away from the control of the heteronym into a quite different area of experience. And this, we will see, is what happens to the other two heteronyms as well: the creation of Caeiro, Reis and Campos on that day in March 1914 was a way of coping with an event without precedent or analogy in Pessoa's life. But, as we will see, they are not a solution for the poet whose quest is for truth at all costs. They are only a stage on the journey towards the shedding not just of the self that is Fernando Pessoa, but of the safety of any nameable self at all.

Ricardo Reis, according to Pessoa, is a disciple of Caeiro. One could say that he is a Caeiro with room made in him for mythology and history as well as Nature, but that would not be quite accurate. He is the heteronym who certainly loses most in translation, for his poems are highly wrought and Latinate in a way which Portuguese can achieve but which English, being much further away from Latin, cannot with any semblance of ease. They are extraordinary poems, the like of which had not been seen in Portuguese verse since Camoẽs, though their translatable content is that of a simple, resigned Stoicism:

Vê de longe a vida.
Nunca a interrogues.
Ela nada pode
Dizer-te. A resposta
Está além dos deuses.

View life from afar.
Ask it no questions.
It can tell you
Nothing. The answer
Lies beyond the gods.   [54]

Like the early Stevens, Reis wages a continuing polemic against Christianity for its call to the unquiet heart:

Vós que, crentes em Cristos e Marias,
Turvais da minha fonte as claras águas
Só para me dizerdes
Que há águas de outra espécie

Banhando prados com melhores horas, –
Dessas outras regiões pra que falar-me
Se estas águas e prados
São de aqui e me agradam?

Ye who believing in Christs and in Marys
Trouble the limpid water of my spring
Merely to tell me
That there are waters of another kind

Bathing meadows in better times, –
Why speak to me of those other regions
If these waters, these meadows
Are of here and now and delight me?

Why should we not be content with the reality that is all around us? Why should we constantly be searching for something else, for *an* answer, for salvation? The poem ends:

Inúteis procos do melhor que a vida,
Deixai a vida aos crentes mais antigos
Que a Cristo e a sua cruz
E Maria chorando.

Ceres, dona dos campos, me console
E Apolo e Vénus, e Urano antigo
E os trovões, com o interesse
De irem da mão de Jove.

Ye who vainly woo what is better than life,
Leave life to believers in older things
Than Christ and his cross,
And Mary weeping.

Ceres, mistress of the fields, be my comfort,
Apollo and Venus too, and aged Uranus,
And the thunderbolts which fascinate
By coming from the hand of Jove.   [52]

(It is interesting to note that the word 'procos' at the start of the penultimate stanza is not Portuguese at all; Pessoa/Reis has coined it for the occasion, basing it on the Latin *procus*, wooer, suitor.)

If Caeiro recapitulates in his verse Rousseauan Romanticism, Reis may be said to recapitulate Parnassianism. It is an amazing achievement for a twentieth-century poet, but it is basically an exercise in antiquarianism. There is something false and unreal about the Stoic stance, which too often emerges in the poems as an elaborate kind of make-believe:

Vem sentar-te comigo, Lídia, à beira do rio.
Sossegadamente fitemos o seu curso e aprendamos
Que a vida passa, e não estamos de mãos enlaçadas.
(Enlacemos as mãos).
· · · · · · · · ·
Amemo-nos tranquilamente, pensando que podíamos,
Se quiséssemos, trocar beijos e abraços e carícias,
Mas que mais vale estarmos sentados ao pé um do outro
Ouvindo correr o rio e vendo-o.
· · · · · · · · ·
E se antes do que eu levares o óbolo ao barqueiro sombrio,
Eu nada terei que sofrer ao lembrar-me de ti.
Ser-me-ás suave à memória lembrando-te assim – à beira-rio,
Pagã triste e com flores no regaço.

Come sit by my side, Lydia, on the bank of the river.
Calmly let us watch it flow, and learn
That life passes, and we are not holding hands.
(Let us hold hands).
· · · · · · · · ·
Let us love each other calmly, with the thought that we could,
If we chose, freely kiss and caress and embrace,
But that we do better to be seated side by side
Hearing the river flow, and seeing it.
· · · · · · · · ·
And if, before me, you take the obol to the gloomy boatman,
I shall have no cause to suffer when I remember you.
You will be sweet to my memory if I remember you thus, on the
    river bank,
A sorrowful pagan maid, with flowers in her lap.   [50]

The sentiment is cloying and unreal; the whole paraphernalia of Lydias, obols, gloomy boatmen and the rest creates the impression of a stage-set rather than real life. There is of course nothing intrinsically impossible about writing a fine poem in an artificial mode – if there were, most Renaissance poetry would have to be dismissed. The trouble here is that the poems present themselves as direct, as the expression of a philosophy of life; there is no tension in the language which would serve as a means of alerting us to its artificiality. We are closer to Huysmans than to Spenser, Marvell or Camoẽs.

However, as with Caeiro, the *persona* of Reis soon starts to blur at the edges. Despite Pessoa's virtuoso control, his loving antiquarianism, there are moments in many of the poems of Reis which belong not to him but to Pessoa-aware-of-Reis:

Nada, senão o instante, me conhece.
Minha mesma lembrança é nada, e sinto
Que quem sou e quem fui
São sonhos diferentes.

Nothing knows me, save the moment.
My memory itself a void, I feel
That who I am and who I was
Are different dreams.   [63]

This poem, significantly, was written in 1930, sixteen years after the creation of the heteronyms. By then they had outlived their usefulness.

The third heteronym, and the easiest to place, is Álvaro de Campos, the 'modern' poet. In 1914 the painter Santa Rita had returned to Lisbon from Paris, bringing with him a copy of Marinetti's *Futurist Manifesto*. In the following year the avant-garde review *Orpheu* was founded, with the avowed aim of giving expression to all that had hitherto been considered inexpressible. The first number contained poems by Sá-Carneiro and 'Álvaro de Campos'. One of these was that 'Triumphal Ode' which Pessoa had written at one go on the fateful night of 8 March. The reaction of the press was as extreme and virulent as any young group of artists could have wished for. Some critics even suggested that the contributors were insane. The truth was more prosaic: they were only producing Portuguese versions of Whitman and Marinetti. Here, for example, are a few lines from another ode by de Campos, also written in 1914, but only published after Pessoa's death:

Vem, Noite antiquíssima e idêntica,
Noite Rainha nascida destronada,
Noite igual por dentro ao silêncio, Noite
Com as estrelas lantejoulas rápidas
No teu vestido franjado de Infinito.

Vem, vagamente,
Vem, levemente,
Vem sòzinha, solene, com as mãos caídas
Ao teu lado, vem
E traz os montes longínquos para o pé das árvores próximas,
Funde num campo teu todos os campos que vejo,
Faze da montanha um bloco só do teu corpo,
Apaga-lhe todas as diferenças que de longe vejo . . .

. . . .

Vem, dolorosa,
Mater-Dolorosa das Angústias dos Tímidos,
Turris-Eburnea das Tristezas Dos Desprezados,
Mão fresca sobre a testa em febre dos Humildes,
Sabor de água sobre os lábios secos dos Cansados.
Vem, lá do fundo
Do horizonte lívido,
Vem e arranca-me . . .

Come, age-old, never-changing Night,
Night born a queen without a throne,
Night inwardly the same as silence, Night
With starry sequins fleeting
In your robe fringed with the Infinite.

Come, dimly seen,
Come, lightly felt,
Come in lone majesty, holding your hands
Limp at your sides, come
And bring the far-off hills close to the trees near-by,
Merge in one field of yours all the fields I see,
Make the mountain one mass with the shape of your body,
Blot out from it all the features I see from afar . . .

. . . .

Come in sorrow,
Mater-Dolorosa to the Anguish of the Timid,
Turris-Eburnea to the Distress of the Despised,
Cool hand on the fevered brow of the Humble,
Taste of water on the parched lips of the Weary.
Come from the remoteness
Of the wan horizon,
Come and pluck me . . .   [19]

There is no reason for such a poem to end. It only stops when the aggressive self gives up. It is poetry of the super-ego, and what it does is to assert the triumph of the self, and with it of machines, war and destruction. But the silence is always there, waiting; the ode tries to shut out awareness of this, but sooner or later it is forced to recognise it. After the initial whirlwind burst of rhetoric even the poetry of de Campos began to acknowledge the existence of this silence – poems like 'In the Terror of the Night', which deal with the horror of the paths not taken, of the words not said; or the poem called 'Birthday', with its desperate cry: 'Stop it, heart of mine;/Don't think! Leave thinking to the head!' Like Pessoa's other attempts to hive off the mystery of the self, with its awareness of non-self and its steady drift towards the ultimate otherness of death, the creation of Álvaro de Campos is doomed to failure. And even more clearly than with Caeiro or Reis we can witness, in the course of the next twenty years, the disintegration of the *persona* of the marine engineer, as poems issue from his pen which have little to do with the image of him so lovingly created by Pessoa and recalled in the letter to Casais Monteiro. In this poem of January 1935, for example, we encounter a wit and irony quite foreign to de Campos, or indeed to any of the heteronyms:

Os antigos invocavam as Musas.
Nós invocamo-nos a nós mesmos.
Não sei se as Musas apareciam –
Seria sem dúvida conforme o invocado e a invocação. –
Mas sei que nós não aparecemos.
Quantas vezes me tenho debruçado
Sobre o poço que me suponho
E balido 'Ah!' para ouvir um eco,
E não tenho ouvido mais que o visto –
O vago alvor escuro com que a água resplandece
Lá na inutilidade do fundo . . .
Nenhum eco para mim . . .
Só vagamente uma cara,
Que deve ser a minha, por não poder ser de outro.
É uma coisa quase invisível,
Excepto como luminosamente vejo
Lá no fundo . . .
No silêncio e na luz falsa do fundo . . .

Que Musa! . . .

The ancients used to invoke the Muses:
We invoke ourselves.
I don't know if the Muses ever came –

It would of course depend who was invoked and how –
But *we* don't come, I'm sure of that.
How many times have I peered
Into the well I fancy that I am
And plaintively cried 'Aah!', hoping for an echo
Yet heard no more than what I saw –
The dim dark brightness of a gleam of water,
Down in the pointless depths . . .
No echo for me . . .
Just an ill-defined face
Which must be mine (if not, whose could it be?).
It's something I can hardly see at all,
Except as clearly as I see
Down there . . .
In the bottom's silence and deceptive light . . .

Some Muse!   [32]

All at once the poetry seems to have woken up. It is no longer merely melancholy, or plaintive, or assertive, but sharp, humorous, cool. There is no reason at all to place it, as Pessoa has done, in the corpus of de Campos's poetry. It belongs rather with the best that Pessoa himself was to write in those last five years of his life and to sign with his own name. With these late poems we feel that he has at last found his true voice. But *whose* voice is that?

Pessoa's poetry had from the start been concerned with solipsism, with the mysteries of appearance and reality, with the paradox of the man dreaming he is a butterfly and waking to find that he is a butterfly dreaming he is a man: 'Dreaming that I slept not, I slept my dream', he writes (under the name of Alexander Search) in one of his English poems; and at the start of a sonnet, also written in English:

The world is woven all of dream and error
And but one sureness in our truth may lie —
That when we hold to ought our thinking's mirror
We know it not by knowing it thereby.

A series of poems written in Portuguese in 1914 elaborate on this theme, sometimes quite hauntingly, as in the sixth 'Station of the Cross':

Venho de longe a trago no perfil,
Em forma nevoenta e afastada,
O perfil de outro ser que desagrada
Ao meu actual recorte humano e vil.

Outrora fui talvez, não Boabdil,
Mas o sue mero último olhar, da estrada
Dado ao deixado vulto de Granada,
Recorte frio sob o unido anil . . .

I come from afar and bear in my profile,
If only in remote and misty form,
The profile of another being, at variance
With this base and human silhouette now mine.

Perhaps in former times I was, not Boabdil,
But merely his last look from the road
At the face of the Granada he was leaving,
A cold silhouette beneath the unbroken blue . . .   [3]

Despite all his efforts, as we have seen, the theme creeps into the poems
of the heteronyms, however inappropriate to them it may be. Occasionally he attempts a long poem in which the elaborated fiction tries to do
the work of image and statement: in de Campos's 'Tobacco-Shop', for
example, the poet's meditation is interrupted by the appearance at the
door of his shop in the house opposite of an 'ordinary person', the
'unmetaphysical Esteves', and we are made aware of the gap between
the dreaming poet and the reality of everyday life; or in Reis's poem
about the chess-players who go on concentrating on their abstract game
while barbarian hordes invade the city and the fighting, looting and
rape go on around them. But most often the tactics are the same: poem
after poem merely talks about the paradoxes of time and existence, self
and otherness. And this is where the importance of the heteronyms for
Pessoa's own development becomes manifest: what the creation of
Caeiro, Reis and de Campos did was to hive off all the strongest temptations of late Romantic poetry and purge the poet of the need to write
in these styles. His final poems, written in his own name, are very close
in spirit to Yeats's 'Circus Animals' Desertion', though Pessoa does
not play with the myth of the poet himself as Yeats was prepared to do.
But we have the same feeling as with late Yeats, that at last, after so
much posturing, we are coming close to the centre, to the secret source
of all the masks.

Before turning to these final poems, however, it is helpful to look for
a moment at the poem which make up the one volume Pessoa published
in his lifetime, *Mensagem* ('Message'). Though, as we have seen, it was
awarded a prize in a competition for the best patriotic poem, and
though it quite obviously deals with the past greatness of Portugal,
I can think of few poems more unpatriotic, or anti-patriotic than these.
For they deal not with Empire but with the loss of Empire, the in-

evitable loss of Empire. Ironically, they are also far more personal than any of the earlier first person poems and reflections:

Mar Português

Ó mar salgado, quanto do teu sal
São lágrimas de Portugal!
Por te cruzarmos, quantas mães choraram,
Quantos filhos em vão rezaram!
Quantas noivas ficaram por casar
Para que fosses nosso, ó mar!

Valeu a pena? Tudo vale a pena
Se a alma não é pequena.
Quem quer passar além do Bojador
Tem que passar além da dor.
Deus ao mar o perigo e o abismo deu,
Mas nele é que espelhou o céu.

O salty sea, how much of thee
Portugal shed as tears!
Because we crossed thee, how many mothers wept,
How many sons prayed to no avail!
How many plighted maids remained unwed
That we might possess thee, O sea!

Was it worth while? All is worth while
If only the soul be not base.
He who would sail beyond Cape Bojador
Must sail beyond the bourn of grief.
God gave the sea its dangers and its deeps,
But in it he mirrored heaven's own face.   [16]

Portugal once had the greatest Empire in the world; now she has practically nothing. But these poems are neither songs of triumph nor of mourning. They merely state the facts: the sea can never be ours, we can never possess any part of the earth, we don't in fact ever possess anything. The themes are taken up again in the untranslatable quatrain that forms an epitaph for Bartolomeo Diaz:

Jaz aqui, na pequena praia extrema,
O Capitão do Fim. Dobrado o Assombro,
O mar é o mesmo: já ninguém o tema!
Atlas, mostra alto o mundo no seu ombro.

Here, on the small strand of the extreme distance,
Lies the Captain of the End. When the Dread has passed,
The sea remains the same: let no one hereinafter fear it!
Another Atlas, he shows the world carried high on his shoulder.

The sea does not change, it endures for ever. But men die, and Empires, and all we thought to hold passes from us. Like the Jew, the Portuguese has felt in his bones the folly of imagining that it is possible to hold on to his possessions. Nevertheless, it is the instinct of man to hold, to possess, to make his own all that is other than himself. Pessoa denies neither aspect of the truth. In these lapidary poems, with their echoes, for English readers, of both 'Marina' and 'The Idea of Order at Key West', though they are less elegiac than either, Pessoa seems for the first time to come fully into his own. The poems of *Mensagem* carry a mythic resonance, but they do not, like those of David Jones or Charles Williams, impose myth on history. Rather, like the novels of William Golding, they press myth out of the solid substance of our own world and the stubborn facts of history. They are resonant with mystery because they are so crystal-clear.

The hardness, the lack of sentiment, the impression that these poems are not spoken or thought by anyone, but have always existed if only we had known how to find them – all this is also in evidence in the non-historical poems written in his own name by Pessoa in the last five years of his life. He has come a long way from Alexander Search, from de Campos and Reis and even Caeiro – but it is doubtful if he would have arrived where he has if it had not been for the engineer, the monarchist and the keeper of flocks:

O poeta é um fingidor.
Finge tão completamente
Que chega a fingir que é dor
A dor que deveras sente.

E os que lêem o que escreve,
Na dor lida sentem bem,
Não as duas que ele teve,
Mas só a que eles não têm.

E assim nas calhas de roda
Gira, a entreter a razão,
Esse comboio de corda
Que se chama o coração.

The poet's good at pretending,
Such a master of the art

He even manages to pretend
The pain he really feels is pain.

And those who read his written words
Feel, as they read of pain,
Not the two kinds that were his
But only the kind that's not theirs.

And so around its little track,
To entertain the mind,
Runs that clockwork train of ours,
The thing we call the heart.   [11]

The poem is called 'Autopsicografia', which I suppose can be translated
as 'Self-Analysis', but where the pseudo-scientific Greek title ironically
conveys the impossibility of the operation. For now the poem does not
merely tell what the poet feels or thinks; it has become a space where
self and other meet, and where the limits of self-analysis are mapped
out. There is no 'self' to analyse, for as we lean over ourselves to
analyse, what we find is a self leaning over, and this will repeat itself
for ever. Nevertheless, an advance has been made. Something has
happened in the course of the poem; something has been, if not understood, at least caught: the poet, figure of all men, in the act of writing,
of thinking, of trying to understand. The mechanical image of the last
stanza works quite differently from the images of ships and cars in de
Campos's Futurist outpourings. It is, after all, only a toy train, going
round and round on its little track. The train is not just an image of
the heart, but of the poem too: the words go round and round the
centre and never get any closer. And yet, strangely, as the reader encounters the poem he discovers that it is *his* heart that is the subject.

The poem as mechanical toy. It is an amazing discovery. With one
gesture a whole world of false postures and lifeless language is swept
away. The lapidary quality of the Latinate poems of Reis has at last
been turned to good use, and the reader finds himself able to move
round each word, each phrase, each stanza, for the joints are clean and
open to view. Yet the poem stands there, resonant, mysterious, ultimately resisting us, though for ever calling us forward to renewed acts
of interpretation and comprehension. It is a mechanical toy we set in
motion each time we start to read and bring to a stop with the last
word: heart.

Two years later came the poem called, simply, 'This':

Dizem que finjo ou minto
Tudo que escrevo. Não.

Eu simplesmente sinto
Com a imaginação.
Não uso o coração.

Tudo o que sonho ou passo,
O que me falha ou finda,
É como que um terraço
Sobre outra coisa ainda.
Essa coisa é que é linda.

Por isso escrevo em meio
Do que não está ao pé,
Livre do meu enleio,
Sério do que não é.
Sentir? Sinta quem lê!

They say that all I ever write
Is but pretence and lies. Not so.
It's simply that I feel
With the imagination.
I do without the heart.

All I dream or live through
All I lack, all that falls short,
Is as it were a terrace
With a view of something more –
And *that*'s a thing of beauty.

So when I write I'm in the midst
Of what is far from me,
Completely uninvolved myself,
In earnest for no reason.
Feelings? They're for the reader!   [12]

The poem is so simple, yet we sense that it deals with what is most mysterious in the acts of writing and reading. Like 'Autopsicografia' it no longer seems to be *about* the paradoxes of the self, but rather to stand as a model (in the sense of a physicist's model) of all such paradoxes. Pessoa no longer seems to be trying to understand or lamenting the impossibility of understanding, but rather to be presenting us with an object and saying: if one sets out on *that* track, this is what is going to happen; if on that, then this. He has recognised, in effect, and made us see, the peculiarity of our relations to language and of communication through language, which has been well described by one writer in this way: 'Only when each of us has had to forgo sight of the other can relation be established.'[4] This emerges even more strongly in what is perhaps the most perfect poem Pessoa ever wrote, 'Between Sleep and Dream', also dated 1933:

Entre o sono e o sonho,
Entre mim e o que em mim
É o que eu me supnho,
Corre um rio sem fim.

Passou por outras margens,
Diversas mais além,
Naquelas várias viagens
Que todo o rio tem.

Chegou onde hoje habito
Â casa que hoje sou.
Passa, se eu me medito;
Se desperto, passou.

E quem me sinto e morre
No que me liga a mim
Dorme onde o rio corre —
Esse rio sem fim.

Between sleep and dream,
Between me and that which is in me,
The Who I suppose myself to be,
An endless river flows.

It passed by other banks,
Diverse and distant,
In those different travels
That every river takes.

It arrived where now I live,
The house I am today.
It passes if I meditate on myself;
If I wake, it has passed away.

And he whom I feel myself to be and who dies
In that which ties me to myself,
Sleeps where the river flows –
That river without end.

This is no longer the river beside which the poet sat dreaming with his Lydia. It is a river without end; always present, yet graspable only through a sense of its absence. And this dialectic of self and river cannot even be voiced except in the poem. The river *is* the poem, or rather, the poem is the river, present now, for us too, the readers, but gone as soon as we attempt to do more than recognise its presence.

When Dante first encountered Beatrice he felt that a decisive event had occurred. He didn't understand, only registered it; understanding would come later. At the time he could only express it in the Latin phrase: *Ecce Deus fortior me, qui veniens dominabitur mihi*. This God, he afterwards recognised, was the God of Love, and we see him appearing again in many subsequent chapters of the *Vita Nuova*. There comes a time, however, when Dante turns to the reader and attempts to explain just how he understands this mysterious being. The God of Love, he says, is an abstraction, a personification of a force which has no name and cannot be understood by the unaided reason. The mark of the responsible poet, however, is his ability to discard allegory and personification when it is no longer needed. So he is going to do away with the God of Love. In his place steps Beatrice, a living woman instead of a poetic abstraction, and for the rest of the *Vita Nuova* and throughout the *Commedia* it is Beatrice or the memory of her which leads Dante forward, out of the Hell of privacy and despair to his vision of God, which is also a vision of what the universe is in itself rather than what it seems to be to the aching will of man. For Pessoa too there was a moment of vision and of submission, and he went on to create his equivalents to the God of Love: Caeiro, Reis, de Campos. But when the time came to discard them it was not in order to turn to a woman of flesh and blood who was at the same time the incarnation of miracle. When Pessoa gave up the safety of the heteronyms, not in order to return to himself, Fernando Pessoa, but to arrive at the point where he could discover himself by finally letting go of all images of self – when that moment finally came he had to do this without the help and guidance of anyone else, without the sense that he was letting go of himself only in order to be worthy of a Beatrice. His only Beatrice was the poem, the poem and the language in which it was to be written. In this he enacts the drama of every major modern artist.

In their acceptance of limitation, in their recognition of themselves as mechanical toys, let us say, rather than as personal lamentations, Pessoa's greatest poems take their place beside the bachelor machines of Duchamp and the twittering machine of Klee. It is poetry such as no one else has written, and it is clearly *our* poetry, as the art of Duchamp and Klee is *our* art, even now, in the last quarter of the century.

And yet. And yet. A whole lifetime of endeavour; the rejection of family and friendship; the dogged pursuit of solitude and of a space in which to create (the space of a city) – was it worth it for a mere handful of tiny poems? There is no need to repress such a question, even if, in the moment of its asking we recognise that it is one to which there is no answer.

Valeu a pena? Tudo vale a pena
Se a alma não é pequena.
Quem quer passar além do Bojador
Tem que passar além da dor.
Deus ao mar o perigo e o abismo deu,
Mas nele é que espelhou o céu.

Or else, if we feel that there is something too Romantic in these lines, a heroism that does not quite strike the right note, let us recall that when Dante met Virgil on the desert plain at the foot of the great hill on which the three beasts had barred his way, and asked who he was, Virgil's answer consisted merely of the information that he was a Mantuan, born under Caesar. It was left to Dante, his reader, to exclaim in wonder and joy at the miracle of the encounter:

'Or se' tu quel Virgilio, e quella fonte,
   che spande di parlar si largo fiume?
. . . .

O degli altri poeti onore e lume,
   vagliami il lungo studio e il grande amore,
   che m'ha fatto cercar lo tuo volume.

Tu se' lo mio maestro, e il mio autore;
   tu se' solo colui, da cui io tolsi
   lo bello stile, che m'ha fatto onore.

Are you then that Virgil and that fountain
which pours forth so rich a stream of speech?

O glory and light of other poets!
May the long study avail me, and the great love
that made me search your volume.

You are my master and my author;
you alone are he from whom I took
the good style that has done me honour.

Notes

1. 'The concern of the Primary Imagination, its only concern, is with sacred beings and sacred events. The sacred is that to which it is obliged to respond; the profane is that to which it cannot respond and therefore does not know . . . A sacred being cannot be anticipated; it must be encountered. On encounter

the imagination has no option but to respond. All imaginations do not recognize the same sacred beings or events, but every imagination responds to those it recognizes in the same way. The impression made upon the imagination by any sacred being is of an overwhelming but undefinable importance – an unchangeable quality, an Identity, as Keats said; I-am-that-I-am is what every sacred being seems to say.' (Auden, 'Making, Knowing and Judging', in *The Dyer's Hand* (London, 1963) 54–5).

2. All translations come from the handy dual-language edition published by Edinburgh University Press in 1971, edited and translated by Peter Rickard, except when I quote from a poem not included by Rickard, when the translation is my own. The number following the poem refers to Rickard's edition.

3. In his excellent introduction to his translations of a selection of Pessoa's poems in the Penguin Modern Poets (Harmondsworth, 1974). Unfortunately there is no Portuguese text on the facing page; this is a great pity because the translations are masterly.

4. George Craig, 'Reading: Who is doing what to whom?' in G. Josipovici (ed.), *The Modern English Novel: The Reader, the Writer and the Work* (London, 1976) 36.

3 Walter Benjamin, 1892–1940

There is no 'essence of Judaism';
there is only: 'Hear, O Israel!'
Franz Rosenzweig

Today, thirty-five years after Benjamin's death, it is neither possible
nor profitable to determine whether he was closer to the Jewish mystical
tradition exemplified by his friend Gershom Scholem, or to the Marx-
ism of Adorno and his Frankfurt colleagues. What comes through
Benjamin's mature writings is the sense above all of a luminously clear-
sighted human being, and I use the term in implicit contrast both to
'hard-headed realist' and 'misty idealist'. Through his work there
shines the same sense of man's place in the world and of his true
potential that one finds in the greatest of his German-Jewish contemporaries, Franz Rosenzweig in particular.

The whole of Benjamin's output testifies to the fact that all his life he
was striving to write the one book that would sum up all his views and
justify an existence which otherwise seemed quite without meaning,
while all the time growing more and more aware that such a book was
an impossible mirage. Not because *he* could not do it, but because *books*
cannot.

The belief that books contain truths, essences, is one that is dear to us.
We take it for granted in fact because it is important to us that it should
be so. Yet not Plato but Adam was the first philosopher, says Benjamin;
truth is not contained in words or sentences or books, but in the living
tradition. It cannot be separated from the unique space and time of
each painting or sculpture, or distinguished from the actual telling of a
story:

> The uniqueness of a work of art is inseparable from its being
> embedded in the fabric of tradition. This tradition is thoroughly alive
> and extremely changeable. An ancient statue of Venus, for example,
> stood in a different traditional context with the Greeks, who made it
> an object of veneration, than with the clerics of the Middle Ages,
> who viewed it as an ominous idol. Both of them, however, were
> equally confronted with its uniqueness, that is, its aura.[1]

This word 'aura' is central to Benjamin's understanding of tradition, and he has many attempts at explaining its implications, while always recognising that it is ultimately extremely mysterious. 'The concept of aura which was proposed above with reference to historical objects', he writes in the essay on 'The Work of Art in an Age of Mechanical Reproduction', 'may usefully be illustrated with reference to the aura of natural ones. We define the aura of the latter as the unique phenomenon of distance, however close it may be. If, while resting on a summer afternoon, you follow with your eyes a mountain range on the horizon or a branch which casts its shadow over you, you experience the aura of those mountains, that branch.' Aura thus depends on a tacit respect for the unique place and time of each experience, and it is utterly destroyed by the placing of an altarpiece in an art gallery for instance, or the reproduction of a particular musical performance on gramophone records.

In the same way as an altarpiece acquires its meaning from the particular place for which it was made and the particular function it was meant to serve, so the traditional story is inseparable from the time and place of its telling, from the gestures and expression of the story-teller. 'The story-teller', says Benjamin, in his great essay of that title, 'takes what he tells from experience, his own or that reported by others. He in turn makes it the experience of those who are listening to his tale.' On the other hand, 'the novelist has isolated himself. The birthplace of the novel is the solitary individual, who is no longer able to express himself by giving examples of his most important concerns, is himself uncounselled, and cannot counsel others.' This mode of argument by opposition is Benjamin's method. We cannot really understand the meaning of aura or of tradition unless we understand that we have lost these things without any hope of return. And we cannot understand *that* unless we are prepared to look critically at the culture in which we live and which we take so much for granted.

What then has caused the decline of story-telling and the triumph of the novel, the decline of wisdom and its replacement by information, the decline of tradition and its replacement by immediate sensation? These things are of course always overdetermined. Benjamin does not try to give *the* answer, or even the answers, but only to draw certain facts to our attention. His method is impressionistic, additive, especially in the essays on Baudelaire and the Paris of the later nineteenth century. He notes that by surrounding themselves with greater and greater material comfort people unwittingly cut themselves off from nature and from other human beings. For example, the installation of gas lighting in nineteenth-century cities increased the safety of the streets, but also removed the sky from human purview much more effectively than even the tallest buildings would have done. Around the middle of that century, too, a number of inventions appeared, all of which had one thing in common: 'One abrupt movement of the hand triggers off a process of many steps.' Think of matches, telephones, cameras. The latter in particular made it possible for an event at any time to be permanently recorded without the slightest effort, and thus, along with the newly developing mass journalism, extended the area of information individuals could store away, but at the expense of wisdom, the sharing of a living tradition.

The belief that truth will be found *in* books has its parallel in the bourgeois' retreat into the privacy of his house, his study, where his leisure hours could be spent surrounded by his possessions:

> Even if a bourgeois is unable to give his earthly being permanence, it seems to be a matter of honour with him to preserve the traces of his articles and requisites of daily use in perpetuity. The bourgeoisie cheerfully takes the impression of a host of objects. For slippers and pocket watches, thermometers and egg-cups, cutlery and umbrellas it tries to get covers and cases. It prefers velvet and plush covers which preserve the impression of every touch ... a dwelling becomes a kind of casing ... for a person and embeds him in it with all his appurtenances, tending his traces as nature tends dead fauna embedded in granite.

This might at first sight seem an eccentric and meaningless catalogue of details, and the Baudelaire essays are full of such passages. But though Benjamin must be more than half in love with the period to write about it in such tender detail, his very attachment to it helps him to see what is really at issue here. The bourgeois, who makes a radical separation between his place of work and his place of leisure, who spends his spare hours collecting and embalming, is in effect engaged in the impossible pursuit of personal immortality. But, as the quoted passage beautifully demonstrates, the result of all his efforts is only to confer upon him and his works the kind of immortality we call fossilisation.

The growth of cities, the development of industrialisation, the enormous increases in the comforts of life – all this has not simply cut man off from his roots. It represents, rather, a positive flight from reality, which means, ultimately, a flight from death. Benjamin does not insist on this but he is quite clear about it:

> In the course of the nineteenth century bourgeois society has, by means of hygienic and social, private and public institutions, realized a secondary effect which may have been its unconscious main purpose; to make it possible for people to avoid sight of the dying. Dying was once a public process in the life of the individual and

a most exemplary one; think of the medieval pictures in which the deathbed has turned into a throne toward which the people press through the wide-open doors of the death-house. In the course of modern times dying has been pushed further and further out of the perceptual world of the living.

However, it is death which gives authority to the story-teller:

> Not only man's knowledge or wisdom, but above all his real life – and this is the stuff that stories are made of – first assumes trans-missible form at the moment of death ... Suddenly in his expressions and looks the unforgettable emerges and imparts to everything that once concerned him that authority which even the poorest wretch in dying possesses for the living around him. That authority is at the very source of the story.

When Benjamin says that death is the sanction of everything the story-teller can tell, that it is 'natural history to which his stories refer back', he means that for the story-teller death is recognised and accepted as a natural part of life, and that life can only be meaningful if we accept the fact that we must all die and that the world will go on. Benjamin's examples come from Leskov and Hebel, but a passage from the Bible will do just as well to demonstrate his meaning:

> And the king said unto Barzillai, Come thou over with me, and I will feed thee with me in Jerusalem. And Barzillai said unto the king, How long have I to live, that I should go up with the king to Jerusalem? I am this day fourscore years old: and can I discern between good and evil? can thy servant taste what I eat or what I drink? can I hear any more the voice of singing men and singing women? wherefore then should thy servant be yet a burden unto my lord the king? Thy servant will go a little way over Jordan with the king: and why should the king recompense it me with such a reward? Let thy servant, I pray thee, turn back again, that I may die in mine own city and be buried by the grave of my father and of my mother. But behold thy servant Chimham; let him go over with my lord the king; and do to him what shall seem good unto thee. And the king answered, Chimham shall go over with me, and I will do to him that which shall seem good unto thee; and whatsoever thou shalt require of me, that will I do for thee. (2 Sam. 19: 33–8).

The story finds its sanction in death precisely because it takes death in its stride. But it is quite otherwise with the novel. The novel enacts death in a desperate effort to exorcise it for both writer and reader.

It uses all its skills to make the reader identify with the hero, and then makes the hero die, either literally or figuratively (marriage or some other passing into a wholly new state), thus revealing to the reader the true meaning of life. 'The novel', says Benjamin, 'is significant, therefore, not because it presents someone else's fate to us, perhaps didactically, but because this stranger's fate, by virtue of the flame which consumes it yields us the warmth which we never draw from our own fate. What draws the reader to the novel is the hope of warming his shivering life with a death he reads about.'

Just as the objects that accumulate in the bourgeois home are withdrawn from the living tradition which can no longer hold them and become objects of aesthetic contemplation, so the hero of a novel is surreptitiously removed from the continuum of life and given an exceptional destiny:

I was born in the northern part of this united kingdom, in the house of my grandfather; a gentleman of considerable fortune and influence, who had, on many occasions, signalised himself on behalf of his country; and was remarkable for his abilities in the law, which he exercised with great success, in the station of a judge, particularly against beggars, for whom he had a singular aversion.

Thus begins *Roderick Random*, and in its confident individualism it can stand for all novels, whatever their subject-matter. Death, however, is less easy to describe than birth. For one thing, it has to be led up to. And how is this done in the great nineteenth-century novels? The author stops the action, puts on a solemn face, prepares himself and us for a big scene. But just how the scene is presented depends on what the author believes we expect of him. The quality of the episode will depend to some extent on current fashion and to some extent on his own taste. In the tale, on the other hand, questions of fashion and taste never intrude – there is neither the time nor the space for them to do so:

So Moses the servant of the Lord died there in the land of Moab, according to the word of the Lord. And he buried him in a valley in the land of Moab, over against Beth-peor: but no man knoweth of his sepulchre unto this day. And Moses was an hundred and twenty years old when he died: his eye was not dim, nor his natural force abated. And the children of Israel wept for Moses in the plains of Moab thirty days: so the days of weeping and mourning for Moses were ended. And Joshua the son of Nun was full of the spirit of wisdom...

What we are witnessing today is the intrusion of taste and fashion in the void left by the collapse of tradition. Benjamin sees clearly what is at issue here:

> Taste develops with the definite preponderance of commodity pro-
> duction over any other kind ... As a consequence of the manufacture
> of products as commodities for the market, people become less and
> less aware of the conditions of production – not only of the social
> conditions in the form of exploitation, but of the technical conditions
> as well ... In the same measure as the expertness of a customer
> declines, the importance of his taste increases – both for him and for
> the manufacturer.

What this means is that taste and fashion can be manipulated. That is why 'the instant the criterion of authenticity ceases to be applicable to artistic production, the total function of art is reversed. Instead of being based on ritual, it begins to be based on another practice – politics.' Thus the themes of Benjamin's Baudelaire book – the apotheosis of the bourgeoisie in nineteenth-century Paris, and the reactions of the one writer who grasped the implications of what was happening – and of the Brecht book – the rise to power of the Nazis and the reactions of Brecht to it – are complementary. Benjamin is in no doubt about the connections between the 'cheerful' pastimes of the nineteenth-century bourgeoisie and the horrors of the Nazi menace, though he never makes the mistake of confusing the one with the other. In both cases what we find is men made rootless by the loss of tradition seeking refuge from the fact of death by withdrawing into the privacy of their homes and surrounding themselves with comforts and artistic treasures or their reproductions, or else by merging with the masses and the State.

Fascism attempts to turn life into aesthetics; the response must be 'to politicise art'. This does not mean making art a tool for propaganda. Quoting a left-wing critic who had argued that 'the *Wilhelm Meister*, the *Grüne Heinrich* of our generation have not yet been written,' Benjamin says: 'Nothing will be further from the mind of an author who has carefully thought about the conditions of production today than to expect or even to want such works to be written. He will never be concerned with products alone, but always, at the same time, with the means of production.' What the modern artist has to do, in other words, is *to make the situation plain*, to reveal what has been lost and to demonstrate how easily taste and fashion have slipped into the gap. In this way bourgeois and Nazi ideology will be shown up for what they are and it will be possible to counter them. This is why Benjamin sees Baudelaire as the first truly modern artist: 'Unlike Gautier, Baude-laire found nothing to like about his time, and unlike Leconte de Lisle he was unable to deceive himself about it. He did not have the humanitarian idealism of a Lamartine or a Hugo, and it was not given to him, as it was to Verlaine, to take refuge in religious devotion. Because he did not have any convictions, he assumed ever new roles for himself. *Flâneur*, apache, dandy, and ragpicker were so many roles to him. For the modern hero is no hero; he acts heroes.' And he who would be a poet has no alternative but to act the poet in full consciousness of what he is doing: 'Baudelaire's poetic output is assigned a mission. He envisioned blank spaces which he filled in with his poems. His work cannot merely be categorised as historical, like anyone else's, but is intended to be so and understood itself as such.'

Brecht, of course, was even clearer about his historical role: 'Brecht is unquestionably the only writer in Germany today who asks himself where he ought to apply his talent, who applies it only where he is convinced of the need to do so, and who abstains on every other occasion.' When he does apply it, he applies it critically.

How does Brecht do this? The finest piece Benjamin ever wrote on Brecht is the first draft of his essay 'What is Epic Theatre?' which was never published in his lifetime. He wastes no time in getting to the heart of the matter:

> The abyss which separates the actors from the audience like the dead from the living, the abyss whose silence heightens the sublime in drama, whose resonance heightens the intoxication in opera, this abyss, which, of all the elements of the stage, most indelibly bears the traces of its sacral origins, has lost its function. The stage is still elevated, but it no longer rises from an immeasurable depth; it has become a public platform... But, as happens in many situations, here too the business of disguising it has prevailed over its proper realization. Tragedies and operas go on being written, apparently with a trusty stage apparatus to hand, whereas in reality they do nothing but supply material for an apparatus which is obsolete... Epic theatre takes as its starting-point the attempt to introduce fundamental change into these relationships.

What kind of change? It breaks up the stream of continuity and allows us to see that events could be other than they are, that history itself could be other than it is. 'Epic theatre is gestural... The more frequently we interrupt someone engaged in action, the more gestures we obtain. Hence the interrupting of action is one of the principal concerns of epic theatre.' Benjamin is well aware of the profound interconnections that exist between the traditional well-made play, the traditional novel, and our notions of history. The 'Theses on the Philosophy of History' help round out his analysis of epic theatre and its role. 'Universal history has no theoretical armature,' runs part of Thesis xvii.

'Its method is additive; it musters a mass of data to fill the homogeneous, empty time. Materialistic historiography, on the other hand, is based on a constructive principle. Thinking involves not only the flow of thoughts, but their arrest as well. Where thinking suddenly stops in a 'configuration pregnant with tensions, it gives that configuration a shock.' This is in effect a brilliantly compressed version of Kierkegaard's critique of Hegel in the *Concluding Unscientific Postscript*. Thesis xviii A has a more Nietzschean ring, though Nietzsche would never have concluded in the way Benjamin does:

> Historicism contents itself with establishing a causal connection between various moments in history. But no fact that is a cause is for that very reason historical. It becomes historical posthumously, as it were, through events that may be separated from it by thousands of years. A historian who takes this as his point of departure stops telling the sequence of events like the beads of a rosary. Instead he grasps the constellation which his own era has formed with a definite earlier era. Thus he establishes a conception of the present as the 'time of the now' which is shot through with chips of Messianic time.

The stopping of history and of the 'flow of thought' is precisely the purpose of Brecht's theatre: 'Epic theatre makes life spurt up high from the bed of time and, for an instant, hover iridescent in empty space. Then it puts it back to bed.' Instead of abetting men in their flight from reality, it reveals to them their potential and their ability to change history. It is didactic theatre, in a sense, but that does not mean that it is solemn. On the contrary, as Benjamin points out: 'There is no better starting-point for thought than laughter; speaking more precisely, spasms of the diaphragm generally offer better chances for thought than spasms of the soul. Epic theatre is lavish only in the occasions it offers for laughter.'

Laughter and shock – these are the effects of modern art. Talking about the parodic element in Proust, Benjamin points out that 'the true reader of Proust is constantly jarred by small shocks.' This is even more true of Baudelaire, who, according to Benjamin, 'indicated the price for which the sensation of the modern age may be had: the disintegration of the aura in the experience of shock.' Kafka too 'divests human gesture of its traditional support, then has a subject for infinite reflection.' Kafka's stories have little in common with the novels of Balzac or George Eliot: 'In the stories which Kafka left us, narrative art regains the significance it had in the mouth of Scheherezade: to postpone the future.'

It is interesting to compare the superficiality of Brecht's dismissal of Kafka with Benjamin's deep understanding ('He was a Jew-boy – one could just as well coin the term "Aryan-boy" – a sorry, dismal creature, a mere bubble on the glittering quagmire of Prague cultural life, nothing more', says Brecht dismissively in conversation with Benjamin). What is so important about Benjamin is the way he was able to bring his profound instinctive sympathy with what one might call the great despairers of modernism, with Kafka and Proust, into the orbit of his understanding of the politico-cultural situation. He was able to do this because he understood the *critical* role played by modern art, and it is this understanding which distinguishes him sharply from dogmatic critics like Lukacs and Leavis, and from the deep ambivalences of a writer like Thomas Mann. Benjamin loved modern art, and he saw that its role in the life of man could be as valuable and positive as in ancient days. But this was only because modern art recognised, as bourgeois art did not, the finality of its break with the past. That is why the way to combat bourgeois ideology is not to write left-wing *Wilhelm Meisters*, but to make the reader or spectator aware of the conditions of produc-tion. Modern art, like historical materialism itself, 'changes the picture of the landscape by naming the forces which have been operative in it'. But such art, an art of process and of irony, is anathema to most critics, whether left or right wing, because it asks them to forsake their dog-matic positions. Brecht, in conversation with Benjamin, puts it in his usual blunt way: 'Production makes them [Lukacs, Gabor, Kurella] uncomfortable. You never know where you are with production: pro-duction is the unforeseeable. You never know what's going to come out. And they themselves don't want to produce. They want to play the apparatchik and exercise control over other people. Every one of their criticisms contains a threat.' This is not just the complaint of the writer against the authoritarianism of the critic. Brecht has put his finger on a very curious but prevalent attitude in modern analyses of culture: that those who are most aware of the breakdown of tradition seem most blind to the fact that modern art, through its radical form, is a vital ally in the attempt to bring this to people's consciousness.

But perhaps the prevalence of this attitude is not so curious. For the Fall consists in the fact that we do not realise that a fall has occurred. Or, in other terms, 'ideology is not a collection of discrete falsehoods but a matrix of thought firmly grounded in the forms of our social life and organised within a set of independent categories ... We are not aware of these systematically generative interconnections because our awareness is organised through them.'[2] There will always be critics ready to tag Virginia Woolf or Robbe-Grillet with the epithets 'élitist' or 'aesthetic', critics for whom 'ideology' is imposed on the naïve masses by wicked capitalists. Benjamin is not of their lot. What he does, without fuss, without unnecessary theory, is in effect to reassert the insights of Kierkegaard and Nietzsche; to reveal the close links of their thought with that of Marx: and to make manifest the relation of the great modernist writers to the critical spirit of these three nineteenth-century thinkers.

It is strange that Benjamin never wrote about Eliot. Eliot should have been Benjamin's author, not Baudelaire or even Brecht. There is an uncanny resemblance between the 'Theses on the Philosophy of History' and 'Tradition and the Individual Talent'. Often it is impossible to tell whether a particular sentence comes from the one or the other: 'For every image of the past that is not recognised by the present as one of its own concerns threatens to disappear irretrievably.' 'Yet if the only form of tradition ... consisted in following the ways of the immediate generation before us in a blind or timid adherence to its successes, "tradition" should positively be discouraged ... It cannot be inherited, and if you want it you must obtain it by great labour.' 'In every era the attempt must be made anew to wrest tradition away from a conformism that is about to overpower it.'

The modern writer's relation to tradition can best be seen by focusing on his attitude to quotation. In the published version of 'What is Epic Theatre?' Benjamin points out that 'interruption is one of the fundamental devices of all structuring. It goes beyond the sphere of art. To give only one example, it is the basis of the quotation. To quote a text involves the interruption of its context.' This aspect of quotation, the feeling that by wrenching it out of its context something extraordinary happens, is reiterated even more forcefully in the untranslated Kraus essay: 'Only the man who questions the present discovers strength in the quotation: not to preserve but to purify ... The only thing to hope for is that something survives this time simply by being torn out of it.' This tells us a good deal more about Eliot than most learned books on the poet's sources. Hugh Kenner comes close to it when he remarks that what is important about Eliot's epigraphs is not what they mean but that they exist. Eliot, Kenner is claiming, needs to start a poem with someone else's voice rather than his own or even that of his *persona*. But, following Benjamin, I think we can go further. We can see in *Prufrock* the failure of the individual voice, no longer a part of a living tradition, to speak at all. Since there is no authority to tell one what needs and what doesn't need to be said, language itself starts to crumble, and 'Do I dare to eat a peach?' and 'Do I dare disturb the universe?' become as meaningless the one as the other, and therefore interchangeable.[3] *Prufrock*, in fact, presents us with a wonderful dramatic portrait of the writer described by Benjamin, 'the solitary individual, who is no longer able to express himself by giving examples of his most important concerns, is himself uncounselled, and cannot counsel others.' Eliot brings out into the open a situation which had existed for three centuries. And, having done that, he is able to move forward. But not yet to speak in his own voice. Rather, he builds up his next poems by juxtaposing blocks of other people's words, either those of earlier writers or of numerous *personae*. This mode of procedure should not surprise us once we have grasped the place of the interrupted gesture in Brecht or Kafka. What is perhaps more surprising, and requires much meditation, is the fact that the only truly *personal* utterance in the whole of the first volume of Eliot's verse is the epigraph that follows the simple two-language dedication: 'For Jean Verdenal, 1889–1915, mort aux Dardanelles.' The epigraph is in Italian, the words addressed to Virgil by Statius when the two poets meet in Purgatory: 'la quantitate/Puote veder del amor che a te mi scalda,/ Quando dismento nostra vanitate/Trattando l'ombre come cosa salda.' (Now you can see the measure of the love which warms me towards you, when I forget our nothingness, and treat shades as solid things.)[4] These words are not in Eliot's native language, and they are not written by Eliot. And yet, miraculously, we feel as we read them that Eliot speaks, and speaks with an authority denied or undercut by every poem in that and subsequent volumes. I am reminded when I read them of Stravinsky's reply to a question put to him by an interviewer in the last years of his life: 'What did you mean, a moment ago, when you declared your disbelief in words?', asked the interviewer. 'Is it a question of their inexactness?' 'They are not so much inexact as metaphorical', replied Stravinsky. 'Not so much another form of notation as an irrelevant and unedifying form. Sometimes I feel like those old men Gulliver encounters in the *Voyage to Laputa*, who have renounced language and who try to converse by means of objects themselves.'

Stravinsky is contrasting the making of music with talk about music, but his words apply just as well to Eliot's own dealings with language. He builds in blocks, he points to what he has done, but his lips are sealed – until, that is, he discovers, in *Ash-Wednesday*, a language akin though not identical to the language of prayer. But that is another story.[5]

'Aura is the unique phenomenon of distance', says Benjamin. The camera records our likeness without returning our gaze. But 'to perceive the aura of an object we look at means to invest it with the ability to look at us in return.' Today aura has everywhere decayed, and, what is worse, we are not even aware of what it is we have lost. The emergence of newspapers, of photography, of gramophone records, as well as the disappearance of most forms of communal life – all are causes and symptoms of this loss. But there is one further reason, not usually mentioned by social historians, and perhaps the most important one of all. This Benjamin describes as 'the desire of contemporary masses to bring things "closer" spatially and humanly, which is just as ardent as their bent toward overcoming the uniqueness of every reality by accepting its reproduction.' This is the proletarian equivalent of the bourgeois desire to collect, wrap up, store away. Benjamin does not make the mistake of sentimentalising the masses: he realises the enormous pull of bourgeois attitudes, the yearning for comfort and pleasure, the desperate search for immortality which affects all classes and conditions of men. It is just because he is so clear-sighted that, like Brecht, he is so keenly aware of the power of the Nazi threat. But his insights apply equally well to present-day society. Had Benjamin lived to witness it, he would not have made the mistake of English and American cultural historians, of calling the 'permissive society' a final breaking away from Puritanism; he would have seen it for what it is, a final apocalyptic manifestation of the Puritan ethos: abolishing distance, abolishing time, merging sensations, merging bodies, seeking oneness with others and with the world – all in a huge effort to blot out the fact that man exists in time and that death will one day claim him.

As Benjamin sees it, what Brecht and Kafka and Proust set out to do was in some way to restore uniqueness and distance to the world. But this too ought to be the task of the critic in relation to the authors he is writing about. Benjamin objects to Max Brod's biography of Kafka because 'Brod's attitude as a biographer is the pietistic stance of an ostentatious intimacy.' This, however, is anything but the attitude of true friendship, for, as Benjamin says in commenting on Brecht's marvellous 'Lao Tzu' poem, 'we learn about friendliness that it does not abolish the distance between human beings but brings that distance to life.' There is no better description of Benjamin's own work as a critic: he does not abolish the distance between us and Leskov or Brecht or Kafka; he brings that distance to life.

Notes

1. 'It is a revelation to compare Menard's *Don Quixote* with Cervantes'. The latter, for example, wrote (Part One, Chapter Nine):

> ... truth, whose mother is history, rival of time, depository of deeds, witness of the past, exemplar and advisor to the present, and the future's counselor.

Written in the seventeenth century, written by the 'lay genius' Cervantes, this enumeration is a mere rhetorical praise of history. Menard, on the other hand writes:

> ... truth, whose mother is history, rival of time, depository of deeds, witness of the past, exemplar and advisor to the present, and the future's counselor.

History, the *mother* of truth: the idea is astounding. Menard, a contemporary of William James, does not define history as an inquiry into reality but as its origin. Historical truth, for him, is not what has happened; it is what we judge to have happened. The final phrases – *exemplar and advisor to the present, and the future's counselor* – are brazenly pragmatic.

The contrast in style is also vivid. The archaic style of Menard – quite foreign, after all – suffers from a certain affectation. Not so that of his forerunner, who handles with ease the current Spanish of his time.' (Borges, 'Pierre Menard, Author of the *Quixote*', in *Labyrinths*.)

2. John Mepham, 'The Theory of Ideology in *Capital*,' *Radical Philosophy*, 2 (summer 1972).

3. I owe this formulation of the problem to Kateryna Arthur. *Eliot/Language*, a pamphlet by Michael Edwards (*Prospice* IV, 1976), came to my attention too late for me to make use of it, but his remarks on Eliot's 'fallen' language express precisely what I was struggling with here.

4. Oddly, Eliot misquotes slightly. Dante writes: 'Or puoi la quantitate/ comprender dell'amor ch'a te mi scalda...'; Eliot's version runs: 'la quantitate/*puote veder* del amor che a te mi scalda...' The difference is minimal.

5. I touch on it in Chapter 7, 'Linearity and Fragmentation'.

4 Saul Bellow

When we think of Saul Bellow's work what we think of is a certain tone of voice, a tone of voice that combines the utmost formality with the utmost desperation. We think of Mr Willis Mosby, diplomat and memoir writer, struggling for breath in the Mexican tombs and saying simply, 'I must get out. Ladies, I find it very hard to breathe.' Or of Herzog, one-time academic and historian of ideas, sitting alone in his crumbling country house and saying into the silence: 'If I am out of my mind, it's all right with me.' But 'think' is the wrong word here. Such phrases are not called up consciously into the mind; they surge into our throats, begging to be spoken, to be released by us into the outside world. And to give way to this impulse (submit to this discipline) is to experience a peculiar pleasure.

Bellow has been described as a great realist; as a follower of Dreiser and the American urban naturalist tradition; as a great fantasist, especially in *Henderson the Rain King*; and as the last of the Yiddish storytellers. But these are ways of shrugging off the demands of that voice, of avoiding its implications by placing it safely in a literary or historical context. Bellow is too important a writer to have this done to him. His style, that tone of voice, emerges as an answer to his most pressing preoccupations, and what we need to do is to see how the two intertwine and reinforce each other, and how they are discovered and made manifest.

Just as, according to Proust, all Dostoevsky's novels could well be called *Crime and Punishment* and all Flaubert's *L'Education sentimentale*, so all Bellow's could be called *Dangling Man*. In each one the protagonist is a dangler, someone who, either through inclination or through the force of circumstances, has drawn back from the rush of the world and hangs in a limbo, trying to make sense of things. But is this possible? We cannot simply step back into a room, a house, even a state of mind, and expect to be freed from the pressures of life. Time crowds us, the past no less than the present asserting its claims; and even space does not seem all that easy to find, especially in a big city. In fact, to step back from the rush of the world is to be made even more aware of the size and violence of what one is trying to avoid. Tommy Wilhelm, in *Seize the Day*, is overwhelmed by the sheer density of the crowd on

Broadway, 'the great, great crowd, the inexhaustible current of millions of every race and kind pouring out, pressing round, of every age, of every genius', and Asa Leventhal, in *The Victim*, speaks for all Bellow's protagonists when he remarks that 'there was not a single part of him on which the whole world did not press with full weight.'

From this seething mass characters emerge – relatives, friends, acquaintances – to argue with the hero, plead with him, or otherwise try to cajole him back into 'the world'. These characters fall into three types, though there is of course much overlapping. The first and least interesting, because offering the least temptation to the hero, are those whom Joseph, in the opening lines of the first novel, calls 'the hard-boiled'; such characters as Simon, Augie March's brother, who, in his determination to get on, marries a bovine heiress and urges his brother to do likewise and 'not to dissolve in bewilderment of choices', but to make himself hard 'and learn how to stay with the necessary, undis-tracted by the trimmings'. Then there are the soft sentimentalists, the believers in what Herzog calls 'potato love', usually women and mem-bers of the family, using emotional blackmail to try and force the hero back into the world. Their power stems from the fact that they appear to stand for values he believes in, yet when they make their claims he can never respond. Is the fault his then? Is he lacking in simple humanity as well as in the drive for worldly power and wealth?

However, the most typical representative of 'the world' in Bellow's novels, its most appealing and dangerous product, is the fast talker, the Machiavel and autodidact, peddler of crisis ethics and solver of the riddles of the universe, the man driven by a violent energy of whose source he is scarcely conscious. His enormous appeal lies partly in this overwhelming energy and partly in the fact that, unlike the other two types, his response to the world is not instinctual but seems to be the result of a real effort to understand. He is thus much closer to the dangling hero, who is himself possessed of unusual energy but who seems to be unable to find a channel in which to direct it, and thus feels it eating into him and destroying him.

The close relationship between the hero and the fast talker is estab-lished as early as *The Victim*, Bellow's second novel. Kirby Allbee, once a casual acquaintance of Leventhal's, comes back years later to pester him with the insistence that Leventhal was responsible for Allbee's losing his job and for his eventual fall into the world of bums and out-casts. Allbee is a sort of Dostoevskian buffoon, ready to abase himself at any moment, bridling up with false pride the next, turning everything into a joke and every joke into an insult. Leventhal is baffled and enraged: ' "Well, you're a crazy, queer bastard," he said. "What's the matter with you? ... One minute you're on the bottom, couldn't be any lower, and the next you're a regular Lord Byron." ' Allbee's strength, like that of Dostoevsky's buffoons, comes from the fact that he has utterly given in to despair, and thus has absolutely nothing to lose. This despair leads not to silence but to feverish talk, and he showers Leventhal not only with hard-luck stories but with all sorts of metaphysical and religious theories:

> Now let me explain something to you. It's a Christian idea but I don't see why you shouldn't be able to understand it. 'Repent!' That's John the Baptist coming out of the desert. Change yourself, that's what he's saying, and be another man . . . . You see, you have to get yourself so that you can't stand to keep on in the old way . . . . It takes a long time before you're ready to quit dodging. Meanwhile, the pain is horrible . . . . We're mulish; that's why we have to take such a beating. When we can't stand another lick without dying of it, then we change.

Leventhal answers dryly: 'We'll see what you are next year', and his scepticism is justified, for Allbee shortly afterwards tries (unsuccessfully, of course) to commit suicide. But it would be wrong to imagine from this exchange that Allbee is incapable of hurting Leventhal. The fast talkers who fill Bellow's books press in on the hero, throwing him into confusion and waiting for him to make a false move so they can pounce and crush him. Augie may well say at the end of his adventures, 'To tell the truth, I'm good and tired of all these big personalities, destiny moulders and heavy-water brains, Machiavellis and wizard evil-doers, big wheels, imposers-upon, absolutists', but the fact is that he has spent most of his life struggling only half successfully to get free of such types. And Tommy Wilhelm, the large, pathetic, middle-aged hero of *Seize the Day*, finds himself reduced to helplessness when the fraudulent Dr Tamkin fastens on him, draining him of his last few dollars even as he lectures him on how a man must live his life: 'The past is no good to us. The future is full of anxiety. Only the present is real – the here-and-now. Seize the day.' Tamkin hypnotises Wilhelm with his patter, his crazy stories about lunatics, crooks, cancer patients, bigamists, Egyptian princesses. The more he talks the wilder his stories get, but just when credulity is strained to breaking point he comes up with a truth that cannot be denied:

> 'In telling you this,' said Tamkin with one of his hypnotic subtleties, 'I do have a motive. I want you to see how some people free themselves from morbid guilt feelings and follow their instincts. Innately, the female knows how to cripple by sickening a man with guilt. It is a very special destruct, and she sends her curse to make a fellow impotent . . . . You're a half-way case. You want to follow your instinct, but you're too worried still. For instance, about your kids –'

Tamkin may only be saying all this to bewilder and confuse Wilhelm while he pockets his money, and the pseudo-medical jargon and general air of authority may only be part of a professional patter, but he does touch on a partial truth. Like all the dangling heroes, Wilhelm *is* a halfway case, a partial believer in the value of instinct and with a sense that he has lost his way and needs to find it again. Yet he also believes in quite different instincts from the ones Tamkin is talking about, though these he is able to formulate only in negative terms, as when he interrupts Tamkin angrily: 'One thing! Don't bring up my boys. Just lay off.' But despite such outbursts both Wilhelm and Leventhal are easy prey for any determined assault on their confidence and values.

There are two reasons for the vulnerability of the dangling hero, and they are deeply interconnected. The first is that, however hard he tries, he is quite incapable of putting up anything positive against the views of life offered to him by those with whom he comes in contact. And these are not only the bums and villains, like Allbee and Tamkin; even someone like Ramona, Herzog's kind and beautiful mistress, is convinced that she understands his real needs better than he does himself: 'She told Herzog that he was a better man than he knew – a deep man, beautiful . . ., but sad, unable to take what his heart really desired, a man tempted by God, longing for grace, but escaping headlong from his salvation . . . .' And Dahfu, the noble king of the Wariri, a man for whom Henderson feels nothing but love and admiration, urges him down into the underground den where he keeps his pet lion, and, when Henderson draws back in instinctive terror at the sight and smell of the great beast, admonishes him:

> You ask, what can she do for you? Many things. First she is unavoidable. Test it, and you will find she is unavoidable. And this is what you need, as you are an avoider. Oh, you have accomplished momentous avoidances. But she will change that. She will make consciousness to shine. She will burnish you.

The difficulty Herzog and Henderson have in countering such arguments stems from the fact that for all they know they may well be true. In fact, they are true: Herzog *is* sad, he *does* long for grace; Henderson *is* in some ways an avoider. Yet both are uneasy with the formulation of the problem; instinctively they feel that it is both true and not true. But their unease cannot be turned into an adequate basis for action, since, as Augie March says:

> How does anybody form a decision to be against and persist against? When does he choose and when is he chosen instead? This one hears

voices; that one is a saint, a chieftain, an orator, a Horatius, a kami-
kazi; one says *Ich kann nicht anders* – so help me God! And why is it
I who cannot do otherwise?

The hero dangles because he won't fit into the world the way people
seem to want him to, but he lacks the drive or egocentricity or madness
of the Protestant hero or the Romantic rebel that would lead him to
create an alternative world. He can't sit still, but he can't find the confidence in himself to make a move. In fact, as the hero frees himself
from the rush of the world, objects start to gain in clarity, but this, far
from helping him to act, inhibits action more and more, for the
multiplicity of detail assaulting his senses only bewilders and con-
fuses him. Henderson feels memories piling into him from all sides till
everything turns to chaos; Herzog, reading the letter in which a friend
reports how his wife and her lover are treating his child, finds the
handwriting keeps getting in the way of the meaning and he has to
struggle to grasp the sense of the words. It is as though he was too close
to the world to make sense of it any more.

No wonder that in a situation like this the hero longs for something
that will restore order and balance to his life. No wonder Joseph cries at
the end of *Dangling Man*: 'Hurray for regular hours! And for the
supervision of the spirit! Long live regimentation!' But is this longing
really very different from that of someone like Allbee? Is it not the
desire to come in out of the limbo in which he finds himself, throw off
the weight of a meaningless freedom, let the world take care of him for
a change? 'Marry me! Be my wife! End my troubles!' Herzog finds
himself saying to Ramona under his breath, and though he is immediately 'staggered by his rashness, his weakness, and by the characteristic
nature of such an outburst', the longing from which it springs is not
something he can simply eliminate.

The Victim, naturally enough, is the fullest exploration of the interconnection of the fast talker and the dangling hero. When we first meet
Leventhal we discover that, though he is not particularly successful in
his public or private life, he at least thinks of himself as one of those
who 'got away with it'. By this he means that 'his bad start, his mis-
takes, the things that might have wrecked him, had somehow combined
to establish him. He had almost fallen in with that part of humanity of
which he was frequently mindful ..., the part that did not get away
with it – the lost, the outcast, the overcome, the effaced, the ruined.'
But to think in this way is already to have closed the gap between the
two groups. Leventhal is like the man who says with relief that he
doesn't have a headache, but only because somewhere at the edge of his
consciousness there lurks the awareness of an incipient headache.
Leventhal is a natural victim; Allbee calls out to something within him

and which at the start of the book he is fighting to keep from himself. Thus on the ferryboat, going to visit his sister-in-law whose child is very ill, he sees a barge spraying paint over the hull of a freighter and the light there seems like 'the yellow revealed in the slit of the eye of a wild animal, say a lion, something inhuman that didn't care about anything human and yet was implanted in every human being too.' This animal quality of the city, corresponding to something animal in man, pulls at Leventhal's heart, unbalancing him; and when to it is added the horror of his little nephew's suffering and possible death, all those forces with which we normally protect ourselves are brushed aside and Leventhal is made to face memories he would rather do without, such as his mother dying insane, which drags with it the recurring fear that he too might one day go mad. Clearly if Allbee had not appeared Leventhal would have had to invent him, for Allbee seems to provide a way of forcing things to a crisis and releasing Leventhal from his tormenting thoughts. 'He kept telling himself, "The showdown is coming",' and what he means by this is 'a crisis which would bring an end of his resistance to something he had no right to resist.'

Yet in spite of everything he does resist. He doesn't let Allbee drag him down; he refuses to let the little boy's death present him with an excuse for some desperate action. He retains his sanity and his sense of responsibility, though not by growing hard-boiled and ceasing to care. And in this he is like Augie and Wilhelm and Henderson and Herzog. They all have reason, and more, to give up, break down, despair, or grow hard, callous, indifferent to the claims of others. Yet they do neither, but weather the blows and trust their initial instincts. In so doing they come to understand both their own motives and the nature of the forces that oppose them. The growth of this awareness is of course gradual, and varies in depth from novel to novel, but the picture that emerges for them is consistent in its broad outlines, from *Dangling Man* to *Mr. Sammler's Planet*. Since much of all the novels is taken up with a delineation of this picture, it is important to step back for a moment and consider its main features.

The first thing to grasp is that things are often not what they seem. This is not to say that one thing hides another, or that men act hypo-critically, as classical analyses of society and behaviour would have us believe. Rather, Bellow's heroes come to see, with Marx and Nietzsche and Freud, that the facts and events of the history of man and the individual histories of men are in effect mute attempts by human beings to express something which they themselves are hardly conscious of. Mr Sammler, miraculous survivor of the Nazi holocaust and one-time friend of H. G. Wells, recognises this fact even in something as ordinary and trivial as his niece's obsession with potted plants in her flat:

This botanical ugliness, the product of so much fork-digging, water-
ing, so much breast and arm, heart and hope, told you something,
didn't it? First of all, it told you that the individual facts were filled
with messages and meanings, but you couldn't be sure what the
messages meant. She wanted a bower in her living-room, a screen of
glossy leaves . . . . Humankind, crazy for symbols, trying to utter what
it doesn't know itself.

In a short story dating from 1949, 'A Sermon by Doctor Pep,' we
find Dr Pep ready to provide an explanation of what it is that drives
humanity in this fashion. Dr Pep is not, of course, to be trusted too
readily, for he is one of Bellow's fast-speaking cranks, but his contrast
of man and animal makes a lot of sense:

> I marvel at the Guiana spider that takes the ant's disguise to perfec-
> tion. But let me suggest to you, listeners, that he comes into the world
> instructed in mimicry and belongs to the cast of the giant creation
> that goes through a performance of days and ages without a falter
> and without a rehearsal. Whereas we, fallible and in need of instruc-
> tion . . . being creatures and more . . . embracing everything with in-
> finite desire . . .

Man is an animal *and* more, yet what that more consists of seems to be
a deep longing to become creature and only creature once again. All
his energy, all his aggression, all his inventiveness, seems to be taken up
with removing that 'and more' from the face of the earth:

> The Walrus was sorry for the poor oysters. The Carpenter ate with-
> out caring. But both of them wept like anything to see such quantities
> of sand. Why did they? Because civilization is never complete
> enough? In dead earnest, it is profound. The sand remains in spite
> of the maids and mops. It creeps back . . . . And were the fierce
> moppers of Auschwitz inspired by their square and polished home
> towns and the pleasant embroidery of the regulated Rhine?

Dr Pep's queer mode of expression makes vivid a truth we find it hard
to acknowledge because it cannot be derived from empirical observa-
tion: human beings have a desperate need to mop up, enclose, control,
bring order out of chaos. And this tendency has been exacerbated by
the events of the last five hundred years, first the Renaissance and
Reformation and then the French Revolution, which removed the
limits within which men had previously lived and gave each man a
freedom which he found difficult to bear. 'We were important enough

then for our souls to be fought over,' Joseph notes in *Dangling Man*. 'Now each of us is responsible for his own salvation, which is his greatness.' So we all dream of greatness, all long to be great lovers, great warriors, even, like Raskolnikov, great criminals. We will do anything to be *something, someone,* and 'the fear of lagging pursues and maddens us. The fear lies in us like a cloud. It makes an inner climate of darkness.'

But what does this fear come from? And why do we find, since the time of the Romantics, this craze for originality allied to a desire to experience as much as possible and as deeply as possible? Why have we come to regard sheer experience as an unquestioned good? Henderson has an answer to these questions in a contrast he draws between man and child:

> The world may be strange to a child, but he does not fear it the way a man fears. He marvels at it. But the grown man mainly dreads it. And why? Because of death. So he arranges to have himself abducted like a child. So what happens will not be his fault. And who is this kidnapper – this gypsy? It is the strangeness of life – a thing that makes death more remote, as in childhood.

In the end it all boils down to this: do we believe the world owes us a living or that it is we who are loaned a life? Behind all the wildness and striving, all the restlessness and anguish, this is the message a dumb mankind is striving to utter: that individuals do not want to die and relinquish their individuality. So they will do anything to silence the little voice of consciousness, the voice that tells them they are separate and distinct from other people and from the world and that one day they will cease to exist while the world just goes on and on. Schlossberg, the wise old Jew in *The Victim*, makes the point with extraordinary clarity:

> Here I'm sitting here, and my mind can go around the world. Is there any limit to what I can think? But in another minute I can be dead, on this spot. There's a limit to me. But I have to be myself in full. Which is somebody who dies, isn't it? That's what I was from the beginning. I'm not three people, four people. I was born once and I will die once. You want to be two people? More than human? Maybe it's because you don't know how to be one.

So death and the fact of death in life and the interconnections of death and responsibility are what the dangling hero finally comes to understand in each of the novels. But understanding alone is never enough. What is still required is for the hero to *feel* the meaning of these words, to grasp that death will come to him too, that not even he (as each of us persists in believing) will be exempt at the final count. Such an awareness can never come from himself alone; there must be an intrusion from the outside world into the world of imagination and desire we each of us construct for ourselves. This can take many forms. In *Herzog* it comes in the form of a minor car accident in which, taking his little daughter out for a drive, Herzog finds himself involved. The incident is both farcical and banal. No one is seriously hurt, but Herzog is shaken by it, and especially by its aftermath, a confrontation at the police station with his furious ex-wife. How could he act like this, he wonders, and show himself in this light to his daughter? The incident seems to bring him down to earth from 'his strange spiralling flight of the last few days'; he can no longer run away from himself; he is at last up against the wall. For all his talk about the ordinariness of life being the important thing and how one must be what one is and ask no questions, Herzog, like the other dangling heroes, has really been engaged in whirlwind activity simply in order to escape from himself and from the way things are. Exactly like Allbee in *The Victim*, or like Ramona's ex-lover George Hoberly, in this novel, who both try to awaken sympathy by acts of deliberate self-destruction, Herzog has been secretly trying to force from life an answer to the question: Who am I? Who am I *really*? The accident and its aftermath serve to free him from this compulsion. He literally bangs into reality. Not hard, but hard enough to remind him of what might have happened, and to make him see how difficult it is to eradicate the notions of crisis and salvation from our minds. We long all the time, however unconsciously, for some decisive event that will change things for ever and show us how from now on we are to lead our lives.

Henderson too has to learn the hard way. When a wood chip flew up and hit him in the face as he was chopping logs, he felt for a moment that here was reality, but the moment passed and things slipped away from him again, until, in despair at the chaos and lack of clarity of things, he decides to take the trip to Africa. There the lessons of the woman of Bittahness and of the noble King Dahfu touch on many truths about himself and the world, and Henderson feels at last that he is coming to an understanding of the central facts. But then instead of The Truth, an answer to life and its problems, something that will still the insistent voice within him that keeps pressing him forward with its *I want, I want, I want*, what does he find? Dahfu, having to catch a grown male lion single-handed (the laws of kingship require it), makes a false move and all Henderson's fears are borne out: in a second Dahfu is mauled by the beast and dies almost at once. So, instead of Truth, Henderson finds death, and where he expected an enrichment of life he is faced with loss. He raises his voice in a great cry of lament:

Oh, the poor guy is dead. Oh, ho, ho, ho, ho! It kills me. It could be time we were blown off the earth. If only we didn't have hearts we wouldn't know how sad it was. But we carry around these hearts, these spotty damn mangoes in our breasts, which give us away.... There'll be nobody to talk to any more. I've gotten to that age where I need human voices and intelligence. That's all that's left. Kindness and love.

Yet perhaps Truth and death, enrichment and loss, are more intimately bound up than we care to think. For it is indeed now that Henderson learns the lesson he had hoped Africa would teach him. Now he feels that 'the sleep is burst and I've come to myself.' You can't win against death, loss, separation. This is the reality he has been seeking all his life but never found with his wives, the lioness, his pigs. It resides neither in the world nor in ourselves, but is the paradox that the longing for a Truth, an answer, is human and natural, but that it will never be appeased, but only denied, again and again and again. So Henderson, on the plane back to civilization, suddenly sees the world and himself as they are and not as we imagine them or would like them to be:

> Other passengers were reading.... But I, Henderson, with my glowering face, with corduroy and Bersagliere feathers ... I couldn't get enough of the water, and of these upside-down sierras of the clouds. Like courts of eternal heaven. (Only they aren't eternal, that's the whole thing; they are seen once and never seen again, being figures and not abiding realities; Dahfu will never be seen again, and presently I will never be seen again; but everyone is given the components to see: the water, the sun, the air, the earth.)

Soon this insight will no doubt slip away from him, but what he has experienced, understood, is that we are fragments and can only ever be fragments. In the other novels the hero is often made aware of this by witnessing sudden death or violence in the streets, in courtrooms, or in hospitals. Both *Seize the Day* and *Mr. Sammler's Planet* move to a climax of understanding as the hero confronts the reality of death. Even Sammler, left for dead among the stinking corpses and miraculously surviving the war to end his days in New York, even he has to be re-awakened to the facts again and again:

> They went down in the elevator, the gray woman and Mr. Sammler, and through lower passages paved in speckled material, through tunnels, up and down ramps, past laboratories and supply rooms. Well, this famous truth for which he was so keen, he had it now, or it had him.

He looks down at the corpse of his nephew, the man who had made it possible for him to come to America, and as he utters the words of lament that come unbidden to his lips, he holds the truth for a moment:

> Remember, God, the soul of Elya Gruner . . . . At his best this man was much kinder than at my best I have ever been or could ever be. He was aware that he must meet, and he did meet . . .

The words, muttered under his breath, lose direction and become in the end only a rhythmic repetition, an assertion of what is: 'For that is the truth of it – that we know, God, that we know, that we know, we know, we know.'

There are, in Bellow's novels, two views of man, or rather, two different conclusions which can be drawn from the same set of facts. The facts are that man is at odds with nature, alien, inauthentic, for ever striving to reach peace, wholeness, oneness with the rest of nature, but never getting there. One response to this is to insist that if man fails then it is his fault, and that what he needs is to be flogged like a mule till he succeeds. Unfortunately the exaltation which usually accomplishes such an attitude soon turns to despair when it becomes clear that man will not be saved once and for all; the flogging then starts to take the form of masochistic self-laceration. For those who hold such views, our imagination has allowed us hints of paradise and what is needed is to turn imagination into reality. This they believe to be possible, given the right degree of fear and dedication on our part. Dahfu, the lovable king of the Wariri (he is lovable because he holds his ideas like a child, wanting to confer them on other people not in order to do them down or get something out of them but only to see them happy), maintains such a view in its extreme form:

> What he was engrossed by was a belief in the transformation of human material . . . the flesh influencing the mind, the mind influencing the flesh, back again to the mind, back once more to the flesh. The process as he saw it was utterly dynamic.

Henderson is impressed but sceptical: 'Thinking of mind and flesh as I knew them, I said: "Are you really and truly sure it's like that, Your Highness?" ' But Dahfu is more than sure:

> 'Although I do not wish to reduce the stature of our discussion,' he said, 'yet for the sake of example the pimple on a lady's nose may be her own idea, accomplished by a conversion at the solemn command of her psyche; even more fundamentally the nose itself, though part hereditary, is part also her own idea.'

There is, however, a second way of responding to the fact of man's alienated state. This is to accept it as an unalterable part of the human condition: this is how we are, divided, self-conscious, full of impossible longings, never free of the burden of daily care and responsibility, and this is how we will always be. It is hard to accept this as something that can never be altered, and, as we have seen, the dangling hero frequently longs to be finished with things once and for all. But because he never gives in to this longing he comes to see the imagination not as something to be transcended, willed into becoming reality, but as man's most valuable possession. For imagination, by allowing us to sense what others are feeling, is the springboard of sympathy and love. When Dahfu tries to convince Henderson that what he needs is to become like the lion, in effect to *become a lion*, Henderson is overwhelmed by the grandeur of the idea, but his common sense forces him to reply: 'If she doesn't try to be human, why should I try to act the lion? I'll never make it. If I have to copy someone, why can't it be you?'

Henderson's fate is to be constantly associated with animals – a fairground bear, pigs, frogs, cattle, lions; and one of the themes of the novel, which it develops from a section of *Augie March*, is the dialectic of our imagination in our relation to animals. We recall the hint Leventhal had of the teeming city calling out to something animal in his nature, and his vision on the ferry of something like the yellow slit of a lion's eye. The lesson Leventhal, like the other dangling heroes, learns, is just this, that we must be sure not to misunderstand our natures. We must not crush our animal instincts, nor grant them covert satisfaction in the pursuit of wealth or power or women; nor, finally, must we commit the folly of trying to extirpate that part of ourselves which is *not* animal in any misguided attempt to turn ourselves entirely *into* animals. For that is not an enrichment of the instincts and the imagination but the guarantee of their final destruction.

Gooley MacDowell, in his 'Address to the Hasbeens Club of Chicago', another early Bellow story, uncovers this dialectic very well:

> How is any man going to account for having closed up in his head, above his teeth and palate and below his hair, what there is? This folding! This isthmus! This finding! That baroque pearl of an inmost thing!... And isn't it maybe the curiosity over these internal discoveries that leads us to have captive animals – eagles in the Park, canaries at home? We keep pets within and without. Imprisoned power. The heart in its cage of bone.

Allbee and Dahfu, though different in practically every respect, come together on this point, that for them man must not hold back but must give in to the animal within, must turn his dreams into reality, whatever the cost. Only then will he be renewed, saved, made radiant. And this is the message of Thea Fenichel, the crazy rich girl who falls in love with Augie March and takes him with her to Mexico to hunt iguanas with eagles. Augie secretly rejoices when the eagle fails to live up to its fierce looks, and though for Henderson the outcome of his experience with wild animals is not comic but tragic, he too is confirmed in his feeling that there is something inherently wrong in men trying to be animals. Like Herzog, Henderson learns from his experiences that the power of the imagination is linked to the power of sympathy and love, and that love means the acceptance of responsibility for ourselves and for those who are dependent on us, especially those who are helpless, like children and animals. And the last we see of him, on his way back to America and his wife, he has a lion cub in a basket and he holds a little lost Persian boy by the hand. 'It is our humanity that we are responsible for, our dignity, our freedom,' Joseph had written in the diary which forms the substance of *Dangling Man*, and that is the truth which all the novels fill out and give meaning to, so that we too, by the end, are aware of and can feel what Joseph meant.

'It has only been in the last two centuries,' Mr Sammler notes, 'that the majority of people in civilized countries have claimed the privilege of being individuals. Formerly they were slave, peasant, labourer, even artisan, but not person.' However, the revolution which occurred at the end of the eighteenth century, and which was a triumph for justice and reason in so many ways, also brought huge problems in its wake: 'Hearts that get no real wage, souls that find no nourishment.... Desire unlimited. Possibility unlimited...'

We have seen the answer to these problems arrived at by the dangling heroes, but there is one vital aspect of the situation we have not touched on, and that is how the writer himself is affected by this situation. For the writer too, liberated from a function as scribe or court poet, seems to have had a burdensome freedom thrust upon him. He is free, it is true, to give rein to his imagination and originality, but what is the nature of this freedom? 'Around our heads we have a dome of thought as thick as atmosphere to breathe', says Gooley MacDowell in his address to the Hasbeens Club of Chicago. 'And what's it about? One thought leads to another as breath leads to breath. I find it barren just to breathe or only to have thoughts.' Words swirl about, and because there are so many of them, and they can be had for the asking, they soon cease to have any meaning. The writer withdraws into his room, freeing himself from the immediate pressures of the world in order to give himself the time and the space to write. But once in his room, what is there except boredom and the merging of days into one meaningless continuity? Bellow's first novel may be about a young man waiting to be drafted, but it is also about any writer at any time, including the writer of *that* book at *that* time.

In response to the historical situation just outlined, writers have made determined efforts to dispense with 'mere literature', to wring the neck of 'rhetoric' and close with the real. And readers and critics have welcomed this, judging novels most often by how close to reality they get, criticising them for being conventional and derivative and praising them for giving us the substance of 'life itself' in all its rawness. Part of Hemingway's popularity was no doubt due to the fact that by dispensing with the formalities of a literary prose he gave the impression of actually getting reality down on the page. But this can of course never be done, and it is easy to see that a writer like Hemingway has many of the characteristics of Bellow's fast talkers, hard-headed salesmen of a home-brewed reality. In fact in one of his rare reviews Bellow talks of Hemingway in these very terms:

> Hemingway has an intense desire to impose his version of the thing upon us, to create an image of manhood, to define the manner of baptism and communion.... When he dreams of a victory it is a total victory; one great battle, one great issue. Everyone wants to be the right man, and this is by no means a trivial desire. But Hemingway now appears to feel that he is winning and his own personality, always an important dramatic element in his writing, is, in *The Old Man and the Sea*, a kind of moral background. He tends to speak for Nature itself. Should Nature and Hemingway become identical one or the other will have won too total a victory.

The writer in the modern age may insist, 'Here I stand; I cannot do otherwise', but for Bellow the nagging question remains: 'Why is it *I* who cannot do otherwise?' Like Augie March, Bellow cannot find it in himself to assert the truth of *his* vision and then impose it on other people. On the other hand the urge to write persists and, like Augie, the writer finds himself faced with 'the double poser' – 'that if you make a move you may lose, but if you sit still you will decay.'

The problem, as always, is to channel one's energies correctly, and, when one acts, to act responsibly. But what does it *mean* for a writer to act responsibly? In *Dangling Man* Joseph has an affair with another woman, but he soon realises that what he is doing is out of character and that 'at the root of it all was my unwillingness to miss anything. A compact with one woman puts beyond reach what others might give us to enjoy.' He recognises that 'a man must accept limits and cannot give in to the wild desire to be everything and everyone to everything and everyone.' But what of the writer? He cannot make a comparable choice because for him there is nothing to renounce. He really is the embodiment of Dahfu's ideal in that whatever he imagines can instantly become reality – in a book. And the problem with this is that there is no pressure, nothing for the writer to press against, to define himself against, nothing except his whim to give a shape to his book. What Joseph does and how he acts depends entirely on Bellow's private decision; he has to make decisions to get the book written, but his very freedom from constraint goes against the implications of the book. The sense of failure Joseph feels at the end must be very close to that felt by his author.

As though recognising this, Bellow, in his next novel, set out to make the limits as tight as possible, taking as his theme the romantic idea of the double. In Romantic literature, as in *The Victim*, the double who haunts the hero is his other, darker self, and when the two come together a crisis occurs which leads to the destruction of the hero. Thus, since the story is synonymous with the consciousness of the hero, the story is itself haunted by the spectre of its own annihilation. Bellow, however, deliberately keeps the context absolutely realistic; he is not going to indulge in Romantic mythology since his overt theme is in effect a form of demythologising. But as a result he, the maker of the book, remains well outside it. Once again he is both too constrained and too free: too constrained by plot and chronology, but too free from any meaningful pressure in his construction of the book. Here, as in *Dangling Man*, we sense that great energy is not finding an outlet. As a result the frequent pain in the chest which afflicts all Bellow's heroes at one time or another is also what the reader is left with. There is a sense of tightness, of constriction, which comes of too much having to be left unsaid because of the way the book is constructed.

In the late forties, however, Bellow started experimenting with ways of loosening up without automatically going soft. The remarkable monologues of Dr Pep and Gooley MacDowell are the first results. And in the novel he was then working on, *The Adventures of Augie March*, he came to the decision that the answer lay in letting the hero speak for himself; the book would not be in the form of a diary or have a third-person narrator, but would go back in one sense to the origins of the novel and have the narrator speak to the reader as to a friend. In this way he clearly hoped to make a break with the moribund (decadent?) European forms of the novel as it then existed, and get back to something genuine, closer to the heart, perhaps more truly American. This is certainly the impression the novel itself seems to want to give, from its opening words:

I am an American, Chicago-born – Chicago, that somber city – and go at things as I have taught myself, free-style, and will make the record in my own way.

However, the freedom which the book flaunts is illusory. For Augie, as we have seen, lacks the Lutheran confidence in his own views which these lines imply. He is passive for all the book's six hundred pages, giving in to this pressure or that for a while and only pulling out when it looks as though he would finally have to commit himself. His is the stubbornness of silent negation, not of confident self-assertion; as a result lines like the above, or other remarks such as 'I have put in my time in the capitals of the world' or 'I am a sort of Columbus of those near-at-hand' sound forced and unreal.

Yet something happens in the course of the book which could not have happened had Bellow not taken the plunge in the way he has. The novel occupies a place in Bellow's development curiously analogous to the one *Molloy* occupies in Beckett's. I say curiously because where Beckett turned to French with *Molloy* in order to escape from the too great freedom of his first two novels, Bellow plunged into *The Adventures of Augie March* to get away from the constrictions of plot and diction imposed on him by *his* first two novels. Both books, however, mark a turning point in their authors' careers, and both exhibit that courage, that readiness to follow where instinct seems to lead, which is perhaps what distinguishes the major from the minor artist.

It is in *Augie March* that Bellow at last discovers his style, and he discovers it by accident, on the way, and where he probably least expected it. For the book comes to life when it focuses not on the banal hero but on those who set out to use him, on the grotesque Machiavels like Einhorn or Basteshaw or Mintouchian. And the reason for this is that our focus here is no longer single but double: we are made to see both the absurdity of these men, with their schemes for running the world, *and* how human and valuable their wild energy is. Where Augie remains shadowy because he is himself the source of light, Einhorn and the other characters, because they are both allowed to speak for themselves *and* looked at by Augie, suddenly come alive:

> I see before me next a fellow named Mintouchian, who is an Armenian, of course. We are sitting together in a Turkish bath having a conversation, except that Mintouchian is doing most of the talking, explaining various facts of existence to me . . .

Note the proximity of the two bodies, so that the physical weight of Mintouchian presses in on the narrator, and the way in which the narrative (this is the start of a chapter) seems suddenly to be free of its dependence on time. Seeing Mintouchian in his mind's eye, Augie can move freely from this specific scene to others and back as the whim takes him. But now the play of Augie's mind itself becomes an element

of the book, not something to be denied or disguised as was the play of
the author's mind in the earlier novels.

If one has to locate the place where the style seems suddenly to find
itself, one ought perhaps to turn to a scene in an earlier part of the
book:

> Einhorn kept me with him that evening; he didn't want to be alone.
> While I sat by he wrote his father's obituary in the form of an
> editorial for the neighbourhood paper. 'The return of the hearse
> from the newly covered grave leaves a man to pass through the last
> changes of nature who found Chicago a swamp and left it a great
> city. He came after the Great Fire, said to be caused by Mrs.
> O'Leary's cow, in flight from the conscription of the Hapsburg tyrant,
> and in his life as a builder proved that great palaces do not have to
> be founded on the bones of slaves . . . . The lesson of an American life
> like my father's, in contrast to that of the murderer of the Strelitzes
> and of his own son, is that achievements are compatible with decency.
> My father was not familiar with the observation of Plato that philo-
> sophy is the study of death, but he died nevertheless like a philo-
> sopher, saying to the ancient man who watched by his bedside in the
> last moments . . .' This was the vein of it, and he composed it ener-
> getically in half an hour, printing on sheets of paper at his desk, the
> tip of his tongue forward, scrunched up in his bathrobe and wearing
> his stocking cap.

Why is this both very funny and very moving? Old Einhorn, like
Augie, represents the best of the American tradition of honesty, self-
reliance and fortitude. But he is not telling us this about himself. It is
not even being *said* of him by someone else. In the forefront is the
bereaved son, writing down the words quickly and elegantly as he leans
over the desk, the tip of his tongue between his lips. That is one barrier
between us and the dead man. But Einhorn's absurd style is a second
barrier. The more he writes the wider grows the gap between the words
going down on paper and the actuality of the dead man. We laugh, but
neither at the pretentiousness of Einhorn nor at the pretensions of his
father. We laugh at the recognition of the fact that there will always
exist a gap between a man and anything, however flattering, that can
be said of him, and we laugh too at the way human beings suffer and
cope with their suffering and know so little about themselves and cling
even at moments like this to their foolish pride in what they believe
they can do well, and are nevertheless capable of deep love.

What Bellow has done here, as well as in Dr Pep's sermon and
Gooley MacDowell's address, is to force the *act of expression* into
greater and greater prominence. He does this by placing highly idio-

syncratic speakers in situations of great formality: the writing of an obituary, the delivering of an address, a sermon. *Seize the Day* is particularly interesting here. For how are we to take Wilhelm? He seems so sentimental, despairing, histrionic. He begs his wife: 'Margaret, go easy on me. You ought to. I'm at the end of my rope and feel that I'm suffocating. You don't want to be responsible for a person's destruction. You've got to let up. I feel I'm about to burst.' Are these not the antics a man like Allbee would go in for? A conversation Wilhelm has with his father about Margaret would seem to confirm this:

> 'Strange, Father? I'll show you what she's like.' Wilhelm took hold of his broad throat with brown-stained fingers and bitten nails and began to choke himself.
> 'What are you doing?' cried the old man.
> 'I'm showing you what she does to me.'
> 'Stop that – stop it!' the old man said, and tapped the table commandingly.... 'Stop this bunk. Don't expect me to believe in all kinds of voodoo.'

Dr Adler seems to be responding with the same sort of horror that Leventhal felt before the antics of Allbee. But there is a vital difference between Wilhelm and Allbee. The latter acted as he did partly out of sheer despair and partly out of the desire to force the world to give him what he felt it owed him. Wilhelm, on the other hand, seems to be acting out some obscure piece of ritualisation, as if by showing on his own body what was happening to his spirit he would reveal something important about what it means to be a man:

> The spirit, the peculiar burden of his existence lay upon him like an accretion, a load, a hump. In any moment of quiet, when sheer fatigue prevented him from struggling, he was apt to feel this mysterious weight, this growth or collection of nameless things which it was the business of his life to carry about.

What does a man do with this burden, the weight of his own being? As the book moves to its climax, Wilhelm is swept into the funeral procession of someone he doesn't know. Looking down finally at the dead stranger, Wilhelm feels the tears welling up, and he makes no effort to stop them:

> Soon he was past words, past reason, coherence. He could not stop. The source of all tears had suddenly sprung open within him, black, deep, and hot, and they were pouring out and convulsed his body, bending his stubborn head.... The great knot of ill and grief in his

throat swelled upward and he gave in utterly and held his face and wept. He cried with all his heart.

A man looks at him and utters the words that sum up the whole book: 'Oh my, oh my! To be mourned like that.' For now at last Wilhelm has found release for his great energy. But what he has *done* is not any action designed to further himself in the world; it is rather a gesture, a ritualised release which is the act of mourning. He cries not for the dead man or for himself, but for Man, that creature of infinite potential who turns his energy against himself and others and can find no way of making good use of the rich desire that is in his heart. The day is finally seized by Wilhelm because he has a sudden overpowering sense that the day can *never* be seized, only its passing mourned. In that ritual action we touch what it is that we are and how we are linked to the world.

There is of course something primitive in such an open exhibition of grief and suffering, and it does not go down too well in our hard-boiled yet sentimental Western society. As Mr Sammler tells the Indian scientist, Dr Lal, Jews are Asians too; despite their Westernisation they retain something of the primitiveness of Asia and the Eastern Mediterranean. But it would be wrong to identify Bellow's new-found style with his cultural or ethnic origins; before being a Jew or an American he is a man and a writer. His style, as we have seen, emerged as the answer to the problems of man's nature and his freedom with which the novels had always been concerned. In the later novels and stories it is simply that the fast talker and the hero have merged, and this has brought with it a new sense of exuberance and release. The hero's histrionics, his peculiar way of putting things, as though he always thought at an angle to the English language, are the result of Bellow's own attempts to find a way out of the crisis in which he found himself, without losing hold of his humanity. Herzog's letters are a symptom of his illness, but they are also what help him through it. Like Hamlet he deliberately exaggerates his condition, 'as if by staggering he could recover his balance . . . or by admitting a bit of madness could recover his senses.'

Instead of trying to sort out the complications beforehand, Bellow lets his characters *express* them. He no longer needs the overt formality of an address or a sermon to give us the sense of the man speaking the words; rather, the whole novel becomes a stage on which the hero struts and shouts, hoping, if his voice and gestures are violent enough, to surprise himself into an understanding of the truth. Here, for example, is Henderson as we first see him:

The facts begin to crowd me and soon I get a pressure in the chest. A disorderly rush begins – my parents, my wives, my girls, my

children, my farm, my animals, my habits, my money, my music
lessons, my drunkenness, my prejudices, my brutality, my teeth, my
face, my soul! I have to cry, 'No, no, get back, curse you, let me
alone!' But how can they let me alone? They belong to me. They are
mine. And they pile into me from all sides. It turns into chaos.

Here, once again, is the familiar pressure in the chest, but this time it
does not grip the reader, only the hero. We laugh at Henderson, that
amazing, ridiculous man, but we also sympathise. And because Henderson is speaking these words, not writing them in a diary or having his
thought paraphrased; because he seems to speak them as they come,
not trying to impress like Augie March or trying to get on with a story,
but following out the strands in his own fashion and coming back to the
main business only when he feels like it, we too, the readers, find ourselves speaking his words. And it is as though, as the words acquire
weight, a tangible reality, are breathed out by us, the pressure on
our chest disappears. Instead of constriction, there is release. Henderson
too of course goes to Africa to silence the voice within him, but what he
learns there is that we are all saddled with speech as with our bodies,
and that it is only through speech that understanding – a certain,
limited understanding – eventually comes.

The title of the novel suggests a Romantic triumph of the imagination, for if human beings can bring about rain then Dahfu is right and
there is no real gap between our desires and the laws of the universe –
the world is what we want it to be, provided we want hard enough.
But surely the title is ironic: Henderson is tricked into becoming rain
king, and the onset of rain clearly has nothing to do with his own
efforts. But is that quite true? The book is so written that as we read on
we start to wonder whether there is not in fact some link between the
religious ceremony that precedes and the coming of rain. We are made
to do two contradictory things at the same time, to recognise the folly
of imagining that the world is subject to our desires, as the title suggests,
and to suspend judgement on the whole question. Far from being
broken by this contradiction, the book in fact makes it possible for us
to hold both views simultaneously.

The crucial moment for Henderson comes when he has to lift the
enormous statue of the goddess of rain. She glitters before him, oiled
and smooth. None of the members of the tribe has been able to lift her.
Henderson steps up close, puts his arms round her, presses his belly
against her, and sinks to his knees. To him she is alive, an opponent
rather than an object, an intimate and friend rather than an enemy:

... with the close pleasure you experience in a dream or on one of
those warm beneficial floating idle days when every desire is satisfied,

I laid my cheek against her wooden bosom. I cranked down my knees and said to her, 'Up you go, dearest. No use trying to make yourself heavier; if you weighed twice as much I'd lift you anyway.' The wood gave to my pressure and benevolent Mummah with her fixed smile yielded to me; I lifted her from the ground and carried her twenty feet to her new place among the other gods.

There is something in this of every schoolboy adventure story. But there is something of the schoolboy adventure story in every novel, though usually it is heavily disguised. Bellow, however, is luminously honest here. He does not pretend that it requires a superhuman effort to lift the idol; it all comes as easily as a dream, as easily as imagining, as easily as writing and reading. Yet we sense also that a very great effort has indeed been made, and that something important though mysterious has been achieved. As we read these lines we experience the pleasureable ease of the imagination while at the same time understanding that the imagination and the world can never be one. Something happens in the course of these lines, and it does not happen to the tribe or the goddess or Henderson himself; it happens to us.

PART II

MODERNISM AND CULTURE

5 English Studies and European Culture

In memory of Martin Wight

No one has ever doubted that English culture forms a part of European culture. There have been moments of nationalist fervour, such as the Elizabethan age or the period of the ballad revival in the late eighteenth century, when Englishmen stressed their native heritage and derided the popularity of Italian melodrama or classical mythology, but the very self-consciousness of such movements is the best proof of the fact that Englishmen have always regarded their literary and cultural heritage as stretching back into a common European past and outward into a common European present. For what is Old English poetry except one branch of Germanic heroic poetry? What is Middle English poetry except one branch of Christian European art? How else can one describe the poetry of Wordsworth and Shelley, of Eliot and Auden, except as part of European Romanticism and European Modernism? It is true that English literature has evolved according to its own native laws to a greater extent than the literature of France or Italy; it is true that there has always been a time-lag between artistic developments on the Continent and in the British Isles greater than can be accounted for simply by the size of the Channel. But no one would question the fact that Machaut was a greater influence on Chaucer than was Langland; Ariosto a greater influence on Spenser than was Chaucer; Cervantes a greater influence on Sterne than was Defoe; Dante and Laforgue greater influences on Eliot than were Tennyson or Arnold. And until the present century there have been few English writers who have not been familiar with the Hebrew Bible and the Greek and Latin classics, whatever their attitudes to their European contemporaries. It would seem perfectly natural then that the study of English at University should take account of these facts and ensure that the distortion of perspective which would inevitably result from the teaching of English literature in isolation be avoided at all costs. This has not, however, been the case in the past, and the reasons for this, whether hidden or overt, are particularly interesting. It may be useful to begin by examining some of the *disadvantages* of studying English in the context of European culture.

There is, to begin with, the problem of language. The growth of the study of English coincided with the decline of the study of Latin. The two phenomena are intimately related. From the Renaissance to the late nineteenth century the academic study of literature was the study of the Greek and Latin classics, and it was conducted – though with declining fervour – in Latin. The growth of English as an academic discipline is the growth of the recognition of the vernacular, and the contemporary vernacular in particular, as a valid object of study.[1] The battle between Ancients and Moderns is as old as the Renaissance itself, and one episode in that battle is embodied in vernacular English literature as the Appendix to Swift's *Tale of a Tub*. But the result of the battle in the present century was that the rise of the study of modern vernacular literature led to the decline of classical studies. The modern student of English is thus rarely trained in the classics and only rarely feels sufficiently at home in another European tongue to be able to master its literature. If, through some accident, such as having lived abroad, he can do this, then he usually opts for a degree in modern languages. Thus to try and integrate English studies into a European context means, for all practical purposes, asking students to read non-English literature in translation.

Clearly it is better to read Dante and Virgil in translation than not to read them at all. On the other hand, unless there is some awareness of what gets lost in translation, this method presents some very real dangers. And, strange as this may seem, the greatest of these is the danger that the work will be *too easily assimilated*.

Let us examine what this means. We all know the present vogue for 'modern' renderings of the great European classics – Homer, Virgil, Horace, Dante. Some of these are extremely good. All of them encourage people to buy and read works they would probably never otherwise have tackled. And yet the very nature of their success is a gauge of the danger I have mentioned. For the fact is that Homer and Virgil and Horace and Dante are *not* modern. In a way one could say that they were important to us precisely because they are not modern, precisely because they are *other* – all that we are not. Although no one today would want to be the Renaissance schoolboy toiling day in day out over Cicero and Seneca, that schoolboy had an awareness, which the modern reader of Day Lewis's translation of Virgil or Ciardi's translation of Dante has not, that these were difficult poets, hard writers who had put a lifetime's effort into their work and would give a lifetime's reading to the diligent reader.

The last thing I want to suggest is that all easy books are bad and that there is virtue in mere difficulty. I am not at all sure that an 'easy' book like Waugh's *Decline and Fall* is not superior to *Finnegans Wake* or Mann's *Joseph and his Brothers*. What I do want to suggest is that the very availability of the great classics in good modern translations, the very proliferation of paperback editions of every single 'great book' in the world, can drug us into an unresponsive assimilation, a blurring of the very real differences between these books and the latest piece of English fiction. Everyone who has spent some time in one of the larger paperback bookshops in the country must have experienced that sinking feeling in the pit of the stomach, that vertigo and nausea in the face of so much literature, all there, all available, and, in the end, all very much the same . . . For there is a satiety of the intellect as well as of the stomach.

One can of course argue that the same problem arises in the reading of the English classics, also available in good modern paperback editions. But here the difference in the language, however small, between even a Victorian novel and a contemporary one, will always remain as a built-in safeguard against too easy an assimilation. We will always feel that we are reading the works of a particular individual, Dickens or Trollope or Thackeray, with his own voice, his own turn of phrase, his own very individual *breath*. And we will unconsciously come to respect this voice, to listen to it and for it and eventually come to recognise it for what it is: the living speech of a man who miraculously lives in us through his books. But reading European literature in modern translation we may too readily see in it nothing but a reflection of ourselves, and therefore get precisely nothing out of it except the satisfaction of having 'got through' one small portion of all the literature that is available.

But can this be avoided? Is it even desirable that it be avoided? Do we not always read the literature of the past only for that which is directly relevant to ourselves now, today? There is a philosophical school, which we might term the historicist school, which argues that since we are living in the present, it is only 'in the present' that we can understand the literature of the past. It is no use asking: 'What does this or that book really mean?', since we can never discover the nature of that 'really'. We can only ask: 'What does this mean to me, now?' Only by facing this fact, the historicist argues, can we get rid of the dead weight of past authority and make use of the literature of the past for our present-day needs; only in this way can literature be taken out

of the hands of those established in power and used as the instrument of
freedom and liberation it really is.

Like most extreme arguments this one contains a partial truth, which
it distorts by presenting it as the whole truth. To read Cicero and Virgil
merely because it is supposed to be 'good for one' is obviously pernicious. But is the alternative to select only those bits of Cicero and Virgil
which immediately appeal to one? Because *we* believe that truth to love
is of far greater value than fidelity to marriage vows should we therefore side entirely with Paolo and Francesca and condemn the Dante
who condemns them? Because *we* find it easier to conceive of a world
dominated by evil than of one in which spontaneous goodness will
occasionally rise up to resist that evil, should we read *King Lear* as a
Renaissance version of Beckett's *Endgame*?[2] If we reply in the negative
to all these questions and point out that we must try and read the
literature of the past in the spirit in which it was written, the historicist
will argue that we are not really reading literature at all. We are merely
substituting certain ideas about Dante or Shakespeare for a true response
to the text. But the historicist does not really go far enough. To his
question: 'What can we know about the literature of the past since we
can never emerge from the prejudices of our own age?', we may reply:
'What do you call the past? Five hundred years ago? One hundred
years? Fifty? Ten? Five? One year? Ten minutes? One minute?'
To put these questions to him is to recognise that what he is arguing
for is not the impossibility of bridging the gap between *cultural epochs*,
but between *any two people*. It is not just the past that I cannot understand except in my (limited and prejudiced) present terms, but any
form of communication that I cannot understand except in my (limited
and prejudiced) private terms. It looks as if the premises of the historicist drive one back into a complete solipsism, a total relativism, which
has dogged philosophy almost from its beginnings, and to which one of
the earliest answers was the best. The whole of Socrates's philosophy
seems to be an attempt to answer just such arguments by showing,
among other things, that if we use language at all it is because some
degree of agreement as to meaning is possible among people. Of course
there will always be those for whom anything less than *total* communication is unbearable, and who would therefore rather have none at all
than only a partial and limited form of communication. Indeed, much
of the most significant literature of the past century and a half has
sprung from just such an impulse, and I will have more to say about that
later. But for the moment it is important to note that since literature
uses language, and since language depends on some degree of social agreement, it can never be either totally assimilated or totally misunderstood.
And this is as true of today's newspapers as it is of Cicero or Virgil.

Perhaps, though, it is the function of art to force us out of our solipsism, to make us understand what it is like to be *other*, and that in this way art differs significantly from other forms of communication. If this is so, then one of the dangers of using modern translations in the academic study of literature is that one loses just this sense of otherness, that one is confirmed in the solipsist position even more strongly than if one had never read more than one line of the original of Dante or Virgil. One of the essential functions of culture, which is to make us understand our past, rather than simply accepting it, or trying to over-throw it, is then in danger of dissolving as past and present merge. It is no coincidence that the extreme historicist position taken up by Heidegger and his pupils coincides in time with the growth of the paperback industry, which is busily feeding modern translations of the European classics to readers avid for culture. From a certain point of vantage one can see that these are two sides of the same coin.[3]

Having examined this first danger at some length we can now deal with the second a little more quickly. In any case, it is really only a variant on the first. Any attempt to deal with more than one literature in a university course makes it inevitable that a choice, a rigorous selection of which books are to be studied, will have to be made. Instead of following a national literature through from its origins to the present day, as one would do if studying only one literature, one is forced to study by means of what the Americans have aptly named a 'great books course'. This involves studying (always in translation, of course), a number of the great books of the Western world, from the *Iliad* to *The Magic Mountain*, via, for example, *Oedipus Rex*, St Augustine's *Confessions*, *The Divine Comedy*, *Phèdre*, and *Wilhelm Meister*.

The dangers inherent in such an approach are obvious. In the first place, who makes the selection? If it is the faculty of the University, they are then put in the position of having to defend their choices, an absurd way to approach literature. If it is the student, then he will naturally choose what has the most immediate appeal, which will be what fits in with ideas he already has, and he will lose the benefit of coming into contact with new ideas. At any rate it will lead to all the anguish of choosing between largely unknown quantities, with the consequent feeling that he should perhaps have chosen differently. Secondly, and more important, this principle of a 'great books course' has the effect of neutralising to some extent what any one author is saying. If you take a book and are told to analyse it; if you are told, moreover, that it is one of the masterpieces of European culture; then the temptation is very strong to look for special, *aesthetic*, criteria, which will validate such a judgement. We all know the tedium of those critical books which go into endless detail about the patterns and relationships within a single work of art, as if this was somehow the *reason* for its greatness.[4] Instead of reading it as the statement of a man or a period, something that might affect our lives if we respond to it, we adopt the attitude of the *connoisseur* towards it. We learn to move among the masterpieces of the past without fear of being touched by them, picking one up here, putting another down there, praising the beauty of each, but totally dead inside to whatever any of them might be saying. The 'great books course', ideally conceived to bring culture to everyone, can easily turn us all into little frozen connoisseurs, able to talk about everything but responding to nothing. For, even more than reading the classics in translation without ever tackling the originals, to read only a choice of great books without reference to the authors or to the age from which they spring is to shut out the claims that others make upon us and to retreat even deeper into the solipsistic 'I'.

ADVANTAGES OF A PURELY ENGLISH COURSE

In the face of this the advantages of a university course where the subject studied is nothing but English are obvious. Added to it is the peculiar richness and continuity of the native tradition, so well described by Sir Maurice Powicke in his little book, *Medieval England*:

> We mean that there is a continuity, rarely to be seen elsewhere, in English history. Properly speaking, there is no medieval and no modern history of England: there is just English history. We have had none of those revolutions which make a cleavage between past and present and are, in the words of the poet, 'as lightning to reveal new seasons'. From time to time we have suffered – suffered terribly – but our land has never been devastated as France and Germany, Italy and Spain have been devastated. Our laws and language have grown and changed continuously and almost imperceptibly. Many of the institutions and local divisions, here and there the actual build-ings and agricultural arrangements of Saxon, Norman, Plantagenet times are still with us – so that, though we know it not, we are in a medieval world. There is a common humanity in our literature, so that Chaucer's pilgrims, the noblemen, clowns, and rustics in Shakespeare's plays, all the people in the *Pilgrim's Progress*, the circle of Sir Roger de Coverley and the ghostly villagers in Gray's 'Elegy', form one big company with the characters in the novels of Miss Austen and Dickens. They are intelligible people: we understand them, and they seem, as it were, to be speaking to us . . .
>
> Everyone who has wandered much about England cannot fail to have been moved by the sense of unity in English history, for our history has been caught and retained by the country-side, so that an English country-side is a harmonious blending of nature and the

works of men. And if he uses his imagination in reflecting upon what he feels and observes, the wanderer cannot but be impressed by the unceasing receptivity of England on the one hand, and by her insular tenacity on the other. The English have absorbed all varieties of foreign influence, yet hitherto they have never been disturbed by them. English history, like the English country, is full of foreign things; they abound, yet they have ceased to be foreign and are part of England; so that even the barrows or burial-places of early man or Germanic kings, even Stonehenge from prehistoric times and the walls of Pevensey from Roman times add a quality always new and subdued to a harmony of tone and to a beauty which have grown old with them.

This was written in 1931 and I doubt if Powicke would feel so confident today about the intelligibility of the characters of Chaucer or Dickens, or about the peaceful and harmonious character of the English country-side. And yet even in these last forty or so years things have changed less than we are sometimes led to imagine. In one of his letters Keats writes: 'I like, I love England. I like its living men. Give me a long brown plain . . . so I may meet with some of Edmund Ironside's descendants. Give me a barren mould, so I may meet with some shadowing of Alfred in the shape of a gipsy, a huntsman or a shepherd. Scenery is fine – but human nature is finer – the sward is richer for the tread of a real nervous English foot.' And this love of the land for itself and for its history can still be seen in writers as diverse as John Cowper Powys, T. H. White, even William Golding, who can hardly be described as sheltering from the burdensome present in an idealised past. The marvellous work of G. H. Hoskins – *The Making of the English Landscape, English Landscapes* – has helped us to 'read' the impact of human nature on English scenery from prehistoric times to the present; and his pupils have furnished us with details of the interaction of history and geography more abundant than Powicke would have dreamt of. And it is still possible, in present-day industrial Britain, to go from one end of the island to the other on foot and keeping off the roads, as John Hillaby did in the summer of 1967 and recorded in his delightful *Journey Through Britain*.

What is important to us, however, is the fact that English literature, of all the Western vernaculars, stretches in a virtually unbroken line from 650 to the present day. To study this literature historically is to be made aware of the ways a national literature can mature and develop, and of the ways in which a literature is always bound to a living language. A work such as C. S. Lewis's *Studies in Words* shows this approach at its best. Here the semantic study of language and the changing meanings of words such as 'silly' or 'good' reveals to us the changing nature of the civilisation and makes us aware of the nature of the very tools we now use in daily speech. Because English is made up of so many diverse elements – Anglo-Saxon, Scandinavian, Latin, French – the study of the language is not only fascinating in itself, but it is also closely related to the social and political changes the country has seen in its long history. The study of the literature of England cannot be divorced from the study of the changing nature of the language, and both are clearly related to the institutions of the country. Thus to spend three years at university studying all this in some depth is not only to understand the otherness of the past, but also its present relevance. It is – or would seem to be – to become truly cultured.

THE DISADVANTAGES OF A PURELY ENGLISH COURSE

I have been arguing a case for limiting the study of literature to English by pointing out first that no one has ever questioned the fact that English culture is a part of European culture, but that from this it does not necessarily follow that English literature ought to be supplanted or even supplemented at university level by the study of European literature. Indeed, I have argued, there are crucial disadvantages in doing this, as well as enormous advantages to be gained from a thorough and historical study of English literature in its social and historical context. Having done this, I should like, for the rest of this essay, to consider some of the disadvantages of such an approach, and to ask whether it is not possible to study English in the context of European culture while avoiding some of the pitfalls I have outlined above.

The main disadvantage of a purely English course is the distortion of perspective which this involves. There is no real danger of our failing to see that Spenser was influenced by Ariosto, or Milton by Virgil, or Pope by Horace. These influences spring at us out of their works, and English studies have always been aware – perhaps too aware – of their importance. No. What I am thinking of is something much less easy to define, a much subtler distortion. One so subtle, in fact, that it tends to pass unnoticed. And therein lies the danger. It is not just that there is a tendency to forget that so much of what was written and read in England until the eighteenth century was written in Latin (and printed on the continent, so that even catalogues of all the books printed in this country give one little or no idea of what was being read); it is not just that from 1066 to the middle of the fourteenth century the official language of England was French. It is that we inevitably tend to regard those areas of English literature which most clearly reflect English culture as being at the core of the English tradition. And those areas are of course the novel of the eighteenth and nineteenth centuries, with its freedom from the constraints of genre and its minute depiction of English society as it found it. This distortion of perspective does not affect poetry so much as fiction, and it does not affect those writers who are most obviously working in a European tradition, such as Spenser and Milton, since it is easy to see that they need to be understood within the context of those traditions. But it does affect those authors who appear to be working in a native tradition, such as Chaucer, Shakespeare and Sterne. There is a strong built-in tendency to read these writers as approximating more or less closely to the norms of the nineteenth-century realist novel, a tendency which has been wittily described as the notion that all literature aspires to the condition of *Middlemarch*.

Let us look first at the example of Chaucer. It has long been customary to see Chaucer as standing at the source of the English literary tradition, and to see him, with Shakespeare and Dickens, as one of the great 'English' writers. The great medievalist, W. P. Ker, was able to make the following statement about Chaucer's own development:

> Chaucer's whole literary career shows him emerging from the average opinion and manner of his contemporaries, and coming out from the medieval crowd to stand apart by himself, individual and free.

Other scholars have endorsed this picture, and have given it more body by distinguishing three periods in Chaucer's development: an early period, which is French and conventional; a middle period, which is Italian and a little more realistic; and the final flowering of his genius, in which he reveals himself as English and thoroughly earthly and realistic. Compared to his mature earthy realism, as exemplified in the Wife of Bath, we are told, the art of the rest of the Middle Ages reveals its aridity, its asceticism, its artificial and conventional nature.

But is this picture accurate? Recent studies have shown that Chaucer's 'realism', no less than his 'idealism', as exemplified by the Knight's and Squire's tales, is traditional and conventional in character.[5] The descriptions of the characters in the General Prologue of the *Canterbury Tales*, far from being individuating and 'novelistic', are now seen to be a careful blend of type and detail, with a cunning use of iconographical motifs as rich in conventional associations as those of Dante and Langland. The Wife of Bath herself presents her case with such a dazzling array of Biblical references that we are at first disposed to take her at her face value; but we soon come to see that Chaucer is as ironic in his presentation of her as he is in his description of the Prioress, and that her parade of Scriptural authorities does more to condemn her in the eyes of the discerning reader than any of her actions.

But does this mean that we are now being presented with another

Chaucer, better in some ways and less good in others, than the traditional image? I think not. What is happening is that we are learning to see Chaucer more clearly. We are learning that the conflict does not arise between originality and convention, but between the good and bad *uses* of convention – or perhaps we could put it another way and say that it all depends on whether a poet uses or is used by the conventions. We can now see Chaucer's growing mastery not as the shedding of conventional elements, but as the mastery of conventions. If one compares, for instance, the *Troilus* of Chaucer with his source in Boccaccio's *Filostrato*, we can see this mastery at work. Boccaccio's poem is written according to the conventions of courtly love: poet and reader accept these conventions as do the characters. But Chaucer *uses* the conventions in order to make a point about the idealism of Troilus alone. The narrator and Pandarus ensure that the audience becomes aware of the fact that it is Troilus who conducts *his life* according to certain poetic conventions which, because they are not shared by the other characters, are seen to be arbitrary and to some extent absurd. Thus when Troilus finds himself for the first time alone (except for Pandarus) with his beloved, he kneels down at her bedside and suddenly, overcome with love, does what the code says he should and swoons. Were the whole poem written within the conventions of the courtly code we would simply accept this as natural and pass on. But this is not Chaucer's method. At once Pandarus rushes forward, admonishes Troilus for his act, strips him, and pushes him into bed with Criseyde. At this point we feel the actual *weight* of Troilus, the mass of his body, in a way we never do in Boccaccio. And the gap between the code and real life, the ideal and the actuality, is brought home to us. Nor is Chaucer's point simply that Troilus is wrong and Pandarus right; as we see later on, the 'realism' of Pandarus is as limited as the 'idealism' of Troilus. Out of the clash of the two the reader is forced to recognise the clichés by which his own life is governed and thus to some extent to free himself from their dominion. The literary conventions, like the convention which is language, allow Chaucer to develop his ironic tale, just as Shakespeare will later make use of the conventions of his own day.

What the example of Chaucer reveals is not just the inadequacy of the old view, but the particular premises of that view. These can be simply defined as those of a *cultural Darwinism*. History, according to this view, moves forward and upward, culminating in the present, and the arts follow the same law. Like all theories, this one has historical roots – in the rational positivism of the eighteenth and nineteenth centuries. Although two World Wars have revealed the absurdity of its liberal optimism, it still has a tenacious hold, especially in the field of art history. Ker's view of Chaucer's development is only one tiny example of it, but it permeates nearly all histories of literature and of the visual arts. Art historians are more aware of its dangers today than are historians of literature. The latter still tend to speak of medieval drama, for instance, as a poor forerunner of Elizabethan drama, or of the prose of Nashe and Greene as a hesitant groping towards the form of the novel as found in Defoe and Richardson.[6]

Nashe provides a particularly interesting example. The most striking thing about his writing is the exuberance of his style, but when we ask what function this style has in his work we are usually given answers that start from the same premises as the traditional novel, which was not born till a hundred years after Nashe. Thus Ian Watt, in his *The Rise of the Novel*, one of the best known books on the subject, writes:

> The previous stylistic tradition for fiction was not primarily concerned with the correspondence of words to things, but rather with the extrinsic beauties which could be bestowed upon description and action by the use of rhetoric.

But these terms – 'the correspondence of words to things', 'the extrinsic beauties . . . bestowed upon description', are clichés of the late seventeenth century, the product of that change of direction taken by European culture after the Renaissance and of which the rise of science, the rise of the bourgeoisie, the development of Calvinism, are all aspects. The words of Ian Watt could have come out of the famous *History of the Royal Society* written in 1676 by Thomas Sprat, and they totally fail to account for Nashe's style. Nashe is not a bumbling forerunner of Defoe. He belongs to a European tradition far older than that of the novel, a tradition which goes back to Lucian in the second century A.D., and runs through Erasmus, Rabelais, Swift and Sterne, and into Joyce, Nabokov and Beckett in the present century. This is a tradition which is less interested in the presentation of character and society and more concerned with the problem of discourse itself: what happens to speech when it gets into books? What happens to words when they get into novels? What distortions inevitably occur when I put my life into a book? These questions, which worry writers like Rabelais and Sterne, do not seem to exist for the traditional novel, which complacently takes its own values for granted and draws a veil over the time and effort required for the creation of art. But they are the very questions we have come to associate with *modern* fiction, with the anti-novel of Joyce or Beckett or Robbe-Grillet. The light-hearted jokes Sterne makes at the expense of a novelist like Richardson are just those which furnish Sartre with his strongest weapons when, in *La Nausée*, he condemns the traditional novel for its 'bad faith'.

But if this is so then a very interesting point emerges. Perhaps the failure of the English academic world to come to terms with modernism

stems from the same source as its failure (until recent years) to come to
terms with the Middle Ages, and with such writers as Nashe and Sterne.
Both are the result of taking the traditional novel as the unquestioned
norm and trying to assimilate all fiction to it. And this in turn is the
result of the implicit acceptance of a cultural Darwinism which is
directly related to the liberal positivism of the last part of the nineteenth century, which is the time when the academic study of English
was taking root. And we are now beginning to see that the major
critical books that have appeared in the last few years owe their
breadth, their understanding of the many literatures of antiquity and of
the Middle Ages, to a thorough assimilation of the lessons of Modernism. Let us glance at two of the greatest of these books, *Mimesis*, by
Erich Auerbach, and *Anatomy of Criticism*, by Northrop Frye, for
among other things what they impart is a notion of European culture.

THE NOTION OF EUROPEAN CULTURE

Auerbach was brought up in the old German philological tradition. He
was a classicist and a medievalist by training, and, like so many others,
he left his native Germany when the Nazis came to power. He wrote
Mimesis, his greatest book, in Istanbul between 1942 and 1945. It is an
attempt to explore the rendering of reality in European writing from
Homer to Virginia Woolf. Auerbach's method is to take a short passage
of prose or verse and subject it to minute syntactic analysis. In so doing
he moves forward from the passage to its immediate context, from that
to the wider context of the author's other works or those of his contemporaries, and from that to the whole culture from which the passage
sprang. Each chapter is thus a remarkable demonstration of the unity
of form and content, not just in what we accept as literature, but in
historical writing, in chronicles, in autobiographies: the syntax is the
age as the style is the man. In dealing with the Bible, Tacitus, Mon-
taigne and Pascal, as well as Cervantes, Shakespeare and Goethe,
Auerbach breaks down the barriers which academics have drawn up
round the term 'literature' and shows us how closely all forms of discourse are linked to the ages that produced them. Naturally he is more
revealing on ancient and medieval authors, not just because he is more
familiar with them, but because his method, which is the absolute anti-
thesis of the old biographical approach, is more suited to the anonymous
author than to the one who deliberately tries to differentiate himself
from his age – to find that 'subtler language' with which men, from the
Renaissance, and especially from Romanticism onwards, have tried to
express that which is unique to themselves.

Auerbach's method, however, as he himself says in his epilogue, was in part dictated by the fact that Istanbul during the war was not the best place to find the kind of 'technical literature' he would have required had he been writing a more conventional book:

> The lack of technical literature and periodicals may also serve to explain that my book has no notes. Aside from the texts, I quote comparatively little, and that little it was easy to include in the body of the book. On the other hand it is quite possible that the book owes its existence to just this lack of a rich and specialized vocabulary. If it had been possible for me to acquaint myself with all the work that has been done on so many subjects, I might never have reached the point of writing.

But earlier, in his chapter on Virginia Woolf, he remarked:

> There is greater confidence in synthesis gained through full exploitation of an everyday occurence than in a chronologically well-ordered total treatment which accompanies the subject from beginning to end, attempts not to omit anything that is externally important, and emphasizes the great turning points of destiny. It is possible to compare this technique of modern writers with that of certain modern philologists, who hold that the interpretation of a few passages from *Hamlet*, *Phèdre*, or *Faust* can be made to yield more, and more decisive information about Shakespeare, Racine, or Goethe and their times than would a systematic and chronological treatment of their lives and works. Indeed, the present book may be cited as an illustration . . .

Thus *Mimesis* itself, he sees, could not have been written without the examples of writers like Joyce and Virginia Woolf, who break up strict chronology, and make all of the past instantaneously present. But that is not its only link with this century. Like the great synthesising works of his art historian contemporaries and fellow exiles, Auerbach is impelled to examine the whole of Western culture as an act of faith and piety in a time when that culture seemed on the point of being engulfed by the barbarity of fascism. Writing in Istanbul as the war draws to an end, Auerbach concludes his epilogue:

> I hope that my study will reach its readers – both my friends of former years, if they are still alive, as well as all the others for whom it was intended. And may it contribute to bringing together again those whose love for our western history has serenely persevered.

Anatomy of Criticism, which was written by a Protestant Canadian rather than a German exile, and which came out in 1957, is a totally different kind of book. Nevertheless, the two have much in common – or rather, they are complementary. Frye argues that there comes a time in every discipline when we cease to add yet more facts to those already existing, and suddenly understand the laws underlying the individual facts. He feels that the pragmatic approach to literature – 'one damn book after another' – should give way to an approach which recognises that literature as a whole has a certain shape, is governed by certain laws. The basic law is that of *displacement*: all literature is the displacement of a central myth which cannot be formulated except through such displacement. Seen in this way literature is no longer a series of objects but a set of forms. Frye thus sets out to write what might be called a generative grammar of literature, in the same way as linguists have attempted to do for language itself. As Roland Barthes,[7] the French critic whose work bears many interesting resemblances to that of Frye, has said:

> Confronted with the impossibility of mastering all the phrases of a language, the linguist decides to set up a *hypothetical model of description*, whereby he can explain how the infinite phrases which make up a language are engendered.

In a similar way Frye endeavours to explain how the infinite works which make up the totality of literature are engendered. The effect of this is rather frightening. What we had thought of as a solid, stable object, is now seen to be only a form, what we had thought of as a 'given' is suddenly seen to be the result of certain kinds of assumption, which vary from epoch to epoch and from country to country. All art operates according to conventions, for it is the conventions that make communication possible, and the more an artist thinks he can do without these the more likely he is to fall a victim to them. The nineteenth-century novel, which imagined it was exploring the world around it or expressing the inmost feelings of the author, is seen to be full of the clichés of romance, the dark passionate evil heroine, for instance, always standing in opposition to the fair gentle good heroine. As Frye remarks: 'When the two are involved with the same hero, the plot usually has to get rid of the dark one or make her into a sister if the story is to end happily'. His examples include Scott's *Ivanhoe*, Fenimore Cooper's *The Last of the Mohicans*, Wilkie Collins's *The Woman in White*, Edgar Allan Poe's *Ligeia*, Melville's *Pierre* (a tragedy because the hero chooses the dark girl who is also his sister), and Hawthorne's *The Marble Faun*.

Frye's book, as we have seen, has much in common with modern linguistics. It also has much in common with the work of Nietzsche,

Freud and Mallarmé, for what it reveals is one of the key notions behind modern developments in the arts and the social sciences, the idea that culture itself is not a 'given', but is man-made and therefore to be explained by reference to men. As Nietzsche realised, the peculiar thing about man is that he is the only animal with a history. But there must be a reason for this, and Nietzsche suggests that what has driven civilisation forward is a feeling of guilt which is initially repressed and projected outwards, the projection then causing further repression, in an ever-increasing spiral. Civilisation itself is thus seen to be a kind of dynamic displacement which engenders further displacement. In exactly the same way Freud saw the cycle occurring in the individual human being. At the same time artists began to see that the norms and forms they had inherited from the past did not correspond to reality itself, but were merely the spectacles through which it had been customary to see reality.

The great discovery of Modernism then is that the past is not a solid mass, weighing down on the present, but is itself in need of reinterpretation in terms of the present. The world is not 'like this'; it is only 'like this when I wear this particular set of spectacles'. In other words, the loss of belief in a transcendental authority eventually led, by the end of the nineteenth century, to a relativisation of all facts. Nothing is given, all is in need of interpretation. It is no coincidence then that it is the Modernist movement in the arts which rediscovers the visual art and the poetry of the Far East, the sculpture of Africa, the songs of the Middle Ages, the music of India. Once the norms of the Renaissance and of the seventeenth century were seen for what they were (only one of a possible set of conventions),[8] it was possible to assimilate and employ art forms which had seemed brutish and barbarian to the eighteenth and nineteenth centuries. Modernism, as Eliot stressed, is thus a rediscovery of the past, and Northrop Frye's book, so medieval in its organisation, is, as he himself is the first to acknowledge, a product of the Modernist revolution. It is important precisely because it brings into the academy the central ideas of the moderns, ideas which, understandably, the academy has never been too willing to face up to.

THE ACADEMY AND THE MARKET-PLACE

Although the university as we know it dates from the Middle Ages, the academic study of literature dates from the Renaissance. The Renaissance is the first of the many European movements which are the result of a peculiar self-consciousness. When Machiavelli donned his Roman toga and retired into his library to read the books of the ancients, he acknowledged, for perhaps the first time, that books are something special, peculiar, apart. And of what use are books? They put us in touch with a past which is nobler than the present, with a classical past which we must strive to emulate. It is this view of culture which academics have seen it as their task to hand down from generation to generation, until we come to Arnold's *Culture and Anarchy*. And it is in reaction to this monolithic, static, and ultimately stultifying view of culture that the historicists I mentioned earlier were rebelling. They wanted none of this piety towards a dead past. In its place they wanted something which would speak to them, to their condition, rather than foist upon them the assumptions and values of a patrician élite. Thus a polarisation was set up, which we can see most clearly at certain periods of turmoil in the history of education, when the public divides into two camps, the conservative patrician academic élite and the radical historicist revolutionaries. Unfortunately, both positions involve a distortion of the complex truth.

The polarisation is already there in the sixteenth century. For what else is the quarrel of Protestants and Catholics except the struggle between those who will accept only their inner promptings and those who will accept only the authority of the Church? And, of course, the argument cannot be resolved on the premises of either side, for both oversimplify the relation between inner and outer, between spirit and letter, freedom and authority.[9] We have heard much recently of student revolutionaries and academic reactionaries; it is perhaps a slight comfort to realise that they were already deep in argument four hundred and fifty years ago.

When Machiavelli put on his toga to go into his study he became a symbol of a crucial change in European thought. As Panofsky has shown, the Middle Ages were not conscious of classical antiquity because they were in a sense at one with it.[10] That is why C. S. Lewis has felt that Gavin Douglas's translation of the *Aeneid* is closer to the original than is Dryden's translation. When people start imitating classical antiquity it means that they no longer feel at one with it – it is separate from them, cut off by the darkness of the Middle Ages, that Gothic and barbarian time. And this view of antiquity, as something different and worthy of imitation, is at the root of all study of the humanities up to the present time. It is against this that those rebel who would have us study nothing but the contemporary and the immediately appealing. There is, however, another answer to the dilemma.

When Shakespeare uses classical myth he does so in a very different way from Milton. With Milton it is a matter of conscious reconstruction. With Shakespeare the gods and goddesses of antiquity are as present as the goblins and pucks of an Elizabethan village. Milton's effort, throughout his life, was directed at keeping at bay the temptations of his native language and of the local myths of England, by shielding himself behind the barrier of a Latinised English and of a classical mythology. When viewed in this light, all his major works can be seen as presenting, at the level of fiction, what is present at the level of the poet's own stance. The temptations of the Lady in *Comus*, of Adam, of Christ, of Samson, are all temptations to yield in some way, and all except Adam reject the temptation through an effort of the will, a steeling of the mind. For this reason we can say that Milton is the first true Renaissance poet England produced, a figure who, like Michelangelo, finds his strength in rejection, denial, and the deliberate imitation of the ancients. In Shakespeare and the Elizabethans, on the other hand, as in the poets of the Middle Ages, all is ease and assimilation, the effortlessness of an art that is simultaneously sophisticated and naïve.[11]

Milton's attitude, when divorced from his heroic vision and his poetic genius, is the attitude of the academy. It is also the attitude of the connoisseur, of the admirer of the beautiful who is careful to see that the beautiful does not touch the deepest springs of his own heart. It is the attitude of Swann, in Proust's novel, who admires all that the past has to offer in the way of lovely things, admires but does not love. For to love means to give yourself up to something, it means to lay yourself open to pain, to suffering, which is the mark of our emergence from the contemplation of our private egos. Marcel recognises this as he recognises that he must love Albertine in a different way from the way Swann loves his paintings:

> But no, Albertine was in no way a work of art. I knew what it meant to admire a woman in an artistic fashion. I had known Swann. For my own part, moreover, I was, no matter who the woman might be, incapable of doing so, having no sort of power of detached observation... The pleasure and the pain that I derived from Albertine never took, in order to reach me, the line of taste and intellect; indeed, to tell the truth, when I began to regard Albertine as an angel musician glazed with a marvellous patina whom I congratulated myself upon possessing, it was not long before I found her uninteresting; I soon became bored in her company, but these moments were of brief duration; we love only what we do not possess, and very soon I returned to the conclusion that I did not possess Albertine.

Two types of art are being contrasted here, and two types of love. The first, which sees *beauty* as the necessary condition, must have a prior set of criteria against which to match the work of art or the woman – only certain kinds of things can be called beautiful; and it guards the object as a precious possession, to be taken out occasionally and contemplated or shown with pride to others. The second, which has *truth* as its condition, strives to enter the otherness of the object while knowing that it can never fully do so. The first is, naturally enough, the method of the academy. Naturally, because the teacher almost of necessity has to neutralise the power of the object if he is to talk about it year in year out; to allow it the power of its otherness would create an intolerable situation. So that built in to the academic treatment of literature is the connoisseur approach, which is, by and large, the approach of the Renaissance to classical antiquity. But it is a falsification of the effects of art, as of life, as the young Marcel perceives. And this explains why artists have for so long felt that academics, however well-meaning and sympathetic, are of the devil's party, and that there must be no truck with them.

In contrast to the connoisseur mentality stands that of the great modern artists, whose output can be seen as a series of raids upon the past in an effort to make that past their own without destroying its unique quality. One has only to think of Eliot's own forays, or of Picasso's extraordinary series of variations on Velasquez's *Las Meninas*, or a work such as Stravinsky's *Pulcinella*, of which the composer said:

> *Pulcinella* was my discovery of the past, the epiphany through which the whole of my late work became possible. It was a backward look, of course – the first of many love affairs in that direction – but it was a look in the mirror, too. No critic understood this at the time, and I was therefore attacked for being a *pasticheur*, chided for composing 'simple' music, blamed for deserting 'modernism', accused of renouncing my 'true Russian heritage'. People who had never heard of, or cared about, the originals cried 'sacrilege': 'The classics are ours. Leave the classics alone.' To them all my answer was and is the same: You 'respect', but I love.

And what is love? It is the acknowledgement by the whole self of the otherness, the uniqueness of the thing loved, as well as the attempt to comprehend that otherness. It draws us out of our limited selves and frees us from the tyranny of either the academy or the market-place, from seeing the past as either frozen and monolithic or as non-existent. And it is precisely this love for the past, for our heritage, that modern art, if we can but learn its lessons, can teach us.

CULTURE AND EUROPEAN CULTURE

There are signs that the lessons are indeed being learnt. A number of impressive works of scholarship which have appeared in the last fifteen years have seen it as their task to recreate the past for us in such a way that we will be able to respond to it with a genuine understanding.

The books of John Jones on Aristotle and Greek tragedy, of V. A. Kolve on the medieval miracle plays, of C. S. Singleton on Dante, have in some way restored the past to us while allowing it its singularity. These are genuine contributions because they do not conceive of culture as an *essence*, as something which we must hug to ourselves to protect ourselves from the philistines, but, on the contrary, as a widening of the horizons, a supplying of the right context in which to understand the past. What they are doing can be explained by an example which Frye gives of a problem of translation:

> It is impossible that a Greek tragedian can have meant by *ananke* what the average English reader means by 'necessity'. But the translator must use some word, and the real difficulty lies in the reader's inability to recreate the word 'necessity' into a conception with the associative richness of *ananke* ... Where are we to find the meanings of words? Sophocles is dead and eke his language, and both at once are buried in dictionaries which give only the translator's equivalent. The meaning of *ananke* must be sought in the meaning of the poetic form in which it is found, in the *raison d'être* of Greek tragedy. Here a knowledge of the historical origin and context of Greek tragedy is necessary, but ... we must eventually move beyond this. Just as we must find the meaning of *ananke* in its relation to its context in Greek tragedy, so we must find the meaning of Greek tragedy in its relation to the context of all tragedy ...

Thus, slowly and painfully, we can overcome the half-truths which say either that the past is irrecoverable and is therefore best ignored or that we must accept what we are told about it.

We must not look at culture as an essence, a thing, but rather as the supplying of a context, the provision both of better spectacles and of a sufficient variety of spectacles to keep us from forgetting that what we see is never seen by the unaided power of the eyes alone. Nearly all misinterpretations are the result of a failure to appreciate the context of a work of art, and for English literature that context must inevitably be European. But of course, as we have seen, just as there is no essence known as English culture, so there is no essence known as European culture. The term culture itself is an Enlightenment term in its modern connotations of tastefulness and civilisation, and we can now see that it is nothing other than a mirror of the aspirations of the century itself. Each age of course recreates the past in its own image, but our awareness of this can allow us to try and nullify it. We can see now, through the work of recent critics as well as of men like Nietzsche, that Homer and the Greek tragedians and the authors of the Old Testament were very very different from eighteenth-century English gentlemen or

German professors. Can we say that they are European at all? But what does European mean? Do we have some set of characteristics which we try to relate to every work we encounter? The answer is that of course we don't. The confusion is a bit like that which Wittgenstein discovered in the discussion of games. There are card games and ball games and other games such as tiddlywinks, which don't use either cards or balls. What unites all of them is not some essence of which they all partake, 'gameness', but rather certain overlapping characteristics, more akin to family resemblances. What is important is not to try and make all games look the same, not to see everywhere only our own reflections in the past. It is the otherness, the strangeness of Greek tragedy that John Jones stresses, and he rightly sees that the first condition of understanding it is an acknowledgement of its alienness. In a similar spirit Robert Lowell explains his love for the classics:

Before going to Kenyon I talked to Ford Madox Ford and Ransom, and Ransom said you've just to take philosophy and logic, which I did. The other thing he suggested was classics. Ford was rather flippant about it, said of course you've got to learn classics, you'll just cut yourself off from humanity if you don't. I think it's always given me some sort of yardstick for English. And then the literature was amazing, particularly the Greek; there's nothing like Greek in English at all ... That something like *Antigone* or *Oedipus* or the great Achilles moments in the *Iliad* would be at the core of a literature is incredible for anyone brought up in an English culture – Greek wildness and sophistication all different, the women different, everything. Latin is of course much closer. English is a half-Latin language, and we've done our best to absorb the Latin literature. But a Roman poet is much less intellectual than the Englishman, much less abstract. He's nearer nature somehow ... And yet he's very sophisticated. He has his way of doing things, though the number of forms he explored is quite limited. The amount he could take from the Greeks and yet change is an extraordinary piece of firm discipline. Also, you take almost any really good Roman poet – Juvenal, or Virgil, or Propertius, or Catullus – he's much more raw and direct than anything in English, and yet he has this block-like formality. The Roman frankness interests me. Until recently our literature hasn't been as raw as the Roman, translations had to have stars. And their history has a terrible human frankness that isn't customary with us – corrosive attacks on the establishment, comments on politics and the decay of morals, all felt terribly strongly, by poets as well as historians. The English writer who reads the classics is working at one thing, and his eye is on something else that can't be done. We will always have the Latin and Greek classics, and they'll never be absorbed. There's something very restful about that.[12]

CONCLUSION

The reading of books does not automatically make us better people. Nor is that a reason for giving up reading books. There are right and wrong ways of using most gifts, and reading is no exception. This is what the academic study of literature can teach us – not how to respond, which is a private matter between the reader and the book, but how to relate that response to the rest of one's life and reading. As Frye points out:

Physics is an organised body of knowledge about nature, and a student of it says he is learning physics, not nature. Art, like nature, has to be distinguished from the systematic study of it which is criticism. It is therefore impossible to 'learn literature': one learns about it in a certain way, but what one learns, transitively, is the criticism of literature. Similarly, the difficulty often felt in 'teaching literature' arises from the fact that it cannot be done: the criticism of literature is all that can be directly taught.

To study English literature in the context of European culture is suddenly to begin to ask the right questions, to see its distance from us but also its contemporaneity. To do this is to make ourselves better readers of those authors who are most in need of readers: those who are writing today. To see English literature in the context of European culture is to be made aware that the past is not a crushing burden of authority but the means of freeing us of our habits and prejudices. It is to take our place as responsible and responsive – that is, active – readers of contemporary literature. That is the least we can do.

Notes
1. See Walter J. Ong, 'The Vernacular Matrix of the New Criticism', in *The Barbarian Within* (New York, 1962).
2. This last example is a reference to the Polish critic, Jan Kott, whose *Shakespeare our Contemporary* shows all the virtues and vices of the historicist position. He gives a marvellous sense of Shakespeare's relevance, but at the cost of distorting a great deal of Shakespeare. Is there a less easy but more reliable path?
3. My discussion of the 'historicist' fallacy is indebted to E. D. Hirsch's *Validity in Interpretation* (Yale University Press, 1967), especially Appendix II, 245–64.
4. E. H. Gombrich, 'Raphael's Madonna della Sedia', in *Norm and Form*

(London, 1965), deals with this problem in connection with a famous painting and its commentators.

5. See especially Charles Muscatine, *Chaucer and the French Tradition* (Berkeley, 1957).

6. There is an enormous literature that could profitably be consulted here. See especially the works of Gombrich, in particular his *Story of Art* and *Art and Illusion*. On the medieval drama see V. A. Kolve, *The Play Called Corpus Christi* (London, 1967). Also useful is William Matthews's essay, 'Inherited Impediments in Medieval Literary History', in *Medieval Secular Literature*, ed. Matthews (Berkeley, 1965).

7. *Critique et vérité* (Paris, 1966) 57. (This is of course an oversimplification both of the linguistic position and of Barthes' own, but not I believe a distortion.)

8. This is not quite true. See Chapter 7, 'Linearity and Fragmentation', for a discussion of the peculiarity of the 'realist' set of conventions.

9. See H. Popkin, *A History of Scepticism from Erasmus to Descartes* (Assen, 1960), especially ch. 1, for the sixteenth-century crisis.

10. See especially three essays in Panofsky's *Meaning in the Visual Arts* (Doubleday, 1955): 'Iconography and Iconology', 'The first page of Giorgio Vasari's *Libro*', and 'Dürer and Classical Antiquity'.

11. I am indebted to A. D. Nuttall's brilliant introduction to *Milton: The Minor Poems* (London, 1970).

12. From an interview in the *Paris Review*, spring 1961.

6 The Lessons of Modernism*

When Vladimir Nabokov was at Cornell after the war he regularly gave a series of lectures on some of the major novels of the past two hundred years. He would devote two lectures to each work. In the first lecture he dealt with the qualities of the book and in the second with its defects. This essay won't have quite that exemplary clarity about it, but it does fall into two main parts, corresponding to what I take to be the two main lessons of Modernism.

But what is Modernism? As I understand it the word refers to that revolution in the arts which took place between 1880 and 1920 and which we associate with the names of Cézanne, Mallarmé, Proust, Joyce, Kafka, Eliot, Schoenberg, Stravinsky, Picasso and Kandinsky. And I want to argue that the lessons of that revolution, correctly understood, have a relevance not only to the arts of the present day, which is obvious enough, but also to what might at first sight seem very far removed from the concerns of a Proust or a Kafka, the teaching of literature and the handling of books in school and university.

Rightly understood, I said, and unfortunately Modernism has not, in the English-speaking world at any rate, been rightly understood. For too long it has been seen as a revolution in the diction of poetry and nothing more. To understand its implications, however, we need to see it as the result of and the reaction to a crisis of authority which affected every sphere of activity in Western Europe and America in the late nineteenth century – political, philosophical, scientific and artistic. At the artistic level this was a crisis of confidence in the authority of the author or creator. Where the Romantic poet had been convinced of the truth and value of what he had to say, his modern counterpart could only see the absurdity of such a posture. Prufrock, the hero of Eliot's poem of 1914, though not himself a poet, speaks here for his creator:

Though I have seen my head (grown slightly bald)
    brought in upon a platter,
I am no prophet – and here's no great matter; . . .

* This is the slightly modified text of a lecture given at the ninth National Association of the Teachers of English conference at York on 27 March 1972.

Prufrock is no John the Baptist, and no Lazarus either, 'come from the dead, come back to tell you all'. There is nothing *special* about Prufrock, or about Eliot either, to justify their utterances – so how should they presume? Presume to act, presume to write, presume to tell other people about the world or how to live their lives. And we recall other writers caught in the same dilemma. Proust filled, from childhood, with the urge to write, and yet incapable of ever getting down to work because he cannot conceive of an adequate subject about which to write. Kafka, pressed by his father and his whole environment to justify his writing or take a job that will allow him to make his mark in the world, and incapable of doing either. The need to write and the meaninglessness of all writing is the paradoxical law under which the modern artist seems to operate.

And out of which he creates his greatest work. For when Proust at last discovers his true subject-matter, that subject-matter is nothing less than the exploration of the impossibility of finding any subject-matter; and Kafka's fictions become the long patient descriptions of his own failures. But these fictions engage us, and make us see that this recognition that the artist is after all a man like the rest of us, with no special prophetic powers, is something which affects us all. We cannot treat the artist as a special case. He is only special in so far as he grasps more clearly than most the real nature of the human condition, which is that of existing in a world where we can nowhere find authority for our actions, our beliefs, even our perceptions. Take the opening sentence of Kafka's *The Trial*: 'Someone must have been telling lies about Joseph K.' Was someone telling lies or not? We read on, expecting to find out. And in a normal novel of course we would. But not here. Is this because Kafka, out of a wilful desire for perversity, is holding out on us? Such charges have of course been made, and not just about Kafka but about any work which remains ambiguous, unresolved, to the end. But they are misplaced. For what Kafka's novel does is to make us question our *assumptions*. When we ask: Was Joseph K. guilty or not guilty? what kind of answer are we expecting to our question? For after all, since Joseph K. is a character of fiction and his adventures have been invented by Kafka, the question really boils down to asking whether Kafka the author has decided that he is one thing or the other. But Kafka is unwilling to take such a decision. Not because he can't, but because he feels it would be perfectly arbitrary – not because it's too difficult, in other words, but because it's too easy. All it requires is the writing down of certain words instead of others – and no one doubts that Kafka can write. But how should he presume?

Let us look at another example, this time from *The Castle*. The hero takes the hands of Frieda, the serving-girl, in his, and remarks: 'Her hands were certainly small and delicate, but they could equally well have been called weak and characterless.' This is a trivial incident, but it must come as a shock to the reader. He feels thrown. Which were they? he asks. But of course what Kafka is revealing here is something we all know intellectually yet continue to ignore in daily life. This is that in order to make any sense of the world around us we have at every moment to adopt certain 'sets', certain ways of viewing, which simply block out those parts of the world which make no sense – or rather, there is a constant adjustment between the 'real world' and our initial hypotheses about it. So long as these are not denied we carry on quite happily, though it is usually not too difficult for us to adjust should they turn out simply not to work. The famous duck-rabbit used by Wittgenstein and Gombrich and the *gestalt* psychologists is a classic example: we can see it as a duck or a rabbit but never as both at the same time (R. L. Gregory's *The Intelligent Eye* is full of splendid examples). But what Kafka does is to wake us up to this fact of perception and thus make us see that what we normally take to be 'the world' is only 'the world as I see it – now'. This is a painful and difficult adjustment to make, since our consciousness continuously rejects the complications which this entails, and Kafka's fictions usually show us the hero gradually overwhelmed by the people who surround him and who do not want to recognise such facts, as well as by his own lassitude. However, for the reader, the work of Kafka is an eye-opener. After reading him one realises how strongly the traditional novel merely confirms us in our conventional ways of seeing and talking.

When I say the traditional novel I mean the kind of fiction which emerged in England in the early eighteenth century with Defoe, and which persists today in the work of such writers as Anthony Powell and Kingsley Amis. The prime allegiance of this form is to verisimilitude: the author enters into a silent agreement with his reader to create a world which will give the illusion of being 'real life'. A world where people will be either guilty or not guilty but never both, where hands will be either delicate or weak, but never both. No traditional novelist could permit himself Kafka's doubts about the precise way to describe Frieda's hands. And we rarely have such doubts in ordinary life. But what Kafka is suggesting is that our decisions that hands or events or people are one thing or another is really a convenience rather than a reality – it simply allows us to get on with things, with the business of living. But living to what purpose?

That, of course, is the question of the moderns, of Eliot and Proust and Virginia Woolf. It is, I am afraid, a religious question. And in asking it they draw attention to the implicit assumptions of traditional fiction. Let me explain what I mean by this – and there is no better way of doing so than by taking Sartre's famous critique of the novel, which is to be found in the opening pages of *La Nausée*. You open a novel, Sartre tells us, and you start to read about a man. He is the hero. He is walking down the road. It is evening. He is free. His whole life is before him, as it is before the reader. And yet the reader *knows* that before the book is over the hero will have lived through certain adventures, made certain decisions, acted in certain ways. His life will now have acquired a *meaning*. And that, Sartre suggests, is why we read novels: because we are hungry for meanings, for lives with meanings, with patterns to them. And, for a while, we enter imaginatively into a meaningful life. And when that novel is over, we pick up another...

Sartre comes back to this theme in his autobiography, *Les Mots*. He recalls a book given to him when he was small, consisting of the fictionalised childhood biographies of famous men. A good example of the genre is the story of the painter Raphael. As a small boy Raphael evinced a desire to see the Pope. Eventually his parents acceded to that request and took him to the square of St Peter's on a day when the Pope and his retinue were to appear. When they returned home that evening the young Raphael was asked: 'Well, did you like the Pope?' 'What Pope?', the future painter replied. 'All I saw was colours.' Now this, as Sartre points out, is pernicious because it robs Raphael of his freedom, it makes of his life a simple task to be carried out without his having to make any choices and sacrifices on the way. It hides the fact that even at the very end of his life Raphael would never know for sure whether or not he was a great painter – let alone a Great Painter. But of course we all desire to know. Sartre himself confessed to this, saying he wished to live at the time as though his life were being recounted by his grandchildren. And it is to this desire that the traditional novel panders, Sartre claims. We cannot live with our own freedom, our lack of certainty, and so we turn to the vicarious meaningfulness of lives in books. Because human kind cannot bear very much reality we prefer to act as though there were an absolute authority for our actions, even our emotions, standing outside and above us, directing us, assuring us that, come what may, at least our lives have a meaning.

Sartre's critique of the traditional novel – which, as we have seen, is not an *aesthetic* critique – had been forestalled by a writer working almost a hundred years before him: the Danish philosopher, Sören Kierkegaard. But where Sartre talked about 'adventures' and novels, Kierkegaard was willing to extend his critique to books at large, or to what he called the sphere of the aesthetic. Kierkegaard wished to draw our attention to the fact that aesthetic objects have a property which makes them absolutely different from the real world, and that we should beware of ever blurring the distinctions between the two. For the simple fact about aesthetic objects is that there are a lot of them, all with an equal claim on our attention. So we can look at one picture in a gallery and then pass on to another, and another, and another. We can pick up a book, dip into it, put it down, pick up another, and so on. Whereas we are only given one life. And that life being subject to time, no two events in it can be exact repetitions of each other. This means that in life we have to make choices (which implies renunciation) whereas in art we do not. The sphere of the ethical, says Kierkegaard, is that of either/or; that of the aesthetic is and/and. That is why Mozart's *Don Giovanni* is the greatest aesthetic work ever created – not only is music the aesthetic sphere *par excellence*, but the subject of the opera is a man who lives aesthetically, not ethically, a man who wants *all* women instead of choosing one.

Now if Kierkegaard is right he is faced with a real problem. For how can he argue his case against books, when he has only books to argue his case with? In Kierkegaard, who wrote a brilliant book *on* authority, we find the first major questioning *of* authority. And his problem is one that has dogged all the great writers of our time: how to convey the sense of the partiality and distortion of books when all one has at one's disposal are books? This explains why the modern novel is an anti-novel, why modern poetry is, in a sense, anti-poetry – 'The Love Song of J. Alfred Prufrock'. For the writer's strategy will be to admit the reader into the imaginative world of the book and then bring him up sharply against the realisation that it is only a book and not the world.

Take, for example, the opening of Nabokov's *Invitation to a Beheading*, a novel he wrote in Russian in the thirties and which he admits is his own favourite among his books. Here is the opening, with a few sentences left out:

> In accordance with the law the death sentence was announced to Cincinnatus C. in a whisper. All rose, exchanging smiles. The hoary judge put his mouth close to his ear, panted for a moment, made the announcement and slowly moved away, as though ungluing himself. Thereupon Cincinnatus was taken back to the fortress ... So we are nearing the end. The right-hand still untasted part of the novel, which, during our delectable reading, we would lightly feel, mechanically testing whether there were still plenty left (and our fingers were always gladdened by the placid, faithful thickness), had suddenly, for no reason at all, become quite meagre: a few minutes of quick reading, already downhill, and – O horrible! ...

The horror here comes from the unexpected conflation of book and life. The death sentence is passed in the very first line, so what else is there to read about? Suddenly the life of the book and the life of Cincinnatus –with which, as novel-readers, we immediately identify – are seen to be synonymous – and the feeling is driven home by the image which forms in Cincinnatus' mind: the leaves of a book, the days of a life. For us this is only one of an infinite number of books; for Cincinnatus it is his one life.

In this way Nabokov overcomes what Kierkegaard would call the irredeemably aesthetic character of books. In William Golding the same effect is achieved by different means. In his work what for most of the book we had taken to be 'reality' or 'the world' is eventually revealed as the product of the obsessive imagination of the hero. In *Pincher Martin* it is the drowning man's refusal to accept the fact of death which creates an imaginary island, an imaginary escape. But Pincher Martin, like the reader, cannot hold out for ever in the face of reality: there will come a time when the book will have to be put down, the assertion of the will relaxed. Even a man's insistent imagination cannot save him from the ultimate reality of death. In *The Spire* Jocelin is slowly forced to recognise that it was perhaps his own pride and not a call from God which drove him to have the huge spire erected on foundations incapable of supporting it. And when he realises this he breaks down and collapses. In both books Golding leads the reader towards the point where the book itself has to be discarded, where it is suddenly seen as itself the product of obsession and guilt, an all too human guilt whose recognition nevertheless means its momentary transcendence. At the end of a Golding novel we are forced out of our comfortable, rational, conscious 'set' and forced to recognise that the world never conforms to our picture of it, and that by imagining it does we conceal the truth from ourselves.

One could go on multiplying examples. Think of Virginia Woolf's *To the Lighthouse*, which, again, moves towards the point of understanding, making us realise that this can never be described, only made, encompassed by the creative imagination of the artist and the recreative imagination of the reader. The 'meaning' of the book lies in that final brushstroke of Lily Briscoe's: 'It was done; it was finished. Yes, she thought, laying down her brush in extreme fatigue, I have had my vision.' She has had her vision, as has the reader, but it is not something that can be removed from the entity of the work we have been reading. In a sense, *that* is the vision – something which the work can never *say*, but only point to (the painting will be put in an attic and forgotten).

When Nietzsche says: 'I am afraid we are not rid of God because we still have faith in grammar', this is what he means: that we are not free of God as a kind of transcendental authority, giving meaning to our lives, so long as we imagine the structure of language to correspond to the structure of the world. So long as we imagine that the world has subjects and objects, past present and future tenses, full stops at the end of sentences. That is why modern art always moves towards silence, away from language, towards the annihilation of language and of the work – ridiculous the waste sad time before and after.

Let me put it another way. For most of our lives we live like a man in a fast train with the blinds down: because everything else in his field of vision is moving at the same rate as him he imagines that nothing is moving. Modernism lifts the blinds and, by revealing the motionless countryside outside, makes us see at what a rate we are travelling. But (to complicate my image) language and consciousness belong on board the train; so that there seems to be nothing outside that we can hold on to which will make us recognise that we are moving. Modernism achieves this by making us suddenly – and momentarily – recognise this fact. In modernism words, after speech, reach into the unknown, and the book, after it is done, reaches forward to that which can never be said in any book.

But if this is the case then a very curious situation arises when such books enter the sphere of culture. For the one person who cannot keep silent, the one person who is committed to speech, is the critic. He belongs to a profession whose business it is to make sense of, pass judgement on, relate books to the society from which they spring and to which they speak. But it is precisely the validity of this mode of speech that modernism questions. Prufrock may not have found the answer, but the women who come and go in the room, talking of Michelangelo, who, with formulated phrase, pin him wriggling to the wall – they most certainly haven't and never will. Modernism almost defines itself by its opposition to such chatter; and yet such chatter is precisely what the critic indulges in. Hence a split develops between criticism and modern art.

One of the great novels of this century, Thomas Mann's *Dr. Faustus*, is in fact an exploration of the nature and meaning of this split, and it derives its peculiar power from the fact that the author, Mann himself, was certainly torn in two by it. Brought up as he was to revere the art of the nineteenth century, with its sense of development, of growth in time, with its optimism and its belief in the links between art and culture – brought up in this way, the music of Arnold Schoenberg must have come as a severe shock to him. Its sense of dislocation, of fragmentation, its disregard of the linear, must have seemed to Mann an affront to humanity. And yet the artist in him recognised that the art of the nineteenth century had rested on an unquestioning belief in authority which could no longer be accepted. There is as much of Mann himself in the figure of Serenus Zeitblom, the cultured academic, to whose lot it falls to talk *about* his friend, the composer Adrien Leverkühn, as there is in the figure of the cold obsessed artist. But behind the figures of Zeitblom and Leverkühn stand those of two nineteenth-century figures, Burckhardt, the academic historian, and Nietzsche, the nihilistic philosopher. And behind them again stand two sixteenth-century figures, Erasmus and Luther. For behind the modern crisis of authority Mann quite rightly saw that earlier one which led to the Reformation and the birth of modern Germany.

Now Erasmus's ironic humanism is also what lies behind our entire academic tradition, whether in the universities or in the schools. And I am not just talking of scholarship, of the rediscovery and loving annotation of the classics. No. The entire basis of scholastic activity, the idea that it is both useful and good to talk *about* texts, to analyse and imitate the ancients, in order to be better citizens of the present, derives from the tradition of Renaissance Humanism, of which Erasmus is a shining example. But when Luther asked Erasmus what all his irony and learning could do in the face of God's wrath, he had no answer.

Now every major critic of the last hundred years has seen himself as in some sense mediating between art and society. Think of Arnold and Burckhardt in the last century, of Leavis and George Steiner in this. They have all held, whether consciously or unconsciously, to precisely those values which modernism challenges. And their reaction to this challenge has been curious and interesting. Either they have ignored the radical nature of modern art and have gone on treating it as no different from the art of the past; or, if they have recognised its radical nature, they have refused to face its implications for themselves, but have instead taken refuge in notions of cosmic catastrophes. Already Mann, in *Dr. Faustus*, was seeing a direct connection between Schoenberg's music and the rise of Nazism – much to the persecuted Schoenberg's anger. More recently, in this country, George Steiner has been the eloquent spokesman of apocalypse, equating in some mysterious way, the silence at the heart of a Webern or a Beckett work with the collapse of Western culture and the atrocities of the Nazis. But such a reading is surely false. It exemplifies what Nietzsche noted at the end of one of his greatest works, that 'man would rather have the void for his purpose than be devoid of purpose'. Man would rather be a prophet of doom than listen to the still small voice which asks him to rethink the bases of his own life.

What I am suggesting is that the liberal humanist tradition has always tended to overvalue the cultural importance of books – that is, the value of books to society rather than to the individual. And I am suggesting that such an overvaluation persists in a Mann or a Steiner, for the discovery that there may be *no* links between culture and reading seems to them to imply the end of culture. But if, instead of taking this tempting apocalyptic line (beautifully satirised by Saul Bellow in *Herzog*), we are prepared to rethink our notion of culture and its relation to books, then we will have learnt one of the fundamental lessons of modernism.

First of all, we must recognise that much art simply cannot be talked about. And of course I oversimplified when I said that such talking about was the prerogative of critics. We are all of us critics as soon as we put down a book and try to explain it to ourselves. Modern art protects itself from such explanation, prods us into an awareness of the distortions which occur when we try to do this. Let us put aside the simple opposition of civilization and barbarism, which is itself the product of a certain kind of civilization, and recognise that there is both a silence of failure and incomprehension *and* a silence of understanding, a silence of destruction *and* a silence of conversion.

But for those of us who are concerned with teaching this poses a real problem. As soon as a book is used in the classroom or the lecture hall it begins to be talked about. What I am suggesting is not that we should ban all such talk. I am only urging that we recognise the kind of destruction that takes place when students are made to analyse a page of a Golding novel, a portion of *The Waste Land*, a poem by Yeats. I think we should recognise that we do a grave disservice to the great modern writers by placing them at the centre of so many syllabuses and spending so much time 'explaining' their work. This leads to the inevitable feeling that once one has understood the meaning of a Greek or Italian epigraph in Eliot, once we have learnt to talk about Time In Joyce, we have 'done' those authors. I think we should push modern works into the hands of students – and not just English works or purely 'literary' works, but the writings of Kierkegaard, of Nietzsche, of Hofmannsthal, Rilke, Proust – and refrain from putting them on syllabuses or talking about them at length in class. For the more we talk about them the deader they will get – and one just has to look around at the cultural life of England today to see that at present they are so dead it is as if they had never been born.

This then is the first lesson of modernism: the recognition that the activities of reading and talking about are not the same. The second lesson is related to this first one, but it is, so to speak, the other side of the crisis-of-authority coin. To understand it let us look again at some of our early examples.

Was Joseph K. guilty or not guilty? we asked, and I suggested that Kafka's answer would be that he had not the authority to say whether Joseph K. was guilty or not. Now the difference between that sentence in a novel and the same sentence found in a newspaper is obvious. For with a newspaper report the problem simply would not arise. To discover whether Joseph K. was guilty or not, or at least whether someone had or had not been telling lies about him, we would simply seek corroborative evidence. But this is precisely what we cannot do with a novel. There, we are at the author's mercy. Let us take a different and clearer example. I read in a newspaper:

As Mr X was crossing the broad High Street of Y he noticed a car hurtling towards him. He leapt aside, but the car swerved and collided with a bus coming in the opposite direction. Two people were hurt, the driver of the car, Mr Z, and . . .

Now suppose I am a close friend of Mr Z. Having read the report I hurriedly ring up the paper and ask for confirmation and additional information about the accident. I am put through to the reporter and he confirms what he has written and tells me which hospital Mr Z is being treated at. Or perhaps he does not know, and I have to ring the police. Eventually I trace my friend. He is not badly hurt, and gives me his version of what happened.

However, suppose I read this in a novel. Here there is nothing I can do if the author is unwilling to supply me with further information. He can even, if he wishes, later repudiate the incident altogether, revealing that the whole thing was a lie on the part of the villain, for example. Whatever the author says, we have to accept it. There is no reason why he could not have written:

As Mr X was crossing the broad High Street of Y he noticed a car hurtling towards him. He flapped his arms twice, rose into the air, and flew away over the housetops. The car swerved . . .

One of the earliest stories ever written, the Egyptian *Tale of Two Brothers* has a slightly similar incident. An elder brother's wife attempts to seduce an unmarried younger brother who lives with them, and, when he resists her, accuses him of attempting to rape her. The younger brother is forced to run away, with the elder in hot pursuit. At this point he prays to Ra for assistance, and Ra places a lake between him and his brother, and fills it full of crocodiles. 'This incident', remarks Northrop Frye in *Anatomy of Criticism*, 'is no more a fictional episode than anything that has preceded it, nor is it less logically related than any other episode to the plot as a whole. But it has given up its external analogy to "life": this, we say, is the kind of thing that happens only in stories.'

What the Tale teaches us is that the main criterion of the traditional novel is not truth but truth to life, or verisimilitude. There is a tacit understanding entered into by author and reader that the author will supply enough 'realistic' information to make his book one into which we can 'enter' and live without disturbance. But this is purely a matter of convenience – there is nothing necessary about it. It is a custom, not a law. And in fact one of the very first novels (or anti-novels) ever written, *Tristram Shandy*, mercilessly burlesques and parodies the custom. The best example of such parody is probably the episode of Obadiah and Dr Slop. Obadiah, the servant, has been sent off to fetch the doctor, for the hero's birth is imminent. Walter, the happy father, is as ever engaged in conversation with Uncle Toby. Suddenly we are told that Obadiah has returned with the doctor. Sterne now makes great play with the fact that there clearly hasn't been time for Obadiah to go the eight miles to the doctor's house and back. He replies that there has: an hour and a half's reading time. But the reader will say that reading-time and 'acting-time' are two quite separate things. Sterne replies with a bewildering discourse on time and Lockean ideas. But he hasn't done yet:

> If my hypercritick is intractable, alledging, that two minutes and thirteen seconds are no more than two minutes and thirteen seconds, – when I have said all I can about them; and that this plea, though it might save me dramatically, will damn me biographically, rendering my book from this very moment, a professed ROMANCE, which, before, was a book apocryphal: – If I am thus pressed – I then put an end to the whole objection and controversy about it all at once, – by acquainting him, that Obadiah had not got above three-score yards from the stable-yard before he met with Dr. Slop: – and indeed he gave a dirty proof that he had met with him, and was within an ace of giving a tragical one too . . .

What Sterne is doing here is in effect saying to the reader: 'All right, if you insist on a realistic explanation – here it is: of course Obadiah did not go all the way to the doctor's house and back in that short span of time. No. He met the doctor when the latter was already practically at Shandy Hall.' And then Sterne invents a wonderful scene with a collision in the muddy lane between the diminutive doctor on horseback and the bewildered Obadiah. In other words it is the need for a realistic explanation which *generates* the comic scene. Sterne teases the reader by both satisfying his desire for realistic explanation and revealing in the process that novels are not imitations of reality or descriptions of events but the arbitrary inventions of individuals sitting alone at a desk, wondering how to go on . . .

I cannot refrain from giving one more example, from another great comic novel, this time a modern one. Watt, the hero of Beckett's early novel of that name, has arrived at the house of his invisible employer, Mr Nott:

> The house was in darkness.
> Finding the front door locked, Watt went to the back door. He could not very well ring, or knock, for the house was in darkness.
> Finding the back door locked also, Watt returned to the front door.
> Finding the front door locked still, Watt returned to the back door.

Finding the back door now open, oh not open wide, but on the latch, as the saying is, Watt was able to enter the house.

Watt was surprised to find the back door, so lately locked, now open. Two explanations of this occurred to him. The first was this, that his science of the locked door, so seldom at fault, had been so on this occasion, and that the back door, when he had found it locked, had not been locked, but open. And the second was this, that the back door, when he had found it locked, had in effect been locked, but had subsequently been opened, from within, or without, by some person, while he Watt had been employed in going, to and fro, from the back door to the front door, and from the front door to the back door.

Of these two explanations Watt thought he preferred the latter, as being the more beautiful.

Where a traditional novelist would have been content to have the door open or shut according to his design for the novel as a whole, Beckett explores *all* the possibilities to great comic effect. Other, vulgar novelists, have verisimilitude as their criterion. Beckett/Watt's criterion is that of sheer beauty, or, as the mathematicians might say, the elegance of a particular solution.

Now the lesson of Sterne and Beckett is that if the novelist is indeed entirely free to do as he will, the criterion of verisimilitude is too lax by far. How long, for instance, should the description of a room be? One line? Five? Twenty-five? How much should an author tell his reader about the prior lives of his characters? Nothing? A little? A great deal? It is just this freedom which made Kafka and Proust despair. But what Sterne and Beckett seem to suggest is that we need other rules than those of verisimilitude, formal rules perhaps, such as exist in chess or football. These rules should govern the composition of a work. And this, indeed, is what a number of modern novelists have been looking for. We can, for example, follow the lead of that strange French writer, Raymond Roussel, who died in 1933, leaving behind a series of published novels, stories and poems, and an unpublished essay called 'Comment j'ai écrit certains de mes livres' – 'How I wrote some of my books.' In this essay he explains his procedure, with numerous examples from his stories. He would take a word which, by the alteration of a single letter, changed into another word: *prune* and *brune*, *billard* and *pillard* ('plum' and 'brunette', 'billiard table' and 'pillager'), for instance. Then he would work out a sentence which could contain either word, but which would alter radically in meaning depending on which word it contained – the key word contaminating all the others, so to speak. Thus: 'La peau verte de la prune un peu mûre' ('the greenish skin of the ripening plum'), and 'la peau verte de la brune un peu mûre' ('the grey-green skin of the ageing brunette'); 'les lettres du blanc sur la bande du billard' ('the letters chalked up on the borders of the billiard table'), and 'les lettres du blanc sur la bande du pillard' ('the missives of the white man concerning the band of the marauding chieftain'). Roussel's task would then be to place one of these phrases at the start and the other at the end of his story, and to write a story that would lead one inevitably from the first to the second. He himself pointed out that this was merely extending into prose what had always been the standard practice of poets. Rhyme in poetry is the formal principle whereby the ending of a word which comes at the end of one line is made to guide the poet towards the ending of a later line. And this, poets have always felt, is not a repressive but a releasing principle – it has allowed poetry to get written which no amount of reliance on inner inspiration could ever have accomplished. In the same way Roussel felt that by submitting to these astringent formal rules he had extended the boundaries of his art in unforeseen ways.

Personally I don't think Roussel's actual stories quite come off, but there is unfortunately no time to go into the reasons for that. What I want to stress here is that they do provide us with an excellent example of one sort of formal game. You can think up others for yourselves. Raymond Queneau, a brilliant and underrated French writer, known over here I suppose only as the author of *Zazie dans le métro*, gives many examples of other devices in his essay called 'Littérature poten-tielle'. He mentions a book called *Gadsby*, written (in English) by a certain Ernest Vincent Wright, and published in 1939. It is 267 pages long and does not use the letter 'e'. Here is a sample: 'It is a story about a small town. It is not a gossipy yarn; nor is it a dry, monotonous account, full of such customary "fill-ins", as "romantic moonlight cast-ing murky shadows down a long, winding country road". Nor will it say anything about tinklings lulling distant folds, robins carolling at twilight nor any "warm glow of lamplight" from a cabin window. No.' Naturally, it couldn't be *yes*.

Queneau himself of course is the author of the marvellous *Exercices de style*, in which the same anecdote is recounted in over twenty different ways, ranging from journalese to five-act Racinian tragedy – none of the 'exercises' lasting more than five pages. In his novels he has devised brilliant and complicated formal rules to achieve a remark-able freedom. It is no coincidence that he is fascinated by mathematics, while Roussel, like Nabokov, spent much time over chess problems. I do not know if chess holds any attraction for Robbe-Grillet and Butor, but they have both acknowledged their debt to Roussel.[1]

None of these writers is using the discovery of the total freedom of the novelist simply to indulge his private whims. Nor are they simply cutting up a traditional novel and asking the reader to put it together again. The newly discovered freedom leads them in search of new and more astringent rules. Their efforts are exactly parallel to those of Picasso and Braque in the great days of Cubism, or of Schoenberg when he set out to find a structure that would replace the sonata form which he realised had, by 1900, been totally exhausted. Yet there is no doubt that all these rules, because they are clearly recognised as man-made and not natural, give to art a greater sense of game, of playfulness, than it had ever known since the dawn of the Renaissance.

Modern art moves between two poles, silence and game. But our concern today is not with modern art as such so much as with the lessons it has to offer us. The first lesson, I suggested, is that we commit subtle but dire distortions by talking about an art that finds its real meaning in the silence beyond the page. The second lesson makes it clear that we should not as a consequence impose merely a silent worship of great works in place of the vocal worship of the past century. It is rather that we should recognise the element of play in all art and seek to release it in the classroom. Now this has of course for a long time been recognised by educationalists dealing with the primary school. But there is still a feeling of unease at the notion of art as game. High seriousness and maturity have for too long been the watchwords, with what seems to me a narrowing and stultifying effect. The lesson of modernism is not just the general one that all art is game. It very specifically opens up again areas of the past which had seemed permanently sealed off: the poems of Skelton and Dunbar, the prose of Rabelais and Nashe and Sterne, medieval lyrics, Anglo-Saxon riddles, the novels of Beckett and Flann O'Brien, the poetry of the Dark Ages and of the Grands Rhétoriqueurs in France and Burgundy in the late Middle Ages.[2] All these works cry out for reading aloud, and they turn the reader into a maker rather than a man of culture or a man of wisdom. By this I mean that they release in us that creative potential which is there in all of us, instead of making us draw back into a view of ourselves as the beleaguered outposts of a declining and threatened civilisation. We too can learn from them how games of art are played, we too can go on to formulate our rules and put together our words. From this perspective the ages of high formal art, the ages of parody and burlesque, of the skilled use of insult and abuse, will come back into their own. We will learn to pay less attention to the purity of our responses, the welfare of our souls, and more to the practice of verbal pyrotechnics. This may not make gentlemen of us, but it can certainly help us to fulfil our human potential.

What I am advocating is of course not new. It corresponds to what in the field of the visual arts we associate with the Bauhaus and the work of Herbert Read in this country: the discovery that it is more fun as well as more profitable to play with blocks of colour rather than go out and laboriously copy a tree or building. It corresponds to what in the field of music Peter Maxwell Davies tried to do when he was teaching at Cirencester. He realised that it was absurd to give children nineteenth-century symphonies to perform. They lack the maturity and depth of feeling to interpret such works, and they lack the technique on the strings. Why not then explore works which have less melody and more rhythm, fewer strings and more percussion? Why not play the music of Stravinsky and of medieval and Renaissance composers, music that is clean in line, short, and clearly articulated, no matter how complex it is? If one substitutes the works of George Eliot, Conrad and Lawrence for nineteenth-century symphonies, one has exactly the programme I am suggesting.[3]

But there is of course a far greater reluctance to think of art as primarily game where words are involved. The teacher of English does inevitably feel himself to be in a privileged position: a hander-down of culture and language, a bulwark against chaos and barbarism. Modern art asks him to relinquish this authority, but, like all authoritarians, he fears that if he does so chaos will ensue, The melancholy history of the past half-century suggests that if he does not do so chaos will most certainly ensue. The two lessons of modernism, the lessons of silence and of game, are hard ones for any teacher, in school or university, to learn. But, once learned, and applied, they could lead to a renewed enthusiasm and excitement in the study of English.

Notes

1. George Perec has written a very funny novel, *La Disparition* (Paris, 1969), which makes do *in French* without the letter 'e' – an even harder feat than in English. See also the little anthology of such explorations published by Gallimard, *OULIPO, la littérature potentielle* (Paris, 1973).
2. See now Paul Zumthor, *Langues, Textes, Enigmes* (Paris, 1974).
3. See now *Sound and Silence: Classroom Projects in Creative Music*, by John Paynter and Peter Aston (Cambridge, 1970). This has grown out of the York University Music Department's Music and Education courses.

7 Linearity and Fragmentation

> My thoughts were soon crippled if I tried to force them on in any
> single direction against their natural inclination. – And this was, of
> course, connected with the very nature of the investigation.
>
> Ludwig Wittgenstein

Thinking about fiction is rather like thinking about time or language.
We all know what these things are but they are somehow so close to us
that as soon as we try to think about them we feel we are going wrong.
Everyone who can read can read a novel, and most of us can, if called
upon, tell a story; but as soon as we try to understand the mechanism
of story-telling a fog settles on our minds and all our words seem to be
made of cotton wool. Take for example the remarks of the brilliant
French critic Jean Ricardou. At the start of his *Problèmes du nouveau
roman*, one of the best books written on the subject in recent years, he
has some sharp and witty things to say about those readers of fiction
who imagine they can cut with the word *knife* or sleep on the word *bed*.
His point is a sound one, but we are reminded of Wittgenstein's remark
about similar errors in our understanding of language: 'The difficulty is
to remove the prejudice which stands in the way . . . [But] it is not a
stupid prejudice.' It is not stupid because it does correspond, somehow,
to an instinctive response, and cannot therefore merely be dismissed as
foolishness.[1]

I want to talk about the fragmented form of works like *The Waste
Land*, *To the Lighthouse*, the novels of Robbe-Grillet. I believe the
fragmentation of form we find in these literary works has much in
common with Cubism and Serialism, that all are responses to the same
needs, the same human needs, in particular the need to escape from
what I will call 'linearity'. So we have to start with an understanding
of the implications of linearity, and we have to start not with works of
art but with our own everyday lives. And we have to start with the
obvious, because it is often the obvious that is most difficult to see and
understand.

I open a book and begin to read. When the book is finished I pick up
another, or write a letter, go to the cinema, play tennis, talk to my

friends. When the day is done I go to sleep and the next day carry on where I left off: go out to work, read a few more pages of my book, visit an art gallery perhaps, and so on. In other words I fill in my days with various kinds of activities, and reading, writing, looking at pictures or listening to music happen to be among them. These activities follow one another in time, but they also help us to pass the time – help us, that is, to ignore the passing of time.

There are moments, however, when something in us rebels against this linear yet timeless existence. It is as if there were unexpected knots which formed, unknown to us, in the smooth rope of our existence. From one point of view all of Freud's work can be seen as the attempt to describe such knots and to account for them. At the simplest level, Freud noted, there are slips of the tongue in everyday conversation, which literally force us to start again if we want to get what we want said. Then there are dreams, which pull us back to the events of the previous day or of our childhood, and sudden stabs of memory, which bring us into touch with areas of ourselves which had laid dormant for years. Finally, there are neuroses of various kinds, from simple anxiety to fully developed hysterical paralysis, all of which assert the fact that some part of ourselves simply wants to stop, to put a brake on this meaningless forward movement. And one does not have to be a slavish follower of Freud to see the value of his insights. For the curious fact about the state I am trying to describe is that though we are completely subject to time, we are completely unaware of time. In fact, we are subject to time precisely because we are unaware of it. Thus Freud could argue that in all three cases – slips of the tongue, dreams, neuroses[2] – the smooth functioning of the organism has been halted by pressure in two opposed directions. On the one hand part of us wants to keep at bay the recognition of time passing, since that would entail a recognition of our own eventual death; on the other hand part of us desperately wants to wake up from a situation in which time is not even acknowledged. This is because in pursuing his linear existence man is in flight from death, but he is also in flight from his own body; the body calls out for recognition, but recognition of the body would entail the acceptance of the world in which that body has a place and thus of the fact that it will one day cease to occupy that place. And none of us, Freud knew, is willing to give up the myth of his own immortality without a struggle.

Several years before Freud another thinker had already begun to explore the curious paradoxes of man's subjection to time. But Nietzsche was more interested in linearity as it manifests itself in history and culture than as it impinges on the individual. Early on in his career he had been struck by the odd fact that man is the only animal with a history. What, he wondered, are the implications of this? What is it that drives man forward into the future even as he builds monuments all round him in an effort to give permanence to the present? The enlightened men of his age had dismissed the belief in God as an ignorant superstition. But, Nietzsche noted, is not the belief in Progress held by these same enlightened men just as much in need of justification as the belief in God? For even the most seemingly disinterested scholarship is based on the implicit assumption that such work is valuable and that, when all the pieces are added together, they will form a meaningful whole. But why should they? The men of the eighteenth and nineteenth centuries had thought they could get rid of God, but all they had done, Nietzsche noted, was to substitute the God of Teleology for the God of Christianity.

For Nietzsche as for Freud civilisation is Janus-faced: it reveals and it conceals. It reveals *as* it conceals. Like the dream or the neurotic symptom, it is a mute plea for help as well as a way of coping with an intolerable situation. When he asks: Why all this industry? Why this frenzied desire for Progress, for accumulation, for culture? – when he asks these questions he does so not in a spirit of mere nihilism, but in order to make men recognise the compulsive and irrational drives that inform even their most normal-seeming activities. And he does not of course exempt himself from his critique. He sees quite plainly at moments that his own polemics against culture are themselves a part of culture and subject to the same criticism. Hence the growing despair of his thought; hence the change from continuous argument, as in *The Birth of Tragedy*, to the fragmentary and aphoristic style of his later books.

Nietzsche sometimes talks about the entire history of the human race and sometimes only about the nineteenth century. Often it is difficult to decide what his target really is. But, as with Freud, this does not lessen the suggestiveness of his insights. Indeed, not only have the events of the last sixty years made it possible for us to be better readers of Nietzsche than his contemporaries could ever be, but developments in historiography and the social sciences, by drawing attention to various aspects of Western society since his day, have made it possible for us to see more clearly the implications of many of his remarks. It is for instance possible to say that in Western Europe before the seventeenth century (and in much of the rest of the world till very recently) man did not live in so completely linear a fashion as he does today. Annual festivals, sacred and secular, ensured a return to the sources, a renewal through repetition. Time was accepted in the public celebration of mythical or historical events; rites of passage marked the key stages of a man's life, so that at each stage he was united both with other members of the community and with the history of his people. To some extent the liturgy still functions in this way for Christians (and Jews) today, but the numbers for whom this is meaningful have dwindled to such an extent that it retains little public or general significance. Sunday, far from being a day of renewal or remembrance, is a curiously empty, isolating day, an unreal hiatus in a life of continuous bustle. And it seems likely that the notion of a work of art as an aesthetic object, existing outside space and time and conferring upon the viewer a contemplative rapture equally free of space and time, only emerged as other, more public modes of escaping linearity, were vanishing.

But there are other, less immediately obvious, though more material ways in which linearity impinges on our history and culture. W. G. Hoskyns, in his *English Landscapes*, quotes the following remarks by John Steane about the changes that came over the village of Helpston during the lifetime of John Clare:

> Clare's vision was limited by the village which was the centre of a road system designed as an internal network to connect different places within the parish. This microcosmic universe was shattered by the work of the rural professional class and the new topography of enclosure was imposed on Clare's world. The ancient internal lanes vanished. Helpston was connected to the outside world with straight roads. The parish now simply became a place on the way to somewhere else. The linear landscape replaced a circular one.

Gombrich has remarked how slow men are to grasp the implications of advances in their own technology and how conservative the design of technology remains. Thus the first trains had carriages that were still built merely as movable rooms. Reading Steane's remarks with hindsight one cannot but be struck by the thought that only a few years later railways would utterly transform not only the landscape of Europe and America, but also man's inner sense of what it meant to travel.[3]

Even more striking is the ease with which Steane's remarks can be applied to changes in the arts. In Fielding and Sterne the chapter is still the basic unit, just as in Hogarth even the rake's 'progress' is presented in separate panels. The plot of *Tom Jones* may be hugely complex, but the book is really like a vast object suspended in eternity, in and out of which the author, with his guest the reader, is free to wander, pausing to examine now this character or incident, now that, and then moving on. In the nineteenth century, however, even in so un-Romantic a writer as Jane Austen, the author has moved into the background, or rather, has suffused himself into the very language of the book, and the chapter has become, like the paragraph, merely the indication of a pause in the swelling continuity of the narrative. In similar fashion the symphony of a Beethoven or a Berlioz has become a single unity, a wide arch stretching from first to last chord, and meant to be experienced as such, instead of a group of discrete movements such as we find in Mozart or Haydn.

There are two important factors to note here. The first is that the nineteenth-century work *leaves no gaps*. A Fielding or a Mozart remind us constantly that they are presenting us with a made world, with something created by them for our pleasure and enlightenment. A George Eliot or a Verdi, by contrast, do their best to make us forget this, to make us enter right *into* the world they have created, to make us suffer and triumph with their heroes or heroines until the novel or opera is over. The second factor, closely connected with this, is what one might call *the tyranny of plot*. An opera by Verdi or a novel by Hardy is good in spite of its plot, though it would of course never have come into being without the extraordinary convolutions and unlikely coincidences which make up the plot. Even so restrained a novelist as George Eliot, in a novel like *Daniel Deronda*, which is in many ways closer to the twentieth than to the nineteenth century, is the victim of a convention of plot formation which she is forced to use without ever quite seeing its implications. Is it likely, for example, that Daniel should discover Mirah's brother with all of London to search in? Is it likely that Mirah's father should chance upon *her*? And is it the slightest bit probable that Daniel should find himself in Genoa and at just the right spot in that city at precisely the moment when Gwendolen is fished out of the water after Grandcourt has drowned? Such absurd coincidences would not bother us in Shakespeare or Fielding, but they do here, precisely because of the novelist's effort to create the impression that the novel is writing itself, that it is 'life', wholly unmediated by the writer or by language.

Kierkegaard, Dostoevsky, Kafka. Three writers who grew up in the great century of the bourgeois family, 1815–1914. Three writers who, whatever their differences, all share the same ambiguous relation to their own fathers. For in all three cases the father *is* the world into which the son has been born, and his acts and pronouncements have the weight of absolute authority. Yet in all three cases the acts and pronouncements of the father can only strike the son as irrational and incomprehensible. Thus the son is torn in two by conflicting needs: the need to obey something in which he cannot believe, and the need to rebel against something which is already planted so deeply inside him that rebellion is tantamount to suicide.

Kafka's is perhaps the most interesting case, because it is the most fully documented and because he was the most fully conscious of the vertiginous implications of the relationship. In his eyes the father stands for the world of progress, solidity, and continuity, a world in which events and actions seem naturally meaningful. Yet his father, he soon discovers, is irrational, arbitrary, and tyrannical. Is his father then only a petty autocrat who has no justification for his acts and pronouncements except his own whim? Or is there a sanction for these which Kafka for some reason cannot see?

The issue soon takes the form (as it does for Kierkegaard): should he marry and become a father in turn, thus appeasing his father and perhaps discovering the sanctions which guide his father, or should he remain true to the stubborn conviction that there is something profoundly immoral about his father's position? He turns the subject over in his diary, and acts out his contradictory impulses in his relations with the women who enter his life. In the great letter he wrote late in life to his father but never sent he says:

> Marrying, founding a family, accepting all the children that come, supporting them in this insecure world and even guiding them a little as well, is, I am convinced, the utmost a human being can succeed in doing at all. That seemingly so many succeed in this is no evidence to the contrary, for, first, there are not many who in fact succeed, and secondly these not-many usually don't 'do' it, it merely 'happens' to them; although this is not that Utmost, yet it is still very great and very honourable (particularly since 'doing' and 'happening' cannot be kept clearly distinct). And finally it is not a matter of Utmost at all, anyway, but only of some distant but decent approximation.

The convolutions of this are typical of Kafka and they reveal clearly his central dilemma: is the ease with which other people lead their lives, marry, beget children, even die, the result of their lack of concern over the distinction between 'doing' and 'happening', or does it only seem so to one who is on the outside, and would the decision to get married, for example, automatically confer meaning upon the event? For it is of course meaning that is at stake here. Kafka's horror of committing himself stems from his profound sense of the sacrilege involved in lending oneself to a mere 'happening', especially if that involves the bringing of other human beings into the world. Yet the doubt always remains that this may be his own fault, that he may be personally excluded from a meaningful world precisely because of his doubts.

Kafka's art, to begin with, is the result of rebellion against the father and the lie of a life lived as though it had a meaning. But almost at once he finds the father installed in the very heart of writing itself. The need for shape, for plot, for a forward movement of some kind, seems to be inseparable from the act of writing itself. And is not the act of writing a prime example of the assertion of will? Further, does not the creation of the simplest fiction perpetuate the lie that all 'happenings' are really 'doings'? But it is in order to escape from such assertiveness, from such lies, that he has turned to writing in the first place. The rejection of the father thus turns into a rejection of himself not just as businessman, or father, but as writer. Hence the profound and quite incurable masochism that pervades every letter, every diary, every story that he ever wrote. The infernal circle has no outlet except death, and one can perhaps now see why Kafka welcomed the sudden flow of blood from his lungs which heralded his impending death. One can also understand why he genuinely wished his own work to be destroyed.

Until the moment of death, however, it was writing which went on holding out to him the only hope of escape. In the first story with which he was fully satisfied (perhaps the only one ever), a father condemns his son to death by drowning and the son carries out his father's orders. The story ends as the son drops off the bridge into the river. By making his art out of the impossible conflict Kafka was able at least to carry on living. But the preponderance of unfinished stories in his *oeuvre* shows that this was no triumph: the conflict ran too deep for words like 'triumph' and 'human spirit' to acquire more than a hollow ring. It was a way of holding out, and the wonder is not just that so much did get written, but that even the tiniest fragments are so rich in echo and reverberation.

Other modern artists have faced the same issues without finding that it cut quite so deep into the fabric of their lives – Eliot, Webern, Picasso, for example.[4] Eliot is particularly interesting in this connection, and it may be worth while to pause for a moment over one of his very earliest poems, 'Rhapsody on a Windy Night'. Five of its six stanzas begin with statements of time: 'Twelve o'clock'; 'Half-past one'; 'Half-past two'; 'Half-past three'; 'The lamp said "Four o'clock..." '. And just as time is here only the ticking of the clock, dividing up the day and night, so space is merely the eternal division of the long street by the regularly spaced street lamps:

> Every street lamp that I pass
> Beats like a fantastic drum,
> And through the spaces of the dark
> Midnight shakes the memory ...

What both the clock and the lamp throw up are fragments of a world: 'Regard that woman/Who hesitates towards you in the light of the door/Which opens on her like a grin...'; 'Remark the cat which flattens itself in the gutter/Slips out its tongue/And devours a morsel of rancid butter.' This seems to be the world of Imagism, but is it? The conclusion shows us why Eliot, for all his surface resemblance to the

Imagists, was never one of them. There is no pleasure for the poet in this fragmentation of the world; on the contrary, this is a vision of meaninglessness which is forced upon him against his will, which he would dismiss if only a meaning could be found that would integrate the bits, but where every impulse towards integration is recognised as a dangerous temptation:

> The lamp said
> 'Four o'clock,
> Here is the number on the door.
> Memory!
> You have the key,
> The little lamp spreads a ring on the stair.
> Mount.
> The bed is open; the tooth-brush hangs on the wall,
> Put your shoes at the door, sleep, prepare for life.'
>
> The last twist of the knife.

Why the last twist of the knife? Because to enter the room, to leave the fragmented vision of the city at night, the awareness of the inconsequential ticking of the clock, the horror of events and moments which do not add up, is indeed to sleep. To sleep as Jonah slept at the bottom of the boat he thought would carry him away from God's insistent summons, the heavy drugged sleep of a man trying to escape awareness of himself. To enter the room is to take part in a falsehood; it is to assert as meaningful a world without meaning; to pause, to recognise its lack of meaning, is at least to make possible the recovery of meaning. As Kierkegaard said, the deepest despair is not to know that you are in despair.

This is the theme of all Eliot's work up to and including *The Waste Land*. Every reader of Eliot has sensed this. And yet as soon as we try to articulate our feelings about his poetry, we fall prey to precisely the temptations he himself is trying to resist. We fill in the gaps, we assert continuity, we impute meaning to the world he describes by searching for a meaning to the poem. Commentary, after all, grew up in response to sacred texts. It twined about the holy words like ivy on the walls of an old house. But Eliot and Kafka write out of a sense of the disappearance of that house. Their art is an effort to make us glimpse a world before sleep catches up with us again. Unfortunately even the best-intentioned commentator takes signs for wonders and turns art, like history, into a golden calf.

The power of Eliot's early poetry stems from its embodiment of a sense of awakening, and that awakening is always frightening since humankind cannot bear very much reality. But there are other, less

anguished responses to the same vision. One of Wallace Stevens's collec-
tions of poems is called *Parts of a World*, and many of the poems included in it repeat the emphasis of the title: 'You said/There are many
truths,/But they are not parts of a truth' ('On the Road Home'); 'The
squirming facts exceed the squamous mind' ('Connoisseurs of Chaos');
'Yet having just/Escaped from the truth, the morning is color and
mist,/Which is enough' ('The Latest Freed Man'). Truth, in Stevens's
terms, implies unity, and truth stops us seeing the world as it is by
imposing a single pattern upon experience. The free man is free of the
burden of truth, the imposition of unity, and so he can see again. 'The
pears are not seen/As the observer wills' he writes in a wonderful evoca-
tion of the Cubist vision, 'Study of Two Pears.' But the most profound
poem on this theme is perhaps the one called 'Add This to Rhetoric'
– profound because it examines the subtlest of all the allies of 'truth',
language. 'I am afraid we are not rid of God because we still have faith
in grammar', Nietzsche had written, and Stevens expresses it like this:

> It is posed and it is posed.
> But in nature it merely grows.
> Stones pose in the falling night;
> And beggars dropping to sleep,
> They pose themselves and their rags.
> Shucks ... lavender moonlight falls.
> The buildings pose in the sky
> And, as you paint, the clouds,
> Grisaille, impearled, profound,
> Pftt ... In the way you speak
> You arrange, the thing is posed,
> What in nature merely grows.

Unconsciously, simply by reporting on what we see, we perform a
mysterious sleight-of-hand: we naturalise culture, culturalise nature.
But even before we sit down to describe, at the moment when we start
trying to make sense for ourselves of what is before us, we distort and
falsify. To recognise the difference between what 'in nature merely
grows' and the way the mind poses, the way words organise, is to be
made aware of what we normally miss. The poem helps us grasp this
by laying bare the purely human, man-made nature of our modes of
articulation: adding this to this to this to this.

Robbe-Grillet is in many ways closer to Wallace Stevens than to any
of his contemporary fellow-novelists. In his fictions he deploys his art
to confound our instinct for linear progression and to deny us our
hankering for 'truth'. This is particularly true of his finest novel, *Dans
le labyrinthe*. It begins like this:

I am alone here now, safe and sheltered. Outside it is raining, outside in the rain one has to walk with head bent . . .; outside it is cold, the wind blows between the bare black branches; . . . Outside the sun is shining, there is not a tree, not a bush to give shade . . .[5]

In *Les Gommes* the action appears to move forward only for us finally to discover that the book has ended where it began; in *Le Voyeur* there is a gap in the centre, where action and meaning ought to be. As with a Cubist painting, the reader is forced to move again and again over the material that is presented, trying to force it into a single vision, a final truth, but always foiled by the resistant artefact: 'It is posed and it is posed./But in nature it merely grows.'

Let us turn from books written within the last hundred years to a long poem composed in the first decades of the fourteenth century. At the start of Dante's *Commedia* the poet, awakening in a dark wood, struggles to escape by clambering up a hill towards the sun, which has just appeared over the summit of the hill, but is forced back towards the wood from which he has just emerged by three beasts who bar his way. However, with the assistance of Virgil, who now appears, he turns his back on the hill and begins to move in a slow spiralling motion, first down to the centre of the cone of Hell, and then up the cone of the purgatorial mount, which is clearly none other than the hill he had first seen and tried to climb. At the top Beatrice appears to him, from the east, radiant like the sun, to name him for the first time in the poem and carry him up to heaven.

Now the essential difference between Dante the pilgrim and the inmates of Hell is simply this: they cannot move out of the circle in which they have been placed, but Dante can. As he descends lower and lower he discovers a greater and greater rigidity in the damned, a physical state which corresponds to their spiritual rigidity. The final, most moving image of the sequence is to be found at the very bottom of the universe where those in the icy circle closest to Satan himself find that even their tears, the physical and spiritual token of life, change and compassion, are frozen on their cheeks and in their eyes, causing them intolerable torment instead of release. In Purgatory, on the other hand, the pilgrims are, like the poet, always on the move. As in life they exhibited enough suppleness to repent, so now they are given enough suppleness to climb the mountain, rising, slowly at first, but with gathering speed as they near the top, until at last, like Dante himself, they leave the earth and enter the manifold circles of the heavens.[6]

The word 'turn' plays a key role in the *Purgatorio*, reflecting the spiritual and physical suppleness of the souls encountered, and it is, as we might expect, usually found in conjunction with the word 'love':

Per lor maladizion sì non si perde,
  che non possa tornar l'etterno amore,
  mentre che la speranza ha fior del verde.   (III, 133–5)

By their curse man is not so lost that eternal love may not return, so
long as hope retains ought of green.

Interestingly, the word 'turn' plays a key role also in Eliot's development as a poet. After the fragmentation of the early poems it seemed
that no way forward was possible. How to write a long poem out of
fragments? It had been done once and for all in *The Waste Land.*
To write a narrative poem in the old Tennysonian or Browningesque
modes was clearly impossible – the last twist of the knife. But it is just
here that the miracle occurred. Eliot, taking Cavalcanti's lines about his
exile, about the impossibility of any return to his homeland, and brood-
ing on them, now found, with Dante's help, a way out of the impasse:

Because I do not hope to turn again
Because I do not hope
Because I do not hope to turn
Desiring this man's gift and that man's scope . . .

The rhythm, like the sense, spirals slowly, returning to the point of
departure as if for reassurance, gradually gathering momentum, until
a whole long poem is generated by the movement. And in the end it is
that movement which allows the semantic transformation to occur, as
the poem moves towards its conclusion:

Although I do not hope to turn again
Although I do not hope
Although I do not hope to turn . . .

It must be clear by now that linearity, fragmentation, the slow motion
of the spiral, are not ways of describing the merely formal properties of
a work, that we are talking about aspects of art and of personality where
questions of form and content, will and choice, are curiously irrelevant.
Was Eliot able to write *Ash-Wednesday* because he had found a faith,
or was his conversion the result of a discovery in himself of unexpected
resources of suppleness made manifest in the process of his engagement
with his craft? Did Dante the pilgrim find his way to heaven because
Beatrice took pity on him and sent Virgil to guide him out of the wood
of error and down to the bottom of Hell, or did she take pity on him
because she discerned in him the desire for salvation? Dante wisely
leaves that question unanswered and we would be well advised to do
the same.

As we might perhaps expect, Wallace Stevens has provided us with his own version of the Dantean experience, and, what is more, he has placed it at the gateway to both his *Collected* and his *Selected* poems, thus underlining its importance in his eyes. It is a short poem called, simply, 'Earthy Anecdote':

Every time the bucks went clattering
Over Oklahoma
A firecat bristled in the way.

Wherever they went,
They went clattering,
Until they swerved
In a swift circular line
To the right,
Because of the firecat.

Or until they swerved
In a swift circular line
To the left,
Because of the firecat.

The bucks clattered,
The firecat went leaping,
To the right, to the left,
And
Bristled in the way.

Later, the firecat closed his bright eyes
And slept.

Just as Dante started by trying to move straight up the mountain, so the bucks try to run forward. But there is always an impediment in the way, barring the direct path. The only way to advance is indirectly. However, when the firecat goes to sleep and nothing need stop the bucks moving forward, the poem comes to an end. It is as though the bucks and the poem could only keep moving at all *against* pressure; the poem ends when the firecat shuts his bright eyes and goes to sleep.

We can see the spiralling mode at work in other major works of the present century, most notably in *A la recherche du temps perdu*. The opening pages of that novel are just such a hesitant backward and forward movement as we find at the start of *Ash-Wednesday*. It is as if we were watching a diver bouncing again and again on the spring board, gradually gaining height, until he is finally ready to take off. Only the gradual, groping, spiralling motion can allow the huge novel to unfold, and even when it does start to move forward it keeps returning to its roots, closer in mode to *Four Quartets* than to *The Forsyte Saga*. And the same is true, despite my earlier remarks, about *Dans le labyrinthe*, which seems to stand in roughly the same relation to Robbe-Grillet's earlier novels as *Ash-Wednesday* does to Eliot's early poetry. Instead of the Cubist fragmentation of *Les Gommes*, *La Jalousie* and *Le Voyeur*, a way forward is discovered, a tentative, hesitant spiralling, which eventually allows the 'I' of the first word to transform itself into the 'me' of the last. Here is that opening paragraph in full:

> I am alone here now, safe and sheltered. Outside it is raining, outside in the rain one has to walk with head bent, hand shielding eyes that peer ahead nevertheless, a few yards ahead, a few yards of wet asphalt; outside it is cold, the wind blows between the bare black branches; the wind blows among the leaves, sweeping whole boughs into a swaying motion, swaying, swaying, that throws its shadow on the white roughcast of the walls. Outside the sun is shining, there is not a tree, not a bush to give shade, one has to walk in the full sunlight, hand shielding eyes that look ahead, a few yards ahead only, a few yards of dusty asphalt where the wind traces parallels, curves and spirals.

The motion of the spiral implies the recognition by the writer of the importance in his life and in the life of the work of the process of creation itself. The act and the time of writing are no longer hidden or repressed, but allowed out into the open, made part of the substance of the work. As a result the traditional relations between form and content, background and foreground, word and object, disappear, and the act of reading, like the act of writing, becomes an adventure, part quest, part prayer.

I am not suggesting, however, that the way of the spiral, the way of turn and return, is necessarily an advance on the way of fragmentation. Both modes (is mode the right word? But what is the right word?) are responses to the deep dissatisfaction felt with linear forms by modern writers, painters and composers. In Eliot and Robbe-Grillet we have seen a movement from fragmentation to spiralling, but in other writers the reverse movement is discernible. After the spirals of *To the Lighthouse* came the fragmentation of *Between the Acts*; after the loops and hesitations of Beckett's *Trilogy* have come a series of works which seem to take a perverse pleasure in the refusal of even that consolation: *Krapp's Last Tape, Imagination Dead Imagine, Lessness, Not I*.

One more aspect of our theme deserves attention. In discussing the response of Kafka and Eliot to linearity I have tried to bring out the sense of betrayal that any 'talking about' engenders. But criticism is precisely the art of 'talking about'. How can criticism countenance the Nietzschean question: why culture? Is not criticism itself the product of culture and committed to it? This perhaps explains the ever-widening rift between modern art and the discourse about art which is criticism. The classic exploration of the nature and consequences of this rift are to be found in Mann's *Dr. Faustus*.

Towards the end of that novel Serenus Zeitblom, the cultured academic to whose lot it falls to write about his friend, the composer Adrien Leverkühn, gives a moving and graphic description of Leverkühn's last great work, 'The Lamentation of Dr. Faustus', and he remarks:

A work that deals with the Tempter, with apostasy, with damnation, what else could it be but a religious work? What I mean is a conversion, a proud and bitter change of heart, as I, at least, read it in the 'friendly plea' of Dr. Faustus to the companions of his last hour, that they should betake themselves to bed, *sleep in peace*, and let nought trouble them. In the form of the cantata one can scarcely help recognising this instruction as the conscious and deliberate reversal of the 'Watch with me' of Gethsemane. And again the Johann's wine, the draught that is drunk by the parting soul with his friends, has an altogether ritual stamp; it is conceived as another Last Supper. But linked with it is an inversion of the temptation idea, in such a way that Faust rejects as temptation the thought of being saved: not only out of formal loyalty to the pact and because it is 'too late' but because with his whole soul he despises the positivism of the world for which one would save him.

Now Zeitblom at moments recognises that his whole book, this biography that we are reading, this monument to his dead friend, may itself be just such a betrayal, a prime example of the 'positivism of the world'. For after all what his biography tries to do is to reclaim Leverkühn for Culture, for history, by showing the close analogies that obtain between the composer's career and the fate of modern Germany. Early on in the book the two friends are discussing art and culture. 'But the alternative to culture', Serenus interjects, 'is barbarism.' 'Permit me', answers Leverkühn. 'After all, barbarism is the opposite of culture only within the order of thought which it gives us. Outside of it the opposite may be something quite different or no opposite at all.'

This is a crucial exchange, for it shows the inability of Zeitblom to grasp what Adrien is saying. Despite his profound understanding of his friend's music, an understanding tinged with horror but none the less genuine, he can only think in the terms he has inherited from the nineteenth century and ultimately, as he himself realises, from his beloved Renaissance. In these terms what stands outside culture can only be barbarism. Adrien, after his brief denial of this way of putting things, never again tries to argue; he withdraws more and more from Zeitblom and gets down to writing his music. Mann, of course, has created both Leverkühn and Zeitblom, both the music and the Professor's response to it. None the less, as the book rises to its climax one has the feeling that he has forgotten Adrien's rejoinder and moved over entirely to the side of Zeitblom, as though, in spite of his insights, his natural inclination to mistrust what was not linear and organic had finally asserted itself. Or perhaps, as his description of 'The Lamentation of Dr. Faustus' suggests, he sensed that there was another way of putting it but felt that as a novelist and user of words, he was for ever debarred from it.

As we have seen in the course of this essay, it is Leverkühn's insights, not Zeitblom's, which are the correct ones. What we have been discussing cannot be reduced to a conflict between culture, represented by nineteenth-century art, and barbarism, represented by the fragmented, non-linear art of this century. Nor can one get round the problems by saying that such art is really a mirror of the barbarism of our time. Such analogies, we must remember, are Zeitblom's, never Adrien's own. The principles of fragmentation and discontinuity, of repetition and spiralling, which we found underlying the works of Kafka, Eliot, Stevens, Proust, Robbe-Grillet, Virginia Woolf and Beckett, do not reveal anything so banal as the final disintegration of the Western Imagination. What they perhaps reveal is the disintegration of a notion of Truth, and of the power of the intellect alone to discover that truth and embody it in works of art, which men had come to take for granted in the centuries following the Renaissance. The fragmented or spiralling work denies us the comfort of finding a centre, a single meaning, a speakable truth, either in works of art or in the world. In its stead it gives us back a sense of the potential of each moment, each word, each gesture and each event, and acknowledges the centrality of the processes of creation and expression in all our lives.

Am I suggesting then that we do without any 'talk-about' – without book reviews, literary criticism, the academic study of literature? No, and for the simple reason that 'talking about' is not the prerogative of the critic or the teacher. It is a perpetual temptation in all our lives as in our reading and writing. I would only suggest that what is important is to learn to wait, to listen in that silence conferred upon the world by art alone:

Tired of the old descriptions of the world,
The latest freed man rose at six and sat
On the edge of his bed. He said 'I suppose there is

A doctrine to this landscape. Yet, having just
Escaped from the truth, the morning is color and mist,
Which is enough . . .

Notes

1. See Jean Ricardou, *Problèmes du nouveau roman*, Paris, 1967, 13; and Ludwig Wittgenstein, *Philosophical Investigations*, para. 340.

2. I am referring here of course to the tripartite division of the *Introductory Lectures*, which in turn refers to the three pillars of psychoanalysis, *The Interpretation of Dreams* (1900), *The Psychopathology of Everyday Life* (1904), and *Three Essays on Sexuality* (1905).

3. Daniel Boorstin, in his 1975 Reith Lectures, sees the same change but from a different angle: 'The great awakening of modern man was finding out that life was not really as repetitious as it had always seemed. . . America was to play a crucial role in that awakening. . . A pilgrim is a religious devotee who journeys to a shrine or a sacred place. Pilgrimage – the characteristic popular travel-institution of the age of Again-and-Again – is of course one of mankind's most ancient and familiar rituals. . . When the first Puritans and Separatists came to New England, they, too, saw themselves as going on a pilgrimage. . . [However] the shapers of American civilisation and the makers of America's influence on the world experience would not long continue to view their American mission in this way. New World experience and New World opportunities would effect a modern transformation. This was the transformation of a world of typology into a world of history.' The emptiness of the American continent, Boorstin argues, thus played a crucial role in the development of a linear view of time and history.

4. Is it fanciful to suggest that this was so because in each case there was a 'good father' to hand, someone who admired and encouraged but did not overshadow, like Pound and Schoenberg, or who had already borne the burden of being the first, like Cézanne? Sadly, one does not feel that Brod was capable of fulfilling either role.

5. I use Christine Brooke-Rose's excellent translation.

6. I am indebted here to T. M. Greene's fine article, 'Dramas of Selfhood in the Comedy', in T. C. Bergin (ed.), *From Time to Eternity: Essays on Dante's Divine Comedy* (New Haven and London, 1967).

PART III

VOICE AND BODY: THE LIMITS OF EXPRESSION

8 Words and Music Today

Though operas go on being written, it must by now be patently obvious that Schoenberg's *Moses und Aron* marks the end of the road. *Moses und Aron* is, among other things, an extended meditation on the possibility of art in general and of opera in particular, and, like so many twentieth-century masterpieces, it forces us to reconsider our own relationship both to the individual work of art and to artistic and cultural history.

Where music is concerned, that history, though full of inner contradictions, can be briefly told. In the Middle Ages music was subservient to the cult, the composer an artisan and decorator, the forms vocal and polyphonic. With the Renaissance a humanisation of music took place, harmony began to replace polyphony and the voice started to be used for the expression of individual feeling. It was not, however, till the birth of Romanticism that music finally changed from being a skill to being an art. In fact it acquired a privileged position as the art most capable of expressing the feelings of men, and with Beethoven we find a dominating subjectivity moulding musical organisation in response to the needs of expression, filling out and expanding both development and variation, which had originally been subordinate elements in the sonata form, until the form itself burst, unable to contain the richness of individual feeling. At the same time the climax of what his own and later generations have recognised as the supreme expression of Romantic hope and belief in the powers of man, the Ninth Symphony, finds Beethoven reaching out beyond the purely orchestral towards the realm of language, man's unique possession. Nor is it surprising to find Beethoven's natural successor, Wagner, discovering his own genius in an utterly new blending of words and music. 'The whole development of music in Germany', Thomas Mann has said, 'strove towards the word-tone drama of Wagner and therein found its goal.'

But the Wagnerian triumph, already tinged with so much melancholy and regret, marks a turning-point in the history of music, comparable to that occupied in literature by *Les Fleurs du mal*. For those who came after, Mallarmé or Schoenberg, Kafka or Webern, unexpected doubts began to creep in. In the place of torrential creativity came the fear of sterility and a deep uncertainty about the validity of the whole enterprise. So long as art is linked to cult such questions do not arise. So long as there is an absolute confidence in the vision of the individual they are kept at bay. But, by the turn of the century, in all the arts, it was being asked: why art? Why the elaborate pretence of art? 'For four hundred years', says the devil in Mann's *Dr. Faustus*, 'all great music has found its satisfaction in pretending. My friend, it cannot go on. The criticism of ornament, convention and the abstract generality are all the same one. What it demolishes is the pretence of the bourgeois work of art.'

Why art, then, except to satisfy the demands of the patrons of the opera houses, the theatres, the bookshops of the Western world? And in what does this satisfaction consist? Partly, of course, in the savouring of the beautiful. But much more in the bolstering up of the belief that there is a meaning to history, to civilization, to life itself. Yet for the man who can no longer find it in himself to accept this, what other solution is there than silence? The art and history of the past hundred years is full of examples of men who have grown silent because they had an insight into the fraud and could not find it in themselves to go on playing the game as though nothing had happened.

Yet, for the artist, the need to create persists, despite the impossibility of creation. The styles of Modernism grow out of the response to this paralysing paradox. In the case of Schoenberg it led to the invention of twelve-note composition, a 'strict style' in which 'every note of the whole composition, both melody and harmony, would have to show its relation to the fixed fundamental series', as Mann describes it. This new rigour restored to Schoenberg and his pupils the possibility of once again creating large-scale works, since form would no longer be dependent on a suspect subjectivity. But it did not resolve the problem of the dramatic union of words and music, and thus the central problem of the relation of music to man and music to truth. The opera *Moses und Aron* is both an exploration of this problem and a kind of desperate solution.

At once we are faced with a startling paradox. The hero speaks. He does not sing. The protagonist of a grand opera and he does not sing? But how, given the subject-matter, could he? To sing would be to turn God's message, of which Moses is the custodian, into a beautiful object, to be admired by the people of Israel and the opera-house audience, instead of a truth to which they must respond. Kierkegaard, in his great essay on *Don Giovanni*, had already drawn the distinction between the world of music, which is both immediate and timeless, and the ethical world of choice and renunciation. For Kierkegaard *Don Giovanni* is the supreme opera, since its hero embodies sheer music, the triumph of erotic immediacy. Yet he recognises that it is only right that the opera should begin and end with the Commendatore, since music cannot survive the stony grip of ethics and responsibility. In *Moses und Aron* it is as though the Commendatore had moved into the centre of the picture. Moses will not compromise. He will not sing when he can speak. Yet without song he cannot reach the people. It is Aaron who has to sing for him, acting as a bridge between God and men. But the bridge proves inadequate, a gross distortion of the truth. The climax comes with the orgiastic worship of the Golden Calf by the people. As George Steiner has rightly said: 'The Golden Calf is both the logical culmination of, and a covert satire on, that catalogue of orgiastic ballets and ritual dances which is one of the distinctive traits of grand opera from Massenet's *Herodiade* to *Tannhauser*, from *Aida* and *Samson et Dalila* to *Parsifal* and *Salome*.' Schoenberg presents the operatic audience with what it wants, and simultaneously reveals that wanting for what it is: decadent, self-indulgent aestheticism, propping up a despairing fear of the void.

The Golden Calf episode provokes a crisis in Moses. He realises that it is not simply song which is false but words themselves. All expression is inadequate, there will always be an ineradicable gap between words and The Word. His last despairing utterance finds its echo in the works of nearly every major modern artist: 'Oh word, thou word that I lack!' And *Moses und Aron* joins Keats's *Hyperion* and Beethoven's Piano Sonata opus 111 as a work whose very incompleteness (Schoenberg wrote the music for only two of the projected three acts) stands as an unanswerable rebuke to every well-made work, every self-satisfied artefact produced in the last century and a half.

The view of cultural history I have outlined above is a familiar one. It is the standard view of those critics and philosophers of art who are heirs to the great tradition of German Romanticism and Modernism. To it we owe the insights of an Erich Heller, a Theodor Adorno, a George Steiner. As a critical and explanatory model it is vastly superior to the liberal positivist view prevalent in the English-speaking world, which, under the guise of objectivity and common sense, peddles a version of cultural history already effectively demolished by Nietzsche and Proust before the First World War. But it is worth noting that though *Dr. Faustus* is a major document in that tradition (and one that I have been able to quote from quite naturally above), Mann seems uneasy with the ways the issues are posed. By making his narrator a parody of a latter-day Humanist he seems to be asking whether the crisis model of history and culture is not itself the product of a specific set of cultural assumptions; whether, in fact, it is correct to speak of culture and music as having come to the end of the road (as I did at the start of this essay), and whether one ought not instead to speak of it as having come to the end of *a* road: that broad road which leads from the Renaissance to the nineteenth century, and along which are to be found most of the works of art with which educated Europeans are familiar today.

We will not find answers to these questions in Mann himself. Like Schoenberg, he is too much a part of European and German culture to do more than glimpse the possibility of alternative attitudes. But let us turn to another voice, one strangely free of the doubts and self-torment to which Mann and Schoenberg are prone:

> An example of a musical antithesis to me in my own time is *Wozzeck*. What disturbs me about this great work and one that I love, is the level of its appeal to 'ignorant' audiences, with whom one may attribute its success to: (1) the story; (2) Bible, child sentiment; (3) sex; (4) brevity; (5) dynamics...; (6) muted brass...; (7) the idea that the vocal line ⟋⟍⟋ = emotion; (8) the orchestral flagellation in the interludes; (9) the audience's feeling that it is being modern.

> Passionate emotion can be conveyed by very different means than these, and within the most 'limiting conventions'. The Timurid miniaturists, for example, were forbidden to portray facial expression. In one moving scene from the life of an early Zoroastrian king ... two lovers confront each other with stony looks, but the man unconsciously touches his finger to his lips, and this packs the picture with, for me, as much passion as the *crescendo molto* in *Wozzeck*.

Thus Stravinsky, in conversation with Robert Craft. And the important fact about Stravinsky, which we are just beginning to recognise, is that his roots do not simply lie outside the German or French musical tradition but outside the whole stream of post-Renaissance European culture. He is rooted not just in the Russian Orthodox Church, not just in the vanished world of nineteenth-century Petersburg, but in an Asian, Tartar world. In his conversations with Craft he recalls the cries of the street vendors of Petersburg, especially those of the Tartars – 'though in truth they did not so much cry as cluck ... Only rarely did they speak Russian, and the low, frog-like noises of their language were an invisible invitation to mockery.' He recalls too the countrywomen of Lzy singing on their way home from the fields in the evening, the peasant music heard in the Ukraine, and the dances at the country fairs. This does not merely help to explain his choice of subject-matter in the early stage works; it also allows us to see how very limited and limiting is our own European concern with expressivity.

Not surprisingly, in his search for texts to set, Stravinsky was drawn not to the European lyric tradition but to Russian popular texts, nursery rhymes and word-games. And here he made a vital discovery, for one important characteristic of Russian popular verse is that the accents of the spoken verse are ignored when the verse is sung. The recognition of the musical possibilities inherent in this fact was one of the most rejoicing discoveries of my life; I was like a man who suddenly finds that his finger can be bent from the second joint as well as from the first.

No wonder Stravinsky rejoiced at this discovery. For suddenly the entire problem which had tormented Romantic and post-Romantic composers vanished. Mann's composer-hero, Adrien Leverkühn, had already noted: 'Abstract it may be, the human voice – the abstract human being if you like. But that is a kind of abstraction more like that of the naked body – it is, after all, more a pudendum.' But Leverkühn, like Schoenberg, was trapped by the paradox that language, or that which the voice must use, is completely removed from the human body. The alternatives are to let the voice erupt into a scream or fade into a sigh, but though all nineteenth-century vocal music moves in the direction of the scream or the sigh, it reaches it at its peril, for no scream or sigh can last more than a few seconds. Stravinsky's joyful discovery, however, gave back to the composer unlimited possibilities for writing vocal music at once abstract and immediate, human and unindividualised. Throughout the rest of his career he was to show a fondness for setting texts in foreign languages, preferably those, such as Latin and Hebrew, at some remove from his potential audience.

As soon as the voice ceases to be thought of as expressing the feelings of an individual, a completely new musico-dramatic form can emerge. Stravinsky recalls, of *Renard*: 'I planned the staging myself, and always with the consideration that it should not be confounded with opera. The players are to be dancing acrobats and the singers are not to be identified with them; ... as in *Les Noces*, the performers, musical and mimetic, should all be together on the stage, with the singers in the centre of the instrumental ensemble.' *Les Noces* is the great work of this period, and Stravinsky's description of what he wanted to achieve is of the utmost importance:

Les Noces is a suite of typical wedding episodes told through quotations of typical talk. The latter, whether the bride's, the groom's, the parents' or the guests', is always ritualistic. As a collection of clichés and quotations of typical wedding sayings it might be compared to one of those scenes of *Ulysses* in which the reader seems to be overhearing scraps of conversation without the connecting thread of discourse. But *Les Noces* might also be compared to *Ulysses* in the larger sense that both works are trying to *present* rather than to *describe*.

Individual roles do not exist in *Les Noces*, but only solo voices that impersonate now one type of character and now another. Thus the soprano in the first scene is not the bride, but merely a bride's voice; the same voice is associated with the goose in the last scene . . . . Even the proper names in the text . . . belong to no one in particular. They were chosen for their sound, their syllables, and their Russian typicality.

What Stravinsky is adumbrating here is, we might say, an alternative modernist aesthetic. Instead of describing, the work *presents*; instead of expressing, the singers *impersonate*. It is an aesthetic which would have been instinctively accepted by all men at all periods of time in every part of the globe – except for that tiny portion of it we call Western Europe, in that minute fraction of time which has elapsed since the sixteenth century. For if *Renard* and *Les Noces* have little in common with Verdi or Puccini or Wagner or Berg, they do have a great deal in common with the music-theatre of Indonesia, China and Japan, with the medieval *Play of Daniel* and with the *Commedia dell'arte*. Like Picasso and Joyce, Stravinsky, overthrowing the moribund conventions of his time, found himself in touch once more with ancient and still vital traditions of art.

Walter Benjamin has acutely observed the crucial function of discontinuity and gesture in Brecht's theatre:

> The task of epic theatre . . . is not so much the development of actions as the representation of conditions. This does not mean reproduction as the theoreticians of Naturalism understood it. Rather, the truly important thing is to discover the conditions of life . . . . This . . . takes place through the interruption of happenings . . . . Epic theatre is by definition a gestic theatre. For the more frequently we interrupt someone in the act of acting, the more gestures result.

This interruption is the theatrical equivalent of Cubist distortion and Joycean dislocation. Its effect is to deny the spectator the comforts of an illusionist mimesis. It pitches him into a world whose space is non-human and where mood is located not inside any one individual but diffused over all the elements. Since the work can no longer be reduced to an anecdote, every element – such as gesture, speech, costume, props – assumes equal significance. What we have here is a *superficial* art, an art which focuses on *surfaces*. When we have learnt to use these words in other than a pejorative way we will have learnt the rudiments of what such an art has to teach.

Now it is often said that a physical and total theatre of this kind is one which must do without words (it was one of the errors of Artaud).

But that is to fall back into an expressionist aesthetic, however nega-
tively. On the contrary, such a theatre rediscovers words, but as the
expression of the total body rather than of consciousness. In a Ionesco
or a Pinter play, for example, speech has a far more important function
than in Ibsen or Shaw. For speech is used not to impart information or
express views, but as a weapon or shield, as an extension of the arm or
the chest, an instrument of survival or aggression. Again, works like
Berio's *Laborintus* II, Stockhausen's *Stimmung* or Lutoslawski's marvellous Michaux settings, do more than treat the voice in startling new
ways. The vocal writing conveys a new sense of space, one which is both
very physical and very abstract, quite unlike that conveyed by Western
music of the past four hundred years. Yet we recognise it with pleasure
as a space our bodies can inhabit. It is a potential space, like that
marked out by the gymnast's body flying through the air, and our
pleasure at experiencing it is pleasure at human potential momentarily
realised, rather than anything known or understood.

In such a situation the role of the librettist becomes less to prepare a
text for the composer to set than to present the composer with ideas
which can generate genuine musico-dramatic works. Since the turn of
the century, in fact, a completely new relation has come into being
between literature and music. *L'Après-midi d'un faune* is pure programme music, but *Estampes* suggests not a specific set of engravings
but the formal problems of engraving in general. We have seen Stravinsky compare the form of *Les Noces* to that of some parts of *Ulysses*, and
the Cyclops chapter of that work lies behind Maxwell Davies's procedure in his *L'Homme armé* Mass: 'In the Joyce', Maxwell Davies
explains, 'a conversation in a tavern is interrupted by insertions which
seize upon a small, passing idea in the main narrative and amplify this,
often out of all proportion, in a style which bears no relation to the
style of the germinal idea...' Not only the Mass in question, but a
great deal of Maxwell Davies's recent music can be traced back to this
passage. The model for Gordon Crosse's second violin concerto is
Nabokov's *Pale Fire*, since the notion of a lyrical core overwhelmed by
a grotesque commentary helped the composer to see how some of his
own preoccupations could best be explored. Examples of such 'borrow-
ings' could be multiplied, but the point I wish to make is clear: artists,
in whatever medium, now look to the other arts to provide them with
structural models rather than with stories, sights or sounds for them to
imitate or embellish. Unfortunately, in England at any rate, composers
have proved better readers than writers are listeners. We await the
playwright or novelist who will take his cue from Stockhausen's *Mantra*
or Harrison Birtwistle's marvellous *The Triumph of Time*, itself already
indebted to Brueghel's painting.

Once one abandons an aesthetic of imitation on expression, the distinction between opera (words subservient to music) and theatre (music subservient to words) disappears. *Les Noces*, Britten's *Curlew River*, Maxwell Davies's *Songs for a Mad King*, Berio's *Laborintus* II, Beckett's *Lessness*, Pinter's *Silence* – all are artistic constructs which create and allow us to experience a new sense of space and time. It does not matter that some are by composers, some by writers. Martin Esslin's radio presentation of *Lessness* and an Aldeburgh performance of *Curlew River* have been among the artistic experiences I recall with most pleasure from the past ten years; I would be hard put to it to say which was the more musical, which the more dramatic.

And yet, it must be said, today no traditions are possible. Each work is a fresh raid on the inarticulate. Britten's attempt to create a tradition of music drama is instructive. Neither of the two church operas that followed *Curlew River* was as good as the first. More important, they were, in a significant sense, redundant. Each new work today seems to require a rethinking of the entire form; each new success remains that and nothing else: one success, against all the odds. In music-theatre, as in drama or fiction, it is an illusion to believe that it is the relative newness of what is being attempted that is the cause of frequent failure.

Nevertheless, a change has started to come over the arts in the years since *Renard* and *Les Noces*. One can at least begin to breathe. The long nightmare of post-Renaissance Europe, that mixture of lunatic pride and unbelievable naïvety, though it gains momentum in many spheres of life, shows signs, here and there, of receding. We will not wake up tomorrow and find it gone. But at least we can, even in London, occasionally enter a theatre or a concert hall and find ourselves in a world where a cleaner air prevails.

9 *The Rake's Progress*

Return! and Love!
The banished words torment.
                Tom Rakewell

He says, later, that his brothers always called him 'the piano tuner,
because I repeated a note that I liked'.
                Robert Craft

No two works of Stravinsky are alike, but *The Rake's Progress* is more
different than most.

As we look back over that amazing list of masterpieces, what strikes
us now is the unity of the entire canon. From *Le Sacre du printemps* to
Abraham and Isaac half a century later the 'feel' of a Stravinsky work
is unmistakeable: that combination of a hieratic, ritualistic style with a
wonderfully lively and witty texture. (The only comparable achievement is the work of the late Yeats.) This is particularly evident in the
stage works. '*Les Noces*', Stravinsky has said, 'presents rather than tells.'
Here, as in *Oedipus Rex*, the music and the stage action *show* a ritual
unfolding, much as a priest might show an icon to the crowd, in André
Boucourechlev's apt analogy. These works eschew expressivity, psychology and mimesis; they do not say 'I am' or 'I wish', but 'It is' and
'It shall be'.

The great exception is *The Rake's Progress*. From 1910 to 1945
Stravinsky had written music that often made use of the past but which
really had little to do with European art since the Renaissance. Like
Eliot and Kafka, and unlike Mann and Yeats, he made the break with
the nineteenth century almost at the start of his career; like Eliot he
forged a radical style out of the fragmentation of the past; like him he
renewed a whole language by so doing; and like him he wrote highly
complex works which are nevertheless immediately accessible – at a
visceral rather than an intellectual level. Yet though Stravinsky knew
and admired Eliot, and indeed later set some of his work, it was not to
Eliot but to Auden that he turned for the libretto to his opera. Auden,
of course, had learnt much from Eliot, but his instinct was very different. Though his subject-matter was just as contemporary as Eliot's and
his range infinitely wider, his approach to art was more traditional, and

deliberately so. He believed that one should use language to *talk about* rather than to *show*; in other words he accepted the human limitations of language and contented himself with making poems that smile at their own inadequacies rather than attempting to break through to some totally new mode of expression.

A good way of describing the difference between *The Rake's Progress* and other Stravinsky works is to say that it stands in the same relation to them as Auden does to Eliot. But why did Stravinsky turn to Auden when he decided that the time had come to write a proper opera, and why did he accept a libretto as far removed as it is possible to get from the sacred joyfulness of *Les Noces* or the hieratic awesomeness of *Oedipus*? Why did he put up with the whimsy of Baba the Turk and the Bread Machine or the triteness of the Epilogue? These are more than rhetorical questions, for we know that Stravinsky was never the kind of composer who gratefully accepts whatever his librettist gives him. On the contrary, one major reason for the success of his theatre pieces is surely that in every case he seemed to know exactly what he wanted from his librettist and made sure he got it. He did not simply ask Cocteau for an adaptation of the Sophoclean tragedy. He knew that he wanted the text to be in Latin, not Greek or French; he knew exactly how he wanted text and narration to relate to each other; he had a very clear idea of the way the work should be staged. And this is as true of *Renard* and *L'Histoire du soldat* and *Les Noces* as it is of *Oedipus*.

Therefore, unless the war, the move to America, and the personal tragedies that beset his life in those years had wrought a total change in him, we must accept the fact that the libretto of *The Rake's Progress* is as it is because that is how the composer wanted it to be. And Stravinsky's own remarks on the collaboration bear this out: he approached Auden with the idea; Auden was enthusiastic and came out to California; in ten days the two of them had mapped out the basic structure; Auden and Kallman then set to work to fill in the detail, and although many fine ideas emerged on the way, the initial shape hardly altered. The truth of the matter is that Auden and Stravinsky were so perfectly in tune with each other – 'I discovered when we began to work together that we shared the same beliefs, not only about opera, but also about the nature of the Beautiful and the Good. Thus the opera was a collaboration in the highest sense', Stravinsky remarked later – that the words only serve to deepen and enrich the initial conception. Paradoxically this means that though the librettists perfectly fulfil their humble role of providing a scaffold for the music, this is one of the few librettos that can be read and enjoyed on its own.

But we have not yet answered the question of why it was that Stravinsky chose this librettist and this form. The answer will only fully emerge when we have examined the libretto in some detail, but it should perhaps be provisionally sketched in here. Each new work of Stravinsky's, like each new work of Eliot's or Picasso's, was a new departure, a unique solution to a problem most of their contemporaries had not even envisaged. None of them was content to repeat or even merely extend the work of the nineteenth-century masters. Though it is possible now to see connections with Tchaikovsky, Browning or Cézanne, in the end these are far less important than the sense we get from their work of the complete abandonment of the Renaissance Humanist tradition for a more primitive and impersonal art. But the abandoned tradition, the tradition of the classical style, of the novel and narrative poem, of imitation and perspective, is not quite a tradition like any other. It is the result of an effort to see man in a human time and space; it presents man not as he is in an absolute way, but as he knows and thinks himself to be in the ordinary course of his life. *Les Noces* and *Oedipus*, like *Prufrock* and *The Waste Land*, are not about the ordinary moments of life. They are, it is true, about ordinary men and women – you, *hypocrite lecteur* – but at extreme moments, when we are taken up into the dance of the universe, when the reality we cannot bear very much of is forced upon us.

But what of those other times, the normal times, celebrated by the nineteenth-century forms? Is the only comment, 'Ridiculous the waste sad time before and after'? *The Rake's Progress* is Stravinsky's attempt to explore these areas of human experience out of which the rest of his music tries to draw us, those areas where man is caught up neither in the primitive dance nor in the sacred procession. More than that: it is about the *relation* of ordinary life to those central moments; about the way in which man, in the normal course of events, turns away from the dance and in so doing denies both reality and himself.

Les Noces and *Oedipus* exist in a timeless world. The celebration of a wedding is an event that takes place outside time; in *Oedipus* the clocks are stopped and for the hero start to run backwards. That is one reason why we feel that these works belong outside our Renaissance Humanist traditions. For time, the ticking of the clock, is the obsessive post-Renaissance theme, finding expression in the legends of Dr Faustus and Don Juan. By the nineteenth century – the Century of Progress, as it is often called – the obsession with time is no longer something to be objectified and expressed; it inheres in the very fabric of society and in the very forms of art. Reading the great novels of the era or listening to Berlioz or Verdi we are bound to recall that this was the great period of the railway: the strong momentum drives one forward; once the plot starts to unfold there is no turning to right or left or ever going back. It is interesting to note that in an eighteenth-century novel the chapters tend to be self-contained units, separate panels; whereas by the nineteenth century they are merely convenient divisions in a swelling narrative. What seems to happen in Wagner is that both the heroes and the music itself start to become aware of the horror of this headlong forward rush, but this awareness only serves to reinforce the sense of the protagonists being caught in a seamless web of continuity. Both heroes and music, in Wagner as in Berg, struggle to free themselves from the web, to deny time and its workings, but it is a struggle which can only end in the destruction of the self: the only way to deny time is to die. Hence our sense that the music itself passionately longs for its own annihilation.

This is where Stravinsky's *formal* solution to the problem of writing an opera is so interesting: rather than seek musical forms 'symbolically expressive of the dramatic content (as are the Daedalian forms in the operas of Alban Berg)', he has said, '*The Rake's Progress* is cast in the mould of an Eighteenth Century "number" opera; the dramatic progress depends on the succession of recitatives and arias, duets and trios, choruses and instrumental interludes . . . In the earlier scenes the mould is pre-Gluck; it tends to crowd the story into *secco* recitatives and to reserve the arias for the reflective poetry. Later the story itself is told and enacted almost entirely in song – in contrast to Wagnerian continuous melody, which consists, in effect, of orchestral commentary enveloping continuous recitative.'

Curiously, what happens here is that an opera which denies the unfolding of time in its form is able to *examine* time and its workings in a way which an opera that lives under the aegis of time (like *Tristan* or *Wozzeck*) never can. *The Rake's Progress* does not ignore the problem of time by devising a form that by-passes the issue, as does *Oedipus*. It had to be Auden and not Eliot who would provide the libretto to Stravinsky's only full-length opera, because in that work Stravinsky wanted to explore the problem of the relation between music and narrative, which is the relation between the ideal timeless world of the imagination and the everyday human world of time and death and such human and social things as promises and wishes. *The Rake's Progress* is thus at once a comment on life and on the genre – opera – in which it chooses to exist.

Les Noces had celebrated marriage as a rite and a sacrament; *The Rake's Progress* charts the consequences of refusing to take part in a sacramental union. The opera opens, like many a Shakespearean comedy, with the praise of a Golden Age:

ANNE

> The woods are green and bird and beast at play
> For all things keep this festival of May;
> With fragrant odors and with notes of cheer
> The pious earth observes the solemn year.

RAKEWELL

Now is the season when the Cyprian Queen
With genial charm translates our mortal scene,
When swains their nymphs in fervent arms enfold
And with a kiss restore the Age of Gold.

Music, which, as Auden says, 'is for everyone and no-one, and is always in the Present Tense', is ideally suited to celebrate the restoration of the Age of Gold. This is the Paradise of the Imagination, when all our wishes are fulfilled. But though it is real in so far as we can really imagine it, it is false in so far as it ignores the facts of space and time in which we live. Opera is, ideally, a wedding of music and words; that is, of imagination and reality. But such a union is impossible, as the greatest operas have always recognised. Monteverdi's *Orfeo*, with which *The Rake's Progress* has much in common, also starts with the celebration of a joyful union which brings with it echoes of a Golden Age, but its central theme is the lament for the loss of that union. In *Don Giovanni* the central issue is the irreconcilable conflict between the immediacy of music, embodied in Don Giovanni himself, and the claims of society and ethics.

In a Shakespearian comedy the ideal of the opening is usually shattered by a father figure who insists on his rights by law to destroy the frail paradise of the lovers. Such comedy usually ends with the father recognising the primacy of Nature over Law and giving his blessing to the lovers. The Maytime of the opening thus returns, reinforced by the trials to which it has been subjected. *The Rake's Progress* begins its re-evaluation of Renaissance assumptions by subverting this basic form. For Truelove, Anne's father, is, as his name implies, not a tyrannical father but one who, unlike Rakewell, loves truly:

TRUELOVE

Tom, I have news for you. I have spoken on your behalf to a good friend in the City, and he offers you a position in his countinghouse.

RAKEWELL

You are too generous, sir. You must not think me ungrateful if I do not immediately accept what you propose, but I have other prospects in view.

TRUELOVE

Your reluctance to seek steady employment makes me uneasy.

RAKEWELL

Be assured your daughter shall not marry a poor man.

TRUELOVE

So he be honest, she may take a poor husband if she choose, but I am
resolved she shall never marry a lazy one.

Rakewell's comment on this is: 'The old fool', but Truelove is no fool,
though he may be a bore. He is asking Tom to recognise that by marrying he is entering a world of responsibility, which means a world where
Time and Money have to be acknowledged and accepted. For time and
love go hand in hand, since love implies commitment in time to another
person; and in our world if two people are to live together at least one
of them will have to give a thought to money. In *Tristan* music and
time are deeply at odds, and music finally triumphs over time in a
death which is also erotic fulfilment. *The Rake*, on the other hand, is
committed from the first to the musical articulation of the acceptance
of time. Time is not denied by the action, but the consequences of such
denial *by the hero* are examined and commented upon, so that the opera
is able to explore the relation of human beings to time in a way *Tristan*
never can.

Tom's response to his future father-in-law is 'I will trust Fortune'.
This sounds very much like the remark of one of Shakespeare's clowns,
and our sympathies, it would seem, should go with him and against
the bourgeois ethics of Truelove. But the central fact about the
Shakespearean clown is that he is alone, whereas Tom has committed
himself in the opening duet to Anne. By this act – singing his love with
the other person is a public act equivalent in opera to taking an oath in
church in real life – he has entered the world of responsibility, and
therefore of time and money, whether he likes it or not. And indeed his
next remark is 'I wish I had money', a sentiment no Shakespearean
clown would ever express. It is quite natural too that the expression of
the wish should bring Shadow on to the stage. Though 'many insist'
that he 'does not exist', yet his task is to carry out such wishes and then
extort the price. In the opera he appears as a parody of a Dickensian
deus ex machina, with his talk of rich uncles and advantageous wills,
and proceeds to whisk Tom off to London.

The first scene is a sort of prelude, since it ends with Shadow address-
ing the audience with the words: 'The Progress of a Rake begins'. It
hovers between the ideal world of Renaissance mythologising and the
practical world of bourgeois capitalist enterprise. The second scene sets
the opera firmly in the eighteenth century – or rather in the late
eighteenth century, for this is not the poised and polished world of the
Augustans but the nervous and anguished world of Dr Johnson and
Diderot, of Hogarth and de Sade; a world which has lost faith in the
ground of eighteenth-century beliefs but has not yet found a vocabulary
to express this, and where there is consequently a tension between the

heavy impersonal style and diction and the sense of desperate uncertainty beneath. This tension comes out clearly in the catechism in
the brothel:

RAKEWELL
　　One aim in all things to pursue:
　　My duty to myself to do . . .
　　To shut my ears to prude and preacher
　　And follow Nature as my teacher . . .

MOTHER GOOSE
　　What is the secret Nature knows?

RAKEWELL
　　What Beauty is and where it grows.

SHADOW
　　Canst thou define the Beautiful?

RAKEWELL
　　I can.
　　That source of pleasure to the eyes
　　Youth owns, wit snatches, money buys,
　　Envy affects to scorn, but lies:
　　One fatal flaw it has. It dies.

Mortality, indeed, hangs heavy over this scene. Shadow can turn the
clock back but he cannot annihilate Time. The philosophy, as in de
Sade, is one of despair; Love's triumphant campaigns are not at all a
fulfilling of nature, for the view of nature expressed here leaves out an
essential element in human nature – and the despair stems from the fact
that it half senses that it does so:

　　Soon dawn will glitter outside the shutter
　　And small birds twitter, but what of that?
　　So long as we're able and wine's on the table,
　　Who cares what the troubling day is at?

　　While food has flavor and limbs are shapely
　　And hearts beat bravely to fiddle or drum
　　Our proper employment is reckless enjoyment
　　For too soon the noiseless night will come.

Dreams are only dreams, the imagination only imagination; man can
glut his senses as much as he wishes but he will not be able to shut out
the thoughts of his own mortality. Where Wagner tried through sheer

willpower to force reality to conform to desire, Auden and Stravinsky
begin with an acceptance of the way things are:

> Sweet dreams, my master. Dreams may lie,
> But dream. For when you wake, you die.

This is why that second scene is so suffused with sadness, a sadness
lifted to a strange height in the wonderful setting of 'The sun is bright,
the grass is green; *Lanterloo, lanterloo,*' which Stravinsky called 'the
most wonderful gift a librettist ever made to a composer', but which is
also one of the most wonderful repayments ever made by a composer to
his librettist. By giving this supremely innocent music to the roaring
boys and whores the composer retrospectively calls into question the
opening duet. As Golding says, there is no innocent work. To portray
innocence is to destroy it. That is why pastoral is such a disturbing
genre. Conversely, by portraying the loss of innocence we may be led to
a rediscovery of it, on the other side of despair, as Tom will do. In
Tristan and *Wozzeck* it is music that dies at the end, as the hero dies,
finally engulfed by the world of reality. In *The Rake's Progress* the
ultimate renunciation happens at the very start, with the composer's
own renunciation of expressivity ('rather than seek musical forms symbolically expressive of the dramatic content...'). Stravinsky accepts
that there is no innocent work, that music cannot by itself portray
innocence or guilt, that it cannot finally convey the feelings of either the
characters or the composer (that is why he says the opera is so bound up
with *Così fan tutte*). Schoenberg, faced with such a realisation, took the
drastic step of having his hero refuse to sing; as always Stravinsky's
solution is at once more and less radical – less radical because all the
characters go on singing away merrily; more radical because his solution
involves a rethinking of the form, not merely the content, of opera.

By siding with Shadow rather than Truelove, Tom has denied Time,
Love, and, ultimately, his own nature. Each of his three wishes draws
him further along the road of denial and despair. Since the two latter
wishes – 'I wish I were happy' and 'I wish it were true' – lead to the
two most arbitrary and whimsical episodes in the opera, the episodes
of Baba and of the Bread Machine, it is worth pausing over them for a
moment.

Both Baba and the Bread Machine look at first as though they would
fill the gap left by the denial of Anne/Love. Both prove illusory. Between
them, however, these two improbable episodes span the major obsessions
of the nineteenth century, the century of Freedom and Progress. In the
first scene of Act II Shadow explains to Tom why he is suggesting a
marriage between him and Baba: 'Come, master, observe the host of
mankind. How are they? Wretched. Why? Because they are not free.
Why? Because the giddy multitude are driven by the unpredictable

Must of their pleasures and the sober few are bound by the inflexible Ought of their duty, between which slaveries there is nothing to choose. Would you be happy? Then learn to act freely. Would you act freely? Then learn to ignore those twin tyrants of appetite and conscience. Therefore I counsel you, master – take Baba the Turk to wife.'

But the *acte gratuit* can never bring real freedom, for there the will acts in a void. Freedom implies responsibility, the acknowledgement that one is bound by one's choices. The argument is not between morality and freedom, as Tom, like de Sade, keeps trying to make it. Nor is it, in musical terms, a conflict between the imposition of order and the indulgence of sensations. It is precisely this sense of responsibility that distinguishes the major from the minor artist in any age.

Tom's third wish is prompted by his dream of the machine that can turn stones to bread. When Shadow shows him the machine of his dreams he immediately imagines that to present this to the world will solve all its problems and will thus be the good deed that can make him deserve Anne's love again. For:

Thanks to this excellent device
Man shall re-enter Paradise
    From which he once was driven.
Secure from need, the cause of crime,
The world shall for the second time
    Be similar to Heaven.

After the Utopia of Freedom, the Utopia of Progress. But the audience has seen Shadow put the bread in the machine in the first place, and thus knows that the 'engine' is a fraud. The effect of this bit of stage-play is difficult to analyse, but I would suggest that what we see in the machine is an analogue of the opera itself, the 'machine' made by Auden and Stravinsky.

The mechanical nature of Stravinsky's music has often been noted. He himself tells us that his problem with *Les Noces* was to find an orchestration that 'would be at the same time perfectly homogeneous, perfectly impersonal, and perfectly mechanical.' This quality is of course one we tend to associate with the hieratic and ritualistic, the one that makes us feel the works 'show' rather than express or describe. But part of the effect comes from an acceptance by the music of itself as only music, the product of sounds made by specific instruments, rather than as a great river carrying the listener off into another world. This music is *made*, rather than simply existing like a force of nature; it belongs to the Secondary, rather than the Primary world, in Auden's terms. In one sense it is no better than the Bread Machine, since it is an 'engine' and a purely man-made and unmiraculous one at that. The paradox here of course is that the insistence on its Secondary nature allows such art to transcend the mechanical, whereas an art which imagines that it is reaching out into the unknown all too often strikes us as expressive only of the composer's own banal obsessions.

The Romantics and the Liberal-Progressives of the nineteenth century were at one in refusing to accept man's fallen nature. They thus railed at society and at man himself for the position in which he found himself. The most profound thinkers of the century – Kierkegaard, Dostoevsky, Nietzsche – realised that it is necessary to start from the premise of man's fallen condition, of the impossibility of innocence. Only in this way could there be any realistic appraisal of man's nature. In recognising this they were of course only touching again on a religious tradition whose greatest exemplars are St Augustine and Dante, and it is to this tradition that both Stravinsky and Auden felt themselves emphatically to belong. In the present age, however, it seems probable that such a tradition can only find its voice through the negation of its opposite. The problem is highlighted in the creation of the figure of Anne in the opera.

Anne's first words after Tom's departure for London set before us the artistic as well as the psychological problem:

No word from Tom. Has Love no voice, can Love not keep
A Maytime vow in cities? . . .
He needs my help. Love hears. Love knows . . .
If love be love
It will not alter . . .

She can only be a presence, as love itself can only be felt as a force, not expressed in words.

Her next appearance, however, in the fifth and central scene of the opera, makes the dilemma most manifest. She has at last found Tom in London, only to discover that he is married to Baba. As he steps out of his chair he recognises her in the gloom outside his house. He reacts guiltily and violently:

RAKEWELL
Anne, ask me, accuse me –

ANNE
Tom, no –

RAKEWELL
– Denounce me to the world, and go;
Return to your home, forget in your senses
What, senseless, you pursue.

At once Anne picks up his word: 'Do you return?' He is shaken: 'I?'
She persists: 'Then how shall I go?' To which he answers:

> You must!
> (*aside*) O wilful powers, pummel to dust
> And drive into the void, one thought – return!

The one thought he cannot face is that conjured up by the word *return*.
Anne is not of course simply talking about a physical return to her
father's house and the country. She is asking him to return *to* her as
well as *with* her. But this is the one thing Tom cannot do. For, in his
denial of time, he is driven on in a frenzied progress *by* time. Only
through his acceptance of time, which would mean his acceptance of
the validity of his vow to Anne, could he find a release from time, and
with that the possibility of return.

In his notes to *New Year Letter*, glossing the line 'Hell is the being of
the lie', Auden makes the following comment, which has a direct bear-
ing on Tom's position:

> It is possible that the gates of Hell are always standing wide open.
> The lost are perfectly free to leave whenever they like, but to do so
> would mean admitting that the gates were open, that is, that there
> was another life outside. This they cannot admit, not because they
> have any pleasure in their present existence, but because the life
> outside would be different, and, if they admitted its existence, they
> would have to lead it. They know this. They know that they are free
> to leave and they know why they do not. This knowledge is the flame
> of hell.

In Dante the damned in Hell cling to their identities in defiance of God,
willing themselves into being and refusing to accept anything outside
their own egos. In the upper reaches of Hell they go endlessly round
and round the same circle, to which they have been condemned by
eternal decree; in the lower reaches they grow more and more fixed to
a single spot, until near the very centre they are frozen in the ice and
even their tears cannot flow. In Purgatory the pilgrims are free of this;
they wind round and round the mountain cone, moving ever upwards
towards the Earthly Paradise. The word *tornare* occurs often in that
canticle, as is fitting where the theme is the celebration of those who
were supple enough to turn to God in repentance before their death.
In Eliot's most Dantean poem, *Ash-Wednesday*, the starting-point is
Cavalcanti's famous lament on his own exile, 'Perch'io' no spero di
tornar giammai', which Eliot first renders as 'Because I do not hope to
turn again'. But the form of the poem is itself a slow, hesitant, gradual

spiralling, and the poem (in contrast to the fragmentation of *The Waste Land* and the other early poems) moves forwards and upwards, until in the last section the opening lines are transformed into:

> Although I do not hope to turn again
> Although I do not hope
> Although I do not hope to turn ...

Stravinsky never changes his style in so radical a fashion. Yet *The Rake's Progress* becomes the place where the exploration of the meaning of turn and return – in psychological and aesthetic terms – is most protracted. To follow it through we now need to move on to the last two scenes.

A year has passed. Shadow, in the graveyard, claims his wages: Rakewell's soul. Rakewell is terrified, and the clock starts to strike the fatal hour. However, Shadow stops it short, as he had done once before in the brothel, and agrees to play a game: for Tom's three wishes, three cards; if he guesses what they are, he is free; if not, he belongs to Shadow.

The first card is picked. Tom, thinking suddenly and unexpectedly of Anne and of her love for him, makes a desperate guess: the Queen of Hearts. The guess is correct. The second card is picked. As Tom struggles to guess, a spade falls beside them, and Tom curses: 'The deuce!' He looks round, sees the cause of the noise, and says calmly:

> She lights the shades
> And shows – the two of spades.

Shadow acknowledges his good luck:

> The two of spades.
> Congratulations. The Goddess still is faithful.

Now comes the final card. Shadow is ironic: 'Think on your hopes.' 'O God,' answers Tom in despair, 'what hopes have I?' As he turns away Shadow picks up the discarded Queen of Hearts and replaces it in the pack. He addresses the audience:

> The simpler the trick, the simpler the deceit;
> That there is no return, I've taught him well,
>   And repetition palls him:
> The Queen of Hearts again shall be for him the Queen of Hell.

By offering Tom the Queen of Hearts again he wishes not simply to trick him, but in so doing to confirm Tom in his servitude to him and to Time, and, by making him deny Anne once and for all, to make him deny any possibility of redemption.

Tom, knowing his hour has come at last, looks away from the spot and sees: 'Dear God, a track of cloven hooves.' Shadow is scornful:

> The knavish goats are back
> To crop the spring's return.

He knows Tom will not believe him, will not even imagine that he wishes to be believed. It is obvious that the tracks are made by his own cloven hooves, denying the return of any spring for Tom – that spring celebrated so joyfully at the start of the opera. But Tom pounces on Shadow's word as Anne had pounced on his:

RAKEWELL
> Return! and Love!
> The banished words torment.

SHADOW
> You cannot now repent.

The word Shadow has spoken has a life of its own – none of our words are exclusively ours, we can never know what echoes they will awake in another mind and heart. This is in part the burden of responsibility in the human use of language: our words only gain meaning and coherence by the meaning and coherence of the lives and thoughts of those who speak them. So now, suddenly, unexpectedly, Tom moves out of Shadow's clutches and into a wholly new world. Out of his mouth come the words: 'Return O love –', and at that moment the miracle happens and the voice of Anne does indeed return, singing

> A love
> That is sworn before Thee can plunder hell of its prey.

Tom listens, spellbound, and then says simply:

> I wish for nothing else.
> Love, first and last, assume eternal reign;
> Renew my life, O Queen of Hearts, again.

And with Tom's acceptance of return and renewal, Shadow vanishes.

But this is not a fairy story. Love can plunder Hell and rob it of its prey, the spirit even of a rake is supple enough to repent at last and turn and return if his lover's love is steadfast. But there is a price to pay. Having betrayed love as he has, he can only find it again, and fulfilled, in madness, just as in *Orfeo* it is only in heaven that Orfeo and Eurydice can be perpetually united once Orfeo has looked back. In this last scene of the opera the echoes of *Orfeo* grow strong again. Tom, who in the opening duet had invoked the figures of Venus and Adonis, now, in Bedlam, believes that he is Adonis and will answer to no other name. Nevertheless, he is lucid about his own errors, and, though greeting Anne as 'Venus' when she comes to visit him, tells her:

> In a foolish dream, in a gloomy labyrinth
> I hunted shadows, disdaining thy true love;
> Forgive thy servant, who repents his madness,
> Forgive Adonis and he shall faithful prove.

But Anne answers:

> What should I forgive? Thy ravishing penitence
> Blesses me, dear heart, and brightens all the past.
> Kiss me Adonis: the wild boar is vanquished.

RAKEWELL
> Embrace me, Venus; I've come home at last.

R. and A.
> Rejoice, beloved: in these fields of Elysium
> Space cannot alter, nor Time our love abate;
> Here has no words for absence or estrangement
> Nor Now a notion of Almost or Too Late.

But reality does have words for 'almost' and 'too late', and though music celebrates the present, in this opera the present attains its poignancy because it is so clearly situated between a past and a future. Just as Orfeo and Eurydice are united only in Heaven, so Tom can become Adonis and shed his earthly self to unite with Venus/Anne only in a madhouse. And since madness, unlike love, cannot be shared, she has eventually to leave him. Here, at the end of the opera, words and music combine to express in miraculous fashion the simultaneous presence of loss and gain, of the fulfilment of desire and its inevitable frustration:

RAKEWELL
> Where art thou, Venus? Venus, where art thou? The flowers open to the sun. The birds renew their song. It is spring. The bridal couch is prepared. Come quickly, beloved, and we will celebrate the holy rites

of love. Holla! Achilles, Helen, Eurydice, Orpheus, Persephone, all my courtiers. Holla! Where is my Venus? Why have you stolen her while I slept? Madmen! Where have you hidden her? . . . My heart breaks. I feel the chill of death's approaching wing. Orpheus, strike from thy lyre a swan-like music, and weep, ye nymphs and shepherds of these Stygian fields, weep for Adonis the beautiful, the young; weep for Adonis whom Venus loved.

The image of Venus and Adonis, which was purely rhetorical and conventional in the opening duet, is now fully placed and accepted. Such an eternal union can be conceived by the human imagination, but it can be achieved only in the timeless world of the stars. On earth our art can only give such longing body, and a responsible art must lament its impossibility. Thus is Romantic longing expressed and put in perspective in some of Stravinsky's most human and haunting music.

The mood of that music is immediately shattered by the sprightly Epilogue. But that too is essential to the overall pattern. Had we been left with the action and music of the ninth scene we would have been tempted to enter fully into Tom's mind and to accept the world of his madness as in some sense the real world. (This is what Maxwell Davies, whose temperament is more akin to a Romantic like Schoenberg than to Stravinsky, does at the end of his *Eight Songs for a Mad King*, when he turns the impersonal spoken lament into the King's howl of anguish, and leaves us with that ringing in our ears.) It is right for this opera that the frame should be deliberately replaced at the end, that we should return from the heavens, from the music of longing and lament, to the light society music of the eighteenth century. What we have seen and heard, after all, the Epilogue reminds us, is only a cunning engine devised by Auden and Stravinsky, ordinary mortals if extraordinary artists both of them. There is no absolute gulf between them and ourselves, only differing degrees of clarity and skill.

I have tried to show how well the libretto of *The Rake's Progress* suits the composer's purpose, and to define a little more precisely what that purpose might have been. I have also wanted to show that this seemingly whimsical and sometimes frivolous work stands as a critique, and not just an alternative, to the 'continuous' opera of Wagner and Berg. That this form corresponded not just to a conscious decision on Stravinsky's part but also to an instinctive mode of composing is hardly surprising. The great artist is the one who is able to objectify his obsessions and, by finding appropriate forms for them, to purge both himself and us. In his diary for 1951 Robert Craft notes that Stravinsky, at about the time of the première of *The Rake's Progress*, remarked that his brothers used to call him 'the piano tuner, because I repeated a note that I liked.' Such a need to go back to the same note or group of notes again and again is characteristic of his music from the start. *The Rake's Progress*, seen in the light of that remark, is perhaps the one work of Stravinsky's which gives a justification in terms of human psychology and of the realities of our world for that obsessional need to repeat and return. It is the piano tuner's answer to the train-driver.

10 Maxwell Davies's *Taverner*: Thoughts on the Libretto

1. 'Jemand musste Josef K. verleumdet haben.' – 'Someone must have been telling lies about Joseph K.' So begins Franz Kafka's *The Trial*. But *had* someone been telling lies about Joseph K.? The phrase, as it stands, is ambiguous. We read on, however, expecting sooner or later to find out the truth. But the novel provides no answer, either for us or for Joseph K. himself.

If an answer was provided by the book, what sort of status would it have? Who would supply it? The author? But where would *he* get it from? The outside world? Inspiration? A direct line to God? In Kafka's writings we are brought face to face with the fact that there is no external authority for our actions or our beliefs. Just as for the author there is no authority to dictate either choice of subject or treatment. And how, indeed, could there be? A vocation implies a call, and a call implies a caller, but Kafka's world remains silent. No voice tells the author how to go about his task, and there is no longer any confidence in the inner promptings of the spirit such as sustained the Romantics. At the same time the urgent desire to write persists.

How then can these two things be reconciled, the impossibility of writing and the necessity of writing?

2. Kafka made his fictions out of the painful exploration of this contradiction. So too, in a different way, did Thomas Mann. With a brilliant grasp of historical realities he set his profoundest exploration of the paradox simultaneously in the late Romantic world he knew at first hand and in the world of the Reformation where, he realised, the crisis of authority had its roots. *Dr. Faustus* is not just about modern music or Nazi Germany or Nietzsche or Luther – it is about all these things at once, for Mann sensed that they were all connected. Behind Adrien Leverkühn, as everyone knows, stands Arnold Schoenberg. But behind Schoenberg stands Nietzsche, and behind Nietzsche, Luther. Behind Serenus Zeitblom, the composer's friend and biographer, stands the greater part of Mann himself; stands Burckhardt, the youthful friend of Nietzsche, who so quickly turned away from him, as if sensing the un-

liveable regions into which his thought was taking him; stands Erasmus.
For the crisis of authority out of which came Cubism and Serialism and
the work of Kafka and Eliot and Borges and Robbe-Grillet was pre-
figured in that first great questioning of authority, when truth and
culture, Germany and Europe, art and the talk about art we call
criticism and scholarship, first came into violent conflict. And, as Mann
clearly saw, when Luther rejected the authority of the Pope and Coun-
cils, putting his trust in his own unaided conscience and the Sacred
Scriptures, he started a bigger landslide than he knew. We are still
living out the consequences.

3. Yet it is not in Germany but in England that the process can most
clearly be seen. For in England events took an exemplary turn. Henry,
rejecting the authority of the Pope, made himself head of the Church,
expropriated the wealth of the monasteries, and started England on the
path to nationalisation and modernisation along which, without too
much optimism, it is still moving. For a while the flowering of culture
in the age of Elizabeth concealed the real impact of Henry's revolution.
But by the late seventeenth century, when the dust of the Civil War
had settled, the pattern was clear, and those virtues were firmly en-
trenched which were to remain paramount till the coming of the First
World War – and beyond. And it is not perhaps too fanciful to see the
eclipse of genuine musical life in this country as the obverse of those
virtues, though such generalisations cannot of course be proved. However that may be, it is not surprising that a young musician, feeling his
Englishness strongly yet repudiating the narrowness and bigotry of the
established musical traditions in this country, should, in the years
following the Second World War, have turned back to the roots of those
traditions to discover the source of his own music. And when it appears
that a great composer of Henry's time, one of the finest late medieval
musicians, unable to square the edicts of the Church of Rome with his
own conscience, turned Protestant, turned Informer, 'repented him very
much that he had made songs to Popish ditties in the time of his blindness', and wrote no more, it is easy to see the fascination exercised by
John Taverner over Peter Maxwell Davies.

4. Taverner, as he appears in the libretto, seems fully justified in his
rejection of Rome. In his very first speech he points out how impossible
it is for him to accept in full consciousness what people had been
thoughtlessly accepting for centuries:

Of one body of Christ is made two bodies, one natural, which is in
heaven, the other, in the sacrament, needs be unnatural, to enter the
mouth in the form of bread, and be disposed of therewith.

What comfort can be to any Christian to receive for a space Christ's unnatural body?

And when the Priest comes in, to give evidence against Taverner, we see how the Church has indeed abused her authority: 'The Priest, fat and bungling, stumbles forward, with leather wine-bottle', says the stage-direction. He asks for a bribe before starting to speak, then, when it is given him, he pronounces:

He is a whoreson corruptor of youth.
He had blasphemous thoughts the Pope is Antichrist,
He refused payment for pardons or kissing saints' relics,
He ate meat on Friday.

Taverner's reply to this is in the heroic mould: 'I must be saved by my faith, not by that of others.' This is the stance of Luther – but it is also, of course, that of those quiet heroes who refused to accept the conventions and traditions hallowed by no authority except time: the stance of Cézanne, of Kafka, of Schoenberg.

5. And yet, though Taverner seems to be so much in the right, the seeds of personal disaster lie in that rejection. At the climax of Act 1 he exclaims in triumph:

There shone about me a light from heaven, and I fell down upon the earth, and heard the voice of Christ, saying, 'Put off thy blindness.'
I am as reborn, His spirit is upon me.
I defend Christ's truth with the sword and the fire, for love of him.
In the name of God the Father, God the Son, and God the Holy Ghost.

But behind him as he utters these words crouches not only the Holy Spirit but Death, who, putting 'his jester's cap on Taverner's head, thrusts his jingling johnny into his hand, and puts his grinning mask over his face.'
What has happened? How has the Jester, Death, usurped this power? How has it come about that the upright Taverner, filled with God's holy zeal, has fallen into those hands?

6. The libretto stresses that the fate of King Henry, and therefore of England, and that of Taverner, run parallel. It may therefore be helpful to turn to Henry to see if his actions can throw any light on what happens to Taverner.

No one has ever doubted that Henry's breach with Rome was dictated first and foremost by private interests. The libretto stresses this aspect of the situation, and also the peculiar mixture of power and vulnerability that belongs to a King. (It is perhaps worth noting the interest in mad kings which runs through the art of this century, from *Ubu Roi* and Pirandello's *Henry IV* to Robbe-Grillet's *L'Homme qui ment*. The reason for this is simple: a madman is someone who insists on being in total control of the world, even if this means shutting out of his consciousness the real world and creating a world of his own; a king already has the power to rule a portion of the real world in any way he likes, though political theorists from Aristotle on never tire of reminding men of the chaos that ensues if kings act irresponsibly. The artist is part madman and part mad king. He appears to have complete power over words, sounds, colours, but at the same time he has no power at all over the world in which other people exist. This is the source of Kafka's anguish. Shakespeare had already used the plight and fantasies of Richard II to explore the extent of his own power over language, and Maxwell Davies wrote the music for the Old Vic production of *Richard II* in 1962.)

In the first scene in which Henry appears, the Jester remarks:

Where the word of a King is, there is power, and who shall say unto him, 'What doest thou?'

While Wolsey thinks to himself:

Often have I kneeled before him the space of an hour or two, to persuade him from his will and appetite, but without result.

And when Henry next appears it is to proclaim:

Our people do hate the Pope marvellously. We have resolved to make no further homage or payment to Rome, for we no longer wish rashly to squander money which is the blood of the State. Therefore we proclaim the absolute abolishment of the usurped power of Rome.

In Freudian terms, which are particularly relevant to this libretto, Henry has finally rejected the power and authority of the Father, and decided to become, in a sense, his own father.

7. If we look at the pattern of Taverner's experience and of Henry's, we see that they do indeed resemble each other very closely. First there is the righteous rejection of authority and the reliance on unaided reason or faith. But, without some external authority, 'who shall know St

Michael, who the Serpent?' Once external authority has been renounced we find no freedom but a new bondage. For we become the
victims of our unconscious impulses, masquerading as reason or faith.
This is plain in the case of Henry, though his very awareness of the
impurity of his motives makes him paradoxically less likely to fall victim
in this way. But it is equally true of Taverner. Another being takes over,
his double, id or superego, who rules over him. For, as Freud rightly
saw, the id or *thing* that is our unconscious transforms itself into a
repressive superego. The task of both id and superego is primarily to
keep from consciousness the fact of its own eventual disappearance –
the fact of death. But, paradoxically again, this is to play straight into
the hands of death, for any denial or repression of reality entails a subjection to it, and the only way to free oneself from it is to recognise it
and learn to accept it. This of course is not an intellectual but an emotive matter. Such 'acceptance' must be understood as something akin
to conversion.

In terms of the individual, subjection to the superego means a life
based on the accumulation of possessions and a denial of the body.
At the level of civilisation it means the growth of a society based on the
accumulation of wealth and knowledge, and a denial of those arts that
are closest to sensation, primarily music. With the rejection of Rome it
thus becomes inevitable that Death the Jester, the double of both Henry
and Taverner, should rule both England and the soul of Taverner.
And this is what we find. The stage-direction at 1. iv. reads:

Death (the Jester) alone, his skull-face only spotlighted. From the
Death's head emerges the face of John Taverner, with eyes closed, spotlighted. The two heads are close together, surrounded by total darkness.

And later in the same scene:

Death bows, and mounts the Cross, ostentatiously, as Joking Jesus.
The Demons place huge rubber nails in his hands, outstretched
against the wood.

And it is Death who utters the last words of that first act, as the soul of
Taverner, 'a coal-black raven with shining red eyes', is consumed in
flame: 'Salvatus! Beatus vir! Resurrectus! Osanna!'

Death's symbol is the Wheel of Fortune, which shows the triumph of
the inhuman over the human, of randomness and necessity over choice
and meaningfulness. Thus it is only right that in the first scene of Act II
the following spectacle should appear before us:

Behind the Council, in a red glow, appears a huge Wheel of Fortune, upon which are counterfeited the following: a King, crowned, at the top, seated; to the left, the same figure, reaching upwards; to the right, the same figure, descending, with crown dislodging .... The Wheel rotates (independently of the figures) in a clock-wise motion, at first slowly, but accelerating, this effected by Death, still in Jester's garb, but unmasked, sitting at the centre of the Wheel; with one hand he pushes the diagonals, with the other holds aloft a large smoking chalice from which emerges the head of a black ape ...

And it is right too that Death's last words, as he makes his blasphemous sign of the cross, should be a Scriptural quotation:

Seest thou these great buildings?
There shall not be left here one stone upon another,
which shall not be thrown down.

Thus is all meaning stood upon its head.

8. If authority is corrupt and fraudulent, it has to be rejected. But if to reject it is to play into the hands of the Jester Death, what is to be done?

The libretto provides no answers, though it hints at one or two possibilities. In the very first scene Richard Taverner, John's father, tells the court that 'His music is witness that he believes'; and Rose Parrowe, his mistress, pleads that 'in this city he fell among thieves, who would rob him of his heart and in its place plant suppositions based on hollow reason, empty of grace.' At the end of the first act she speaks again, this time to Taverner himself, reminding him that

It is not given you to understand divine nature, except it be implied in your creation, through your songs for the Church.
So be content, for in denying this, you betray us, the only divine in you.

Reason alone can never understand, Rose argues. To put our trust in reason is to mistake our nature. Human beings can never understand, they can only *make*, and in such making reveal the God who is in us all. Insistence on one's reason is a form of pride, the cardinal sin for which Satan fell.

Once again the parallel with later artistic movements is plain: the pride of the Romantic artist, imagining *he* can legislate for mankind; and the reaction to such pride in a Webern, a Stravinsky, an Auden, insisting that the artist creates only secondary, not primary worlds, that it is his humble task to make rather than to convey some prophetic message. The motto here might come from one of the great central cantos of Dante's *Commedia*:

> Ogni forma sustanzïal, che setta
>   è da matera ed è con lei unita,
>   specifica virtù ha in sé colletta,
> la qual senza operar non è sentita,
>   né si dimostra mai che per effetto,
>   come per verdi fronde in pianta vita.

Purgatorio 18: 49–54

> Every substantial form being both distinct from
> matter and united with it, holds within itself a
> specific virtue, which is not perceived except in
> operation nor is ever demonstrated but by its
> effect, as life in a plant by green leaves.

Very Stravinskian this, the cold austerity of the Aristotelian anti-essentialism suddenly burgeoning in the wonder and naturalness of that last phrase: 'come per verdi fronde in pianta vita.'

9. It is surely no coincidence that the most Stravinskian piece Maxwell Davies has written is a setting of the great hymn to the Holy Spirit, *Veni Sancte Spiritus*. There is no better expression of the healing and unifying power of the spirit of God than the latter part of this medieval poem:

> Lava quod est sordidum,
> Riga quod est aridum,
> Sana quod est saucium;
>
> Flecte quod est rigidum,
> Fove quod est frigidum,
> Rege quod est devium.
>
> Da tuis fidelibus
> In te confidentibus
> Sacrum septenarium.
>
> Da virtutis meritum,
> Da salutis exitum,
> Da perenne gaudium.

Yet Maxwell Davies's true centre lies elsewhere, though it was only in the course of the 1960s that this became clear. The serenity of a faithful son of the Eastern Church does not come naturally to him. The words of Taverner go on troubling him: 'I must be saved by my own faith, not by that of others.' There is in fact more of another Russian behind the libretto, one regarded with a certain amount of distaste by the Europeanised liberal milieu to which Stravinsky (like Nabokov) belongs: Dostoevsky. Here in *Taverner* we find the same intense febrile world, the same propensity of man to succumb to his own devils and to turn on the Father and destroy him in an act which is very close to self-destruction as in Dostoevsky's novels, those great fictional explorations of the paradoxes of reason and faith. We are in a world which springs out of the torment of having to live out an impossible paradox: the refusal to recognise any authority and the awareness of the suicidal nature of such a refusal.

10.   How can such a paradox be contained? The answer takes us to the heart of the libretto and of Maxwell Davies's world, and it can be given in one word: *parody*. For parody is the assertion of the primacy of process over product, of making over knowing. It is the assertion of the freedom of man in the face of destruction and despair: the uniquely human freedom to articulate. In Puritan England the Jester Death triumphs and music is destroyed. In Henry's England the Jester triumphs and Taverner denies his creative impulses, dries up, turns informer and then butcher. Id and superego triumph over ego and the opera ends with Taverner falling 'prostrate before the pyre' to which he has condemned his fellow human beings. But on the stage in 1972 the *dramatisation* of the triumph of Death the Jester asserts the triumph of life and art. Antichrist, obscenely grinning, moves into the centre of the stage, but the dramatisation of Antichrist is the triumph, if not of Christ, then at least of that creative principle of which Christ, according to Rose Parrowe, is the root. As in Thomas Mann's *Death in Venice* or Nabokov's *Lolita*, the articulation of the hero's failure, despair and disintegration reveals the ultimate triumph of art, of the human over the inanimate, of ego over id ('Where *it* is there shall *I* be', Freud had written late in life of the aims of psychoanalysis).

Such a triumph is typical of much of the art of our time. Think of Dostoevsky's *The Devils*, of the paintings of Francis Bacon, of *Moses und Aron*. It is only people who neither read nor look nor listen who complain that such art is 'obscene' or, at best, 'depressing'. The reverse is true, for it is perhaps only such art which is completely satisfactory, for only it faces up to the destructiveness in ourselves and asserts, by its simple existence, that such destructiveness can be overcome by a creative power for which the only word is love. And that, of course, does not make it any less terrible to contemplate.

11. Kafka wrote a parable called 'The Truth About Don Quixote'. It runs like this:

Without making any boast of it Sancho Panza succeeded in the course
of years, by devouring a great number of romances of chivalry and
adventure in the evening and night hours, in so diverting from him
his demon, whom he later called Don Quixote, that his demon
thereupon set out in perfect freedom on the maddest exploits, which,
however, for the lack of a preordained object, which should have
been Sancho Panza himself, harmed nobody. A free man, Sancho
Panza philosophically followed Don Quixote on his crusades perhaps
only out of a sense of responsibility, and had of them a great and
satisfying entertainment to the end of his days.

Maxwell Davies's demon is called Antichrist, and it is fitting that
his short work of that name should have become established as the
'signature-tune' of his group, The Fires of London. The libretto of
Taverner makes plain the origins and lineaments of Antichrist.

12. Antichrist is both Death and a Jester, and he is the central figure of
Taverner. The opera simultaneously charts his triumph and exorcises
him. Yet a reading of the libretto alone leaves one uneasy. Thematically
the Jester is central; formally not. It is possible that music and staging will
resolve these contradictions; here I am concerned only with the libretto.

Part of the problem seems to be that there is actual pressure from
within the work for the entire action to take place inside Taverner's
mind. (The stage directions at II. i. suggest that what we are seeing on
the stage is Taverner's nightmare.) On the other hand the presence of
King and Cardinal, and the fact that Taverner himself really did exist
in history, make it impossible for this to happen. Thus part of the
libretto seems to pull dramatically in the direction, if not of *Anne of the
Thousand Days*, at least of *A Man for all Seasons*: that is, towards the
presentation in theatrical terms of episodes from English Tudor history;
while part of it pulls dramatically in the direction of *Wozzeck* or
Erwartung: that is, towards the presentation in theatrical terms of what
is essentially a private, internal crisis. This is particularly obvious in the
handling of time. The opera is strung out in two acts, eight scenes.
Many years clearly elapse between the first and last scenes, since
Henry's Reformation has not started in the first and is well under way
by the last. Yet the composer seems to take every available opportunity
to discard continuity altogether, and to turn stage time into internal
rather than historical time, And, indeed, this is to be expected, since the
centrality of parody in his work makes clear his contempt for the linear
and realist conventions of nineteenth-century art, of which Grand
Opera – all plot and clappable arias – is the apotheosis. But it highlights
the unresolved conflicts within the libretto. Perhaps in the writing of it
the Jester has triumphed just a little more than the composer knew.

13. One can count on the fingers of two hands the successful operas of this century. Most often they have not been operas at all but something else: *Oedipus Rex*, a dramatic oratorio; *Curlew River*, a mixture of miracle and Noh plays; *Punch and Judy*, ancient Greek drama in the guise of popular puppetry. All, at any rate, depend for their success on their total rethinking of the genre. For any serious composer there is always the old problem: why should anyone sing what can perfectly well be spoken? Maxwell Davies's *Eight Songs for a Mad King* solves the problem beautifully, since there is excellent dramatic reason for the King to sing as he does. But as soon as one moves away from one person to two or more, the problem arises with real urgency. One person can make the world in his own image and draw the audience in after him (*Erwartung, Revelation and Fall*). But two people imply a world in which both exist, a time which they both share. The central problem for dramatists this century has been to find a form of stylisation that will allow such a world to be created, both removed from the 'ordinary' world of the spectator yet clearly related to it. With this problem overcome the dramatist can be as abstract or absurd as he likes. (This is why Brecht, Ionesco and Beckett are great playwrights, while Camus, Sartre and Osborne are merely interesting commentators on the times.) *Oedipus Rex*, *Curlew River*, *Punch and Judy*, all work because of the assurance with which the stylisation is handled, the elegance with which the new rules are defined. Such assurance has always come naturally to Stravinsky, who has for this reason scored more theatrical successes than all other modern composers put together.

14. The forces that drove Maxwell Davies on from *Veni Sancte Spiritus* to *St. Thomas Wake* are the same ones that have made it difficult for him to find an elegant solution to his dramatic problems. Unlike Stravinsky and Birtwistle, he cannot find it in him to rely on distancing conventions. His roots are deep in Romanticism and in German music, which is only another way of saying that his problem has always been to render the *cry* articulate rather than to transmute it into a more formal scheme. It seems clear in retrospect that sooner or later he would write *Revelation and Fall*, *Eight Songs for a Mad King* and *Vesalii Icones*. But in all these works the focus is on one figure and one figure only – double of the artist if you like, but of the spectator too. In the libretto of *Taverner* I think one finds traces of the struggle to reach that degree of direct expression of the animal scream of the heart without the immediate disintegration of the music. The opera and the long years spent on it surely made the later works possible. Whether it can stand beside them only a visit to Covent Garden will reveal. But let us remember: few works could.

11 Two Moments in Modern Music-Theatre

The upshot of all these reflections is that I have only to let myself go!
So I have said to myself all my life – so I said to myself in the far-off
days of my fermenting and passionate youth. Yet I have never
fully done it. The sense of it – of the need of it – rolls over me at
times with commanding force: it seems the formula of my salvation,
of what remains to me of a future.

Henry James, *Notebooks*

Art, for instance, we might call the high school of patience in
impatience.

Thomas Mann, *Lotte in Weimar*

The two moments of which I wish to speak occur at or near the end of
two of the most beautiful and successful music–theatre works to have
been written in England since the war: Britten's *Curlew River* and
Maxwell Davies's *Eight Songs for a Mad King*. Both are moments when
music and language transcend or seek to transcend their natural limitations, and to focus on them may help us to understand not only the
particular problems facing the composer of music drama, but also the
general laws that govern the limits of all artistic expression. To focus
properly on those two moments it will of course be necessary to step
back and take in other works by the two composers in question. I will
start with Maxwell Davies.

I

When Edvard Munch felt that 'loud unending scream piercing nature',
the question for him was how to get it down on canvas. Only thus could
the anguish be at least temporarily exorcised. It is true that he might
never have heard the scream if his art had not been ready for it.
Nevertheless, the search for the right image was a long one, and, when
he finally created it, it was, of course, quite unlike anything he or
anyone else could have predicted. That is the essence of important
moments in the history of art. In the lithograph of 1893 a wormlike
figure rises out of swirling black and white lines, mouth open to swallow

or emit, little paw-like hands pressed against the sides of the elongated head where ears might be expected to be. It does not matter that the figure in no way resembles anything we have ever seen before. We know what it is feeling, and we know that there are no words with which to describe it. For this is not the scream of a man in pain. It is a scream which yearns to break all barriers, the scream of the child for the breast, of the defenceless animal when the predator pounces, of the mother at the death of her son. It is a loud annunciation of the Fall. At the same time it is a desperate attempt to overcome the Fall. For the short period of its duration contact is established with the alien world, loss and separation denied.

It may seem odd that it is in painting that the scream has found its most perfect artistic expression, but a little thought will show us that this is only to be expected. For the scream annihilates consciousness and time, and language exists only in time, is synonymous with consciousness. Modern literature and music, and in particular modern drama and music-drama flirt with the scream, but they embody it at their peril. Since Wagner at least composers have been drawn nearer and nearer to the edge, as if to see how near they could get and yet allow their music to survive. Practically every work of the second Viennese school is, we could say, a sublimation of the scream. Sublimation, however, is the operative word. One might think that one or other of these composers, since none of them was noted for his lack of daring, would have tried to let loose a naked scream upon the stage or concert platform. Yet none of them ever quite does so. For that we have, as far as I know, to wait until the 1960s and two remarkable pieces by Peter Maxwell Davies.

The first of these, *Revelation and Fall*, was completed in February 1966 to a commission by the Koussevitzky Foundation. It is scored for sixteen instrumentalists and soprano. The instrumentalists play flute doubling piccolo; oboe; clarinet doubling bass clarinet; bassoon, horn, trumpet, trombone, harp, percussion; and string quintet. Various instruments have individual amplification systems in certain passages, and some of the instruments were specially made to the composer's specification. These include such things as a metal cylinder with protruding steel rods of various lengths and a resonant metal sheet. Also used are handbells, a glockenspiel, an oil drum, a knife-grinder and a railway guard's whistle.

This may sound like the familiar array of tools for any composer out to shock, and the violence of the piece is indeed shocking. However, with every major artist, what appears at the time as totally new and often arbitrary is later seen to have had its seed in the author's earlier work. At the same time, without the courage to plunge into the unknown, that seed would not have sprouted. *Revelation and Fall* is both an extension of what Maxwell Davies had been writing before it and a major breakthrough. What he seems to have discovered in the course of composition is that it is possible to make sounds more barbarous, more violent and unearthly, than had hitherto been thought possible or per-missible, and yet to retain total control and for something on half an hour. As always in moments of breakthrough, the rules which had guided the forms of artistic expression until that moment were suddenly seen to be arbitrary and needlessly restrictive. As with Joyce and *Ulysses*, one has the impression here of assisting at the moment when one man suddenly saw *that it was possible to do it in another way*! The sounds produced by the sixteen instrumentalists can truly never have been imagined by anyone until that moment, unless it was by Thomas Mann in the later pages of *Dr. Faustus*.

What allows the piece to exist for as long as it does is of course the fact that it is the setting of a poem. In this case it is a prose poem, written by Trakl in 1917, shortly before his death. As in some of Maxwell Davies's earlier work, notably the Leopardi fragments, what seems to have fired the composer's imagination is the possibility of juxta-posing an ultra-Romantic text with a very strict and un-Romantic mode of musical construction. In the music there is a good deal of 'period' colour, including specific references to Schoenberg and even to Lehar, but, as the composer has said, 'on a deeper level it represents a marked extension . . . in the use of late medieval/Renaissance composition tech-niques. Particularly in the complexity of rhythmic relationships between simultaneous "voices", in the use of *cantus firmus* with long melismas branching out, and in the use of mensural canon, the work is more un-compromising and more demanding on the players.' As in the works of Leverkühn described by Thomas Mann, the very rigour of the form makes the expressiveness that much more violent.

Trakl's apocalyptic poem, though banal, seems to have released in the composer areas of violence and aggression he had not previously known how to tap. The banality itself is not an incidental feature, but an essential factor, in both poem and composition. For, reading the poem, one feels that for Trakl the real drama is being played out not in the work itself, but in the relation of words to meanings, of the speaker to what he says; and this Maxwell Davies seems to have sensed and multiplied a hundredfold. Here is the poem, in Stephen Pruslin's deliberately flat translation:

I sat in silence under the charred beams of an abandoned inn, alone with my wine. A glittering corpse leaned over the dark pool and a lamb lay dead at my feet. Out of the dissolving azure stepped the pale form of the Sister, and so spoke her bleeding mouth: stab of the black thorn. Ah still resound to me the silvery arms of wild tempests. Let blood flow from moonlit feet and blossom on nocturnal paths where the screeching rat rushes. Flare, you stars, in the vaults of my brow, and my heart will peal gently into the night. A crimson spectre broke into the house with flaming sword, but fled with a snowy brow. O bitter death.

And a dark voice spoke from within me: in the nocturnal forest I broke my steed's neck, for madness leapt from his crimson eyes; the shadows of elms fell on me, the blue laughter of the spring and the black coolness of night. I was a wild hunter in a snowy wilderness; in a rocky wasteland my face dissolved.

And shimmering, a drop of blood fell into my lonely wine; and when I drank, it tasted bitterer than opium; and a dark cloud surrounded my head, the crystalline tears of fallen angels; and gently blood ran from the silver wound of the Sister and fell on me in a fiery rain.

The very banality of the language and the stereotyped nature of the imagery convey the poet's own disgust with a language which cannot come near to conveying the unique horror of his vision. Not only is there no coherent objective correlative for the *angst* which the poet obviously feels; the *angst* itself is partly the result of the fact that no such correlative can be found. The poem is the expression of extreme anguish at the inexpressibility of experience.

What does Maxwell Davies do with this? All his efforts are designed to open up even further the gap between what can be said, and what is felt. This can be done both dramatically and musically. First of all he will *show* us the apocalypse in the person of the singer, who appears before us, dressed in a nun's costume, a red flower at her breast. At first the tone and line of her voice follow the familiar patterns of Schoenbergian expressionism, though Maxwell Davies has always been prepared to slow music down until it is almost static. Though at first we are startled by some of the noises that come from the small orchestra, we soon relax and sink into the warm slow web of sound emitted by the singer. As often in Mahler, we are lulled almost into forgetting the music or the meaning of the words, released into private reverie: 'Fliesse Blut von den mondenen Fussen ... Let blood flow from moonlit feet and blossom on nocturnal paths where the screeching rat rushes. Flare, you stars, in the vaults of my brow, and my heart will peal gently into the night ...'

Then, suddenly, the singer leans forward, picks up a loud-hailer which had been lying unnoticed beside her, and screams into it with all her might. The effect is immediate and horrific. It is totally physical and indescribably violent. And it heralds a few minutes of absolute frenzy. The instruments grind and screech, whistle, crash and whine, and the voice runs shouting, laughing, whimpering and giggling over the next few lines: 'Einbrach ein roter Schatten mit flammendem Schwert in das Haus, floh mit schneeiger Stirne. O bitterer Tod.'

After this there is no going back. Something has occurred on stage from which the audience cannot recover. The rest of the piece is coloured by the purely physical assault of that scream and its aftermath. Even when the work is over it is the sheer physical impact of those moments which colours everything.

The piece is indeed a breakthrough. It contains the seeds of much that Maxwell Davies was to write in the next four years. And yet I have the feeling that theatrically it doesn't quite work. Once the initial shock is over the effect seems merely titillating. And the reason for this is not difficult to find. It lies primarily in the absence of motivation: since Trakl has found no coherent objective correlative for his *angst* there is no good reason for the introduction of a dramatised singer. The poem as it stands is not spoken by the nun, she merely appears in it. There is thus no reason for her to appear on the stage, except that she provides a shocking image. But this is only a symptom of a deeper fault.

In the stage work the amplifier and the scream produce an effect of unmotivated panic. This is perhaps being faithful to the text. But the crucial point is that there is an absolute discrepancy between the scream itself, sudden, irreducible, unrepeatable, and the fact that it is after all emitted by a singer on a rostrum. Clearly it has been rehearsed and equally clearly it will be emitted again at just this point the next time the work is played. But the whole impact of a scream lies in the fact that we feel it to be a bursting of time and place: the definition of a scream could almost be that it cannot be repeated. Thus instead of escaping at last from the lies of art into the truth of the scream, the piece merely devalues the scream by turning it into art. The gap between singer and audience, which the scream was meant to bridge, is only widened. Instead of making at last for direct communication, it merely becomes an example of the author's contempt for and desire to humiliate, his audience: 'Even this, which you thought was genuine, is only another of my tricks', it seems to be saying. But such contempt is always suspect. It usually springs from a feeling of helplessness and lack of contact, and usually has as its unspoken refrain: 'If that is what you think of me, *this* is what I think of you.' The attempt to reach out directly through the deployment of the scream thus not only fails; it reinforces our sense of the singer's – and the composer's – total isolation: a man calling out in the middle of an empty desert.

Revelation and Fall was followed within less than a year by *Eight Songs for a Mad King*. Though this is perhaps not as inventive musically as the Trakl setting, it works *theatrically* in a way the other never does.

Why this should be so is at first not easy to see: here again we have a solo singer plus a small group of instrumentalists, and here too, though the ensemble is much smaller, we seem to be touching the limits of expression as we listen to the cries, laughter, whimperings and giggles of a character who has crossed the threshold of sanity. Yet the effect is radically different.

Does the piece come off because the singing is even more extreme than in *Revelation and Fall*? I think not. The roots go much deeper than that. To begin with the later work has the advantage of a marvellous set of dramatic poems by Randolph Stow, the Australian poet and novelist. But the difference is not merely that between Trakl and Stow. Or rather, Stow is not a better *poet* than Trakl. What is of decisive importance is that Stow has provided the composer with a genuine drama. A stage illusion is created. Stow tells a story where Trakl merely created an atmosphere. On the stage are the six instrumentalists, each enclosed in a cage. They are the birds of George III, to whom the King, now mad, chirps, whistles and sings, in the hope that they will sing back to him. The King walks about between them, encased in a white straight-jacket. Sometimes his attention is wholly captured by the birds; at other times he talks in his imagination to Fanny Burney, to his wife, to his subjects. Finally, in despair and anger, he seizes the violin from its cage and breaks it. This is the moment of crisis. Breaking it, he kills the bird, and in so doing kills his mad self. He emerges, for the first time, in full consciousness of his own state, where previously he had hidden behind a veil of imagination, self-pity and facetiousness. He steps forward to address us, the audience, his subjects. He no longer sings – that belonged with his old, dead self. He delivers an obituary of the King, starting quietly, speaking clearly and simply as anyone might do. But as the speech develops he starts to identify with the dead monarch, until, at the words: 'Poor fellow, I weep for him. He will die howling. Howling.' – the King's voice does indeed turn into a howl. The drum, which symbolises the warder, now strikes up, grows louder and louder, and accompanies the still howling King from the stage. The work is over.

As soon as the King opens his mouth for the first time we realise that we have entered a world hitherto excluded from the realm of artistic expression. For the King sings like a man who is deaf to his own voice. The sounds that come out of his mouth appear to be totally out of his control, they slide wildly from register to register, rise to a shout, fall to a whisper, all in the course of a single word. It is an amazing conception and an amazing feat for any singer to accomplish. (It was written for the South African actor and singer, Roy Hart, though it has since been successfully performed by a number of other artists.) It makes one suddenly feel that modern music, which has never been very kind to the voice, though, paradoxically, it has from the beginning been very dependent on written texts to sustain it, has here found its perfect dramatic vehicle.

Now as soon as the King opens his mouth a strange thing happens to us, his audience. We don't, as we would normally do at a concert or a recital, sit back and *listen* to him; in a way there is nothing here to listen to – this is not 'music,' it is too raw, too painful, too direct. What we do is feel *with* him. We are immediately bound into a stronger unity with the mad King than could ever be achieved by mixed or multi-media shows, for the most basic of all theatrical emotions has been tapped: empathy. Our response to the grotesque nun of *Revelation and Fall* was one of uneasy laughter and then horror; our first response to the sight of the instrumentalists in cages was of doubt – 'What's he up to *now*?' But all that is forgotten. We don't tell ourselves how good the music is, or how extraordinary the conception, or how terrifying the sounds the composer has extracted from the tiny ensemble. We enter the fiction, we live the King's anguish and his pain. And so, oddly, the effect of distancing which is achieved by the spoken words of the last song, by the King's address to us across the space that divides stage from auditorium, is the final example of unification. For the King's solitude is our solitude.

On record the *Eight Songs for a Mad King* does not really work. The King is too close. His horrifying, uncontrolled deaf man's voice is right there in our ears, inside our heads, and, paradoxically, what happens is that we start to think of the work as merely an expressionist virtuoso piece, with composer and performer squeezing as much violence out of the human voice as they can. One needs the stage, the distance between audience and character, one needs to see the King, small against the giant cages, in order to sense the pathos of his condition. This is not to say that we need the illusion of reality – we never for a moment imagine that this really *is* George III, or even a madman imagining he is George III. The instrumentalists are there, after all, in full view, and they are hardly likely to be mistaken for birds, even by the most short-sighted members of the audience. But this is not the point. We only need a minimum number of clues – of cues – to feel ourselves into any situation, as all primitive and Eastern drama instinctively understands. Just as a mask is in fact a much more powerful source of empathy than a realistically portrayed human face – think of Munch and the scream again, or Klee, or Francis Bacon – so a few people and a text that is integrated to the needs of the composer are quite enough to ensure the audience's identification with the hero. The 'libretto' of the *Eight Songs* provided Maxwell Davies with exactly what he was looking for at the time, and he took full advantage of it.

The sixth song is made up entirely of George III's own words, skilfully put together by Randolph Stow:

> I am nervous. I am not ill
> but I am nervous.
> If you would know what is the matter with me
> I am nervous.
>
> . . . .
>
> I hate a white lie!
> If you tell me a lie,
> Let it be a black lie.

The song starts with nervous, febrile music on percussion and strings, after which the King starts to speak; but at 'If you would know what is the matter with me' the voice breaks and the parodic element in the accompaniment surfaces powerfully with ironic echoes of Handelian arias. As the last words are almost spat out that is cut short and replaced by a soft, oversweet melody on the piano. All music till that moment, we suddenly feel, has been a form of white lie, a lie which sweetly pretends that it is nothing of the sort; this is the first of the 'black lies', a lie that recognises itself as such and makes sure you do so too. And, despite the horror it engenders, this awareness also brings with it a kind of relief.

Song seven follows at once, introduced by that sentimental piano music, and it opens with the line 'Comfort ye . . . my people' which inevitably brings echoes of some of the greatest 'white lie' music ever written; but that is immediately disrupted by a violent bout of twenties jazz. It is at this point, as the accompaniment seems to get more and more out of hand, adamantly asserting its inability to 'accompany' the words of the King, that the wringing of the 'bird's neck' occurs, followed by the King's sudden awareness of who and what he is. It is now that he steps forward and speaks the words of the last 'song' with dignity and simplicity: 'The King is dead. A good-hearted gentleman, a humble servant of God . . . Poor fellow, I weep for him. He will die howling. Howling.'

Stravinsky would have ended the piece with a rhythmic coda after the King's spoken words. He would never have allowed the 'howl' *spoken* by the King to become an *actual* howl. His endings are like those of Shakespeare's comedies, integrating the performers in a dance or feast. Our instinct at the end of a Stravinsky work is to join hands with our neighbours in the audience, or at least to do so symbolically by clapping. Maxwell Davies on the other hand, removes the King from the stage, isolates him from us and isolates each of us in the auditorium. Stravinsky would know that the word 'howl' can never merge with a real howl in a work of art, and he builds such knowledge into his music. Maxwell Davies knows that we long for the word and sound to merge, we long to rise beyond the black lies of art to a direct articulation of feeling, and he dramatises that longing in his play of mad George III. Instead of breaking down the barriers between stage and audience by a reinforcement of convention, as Stravinsky does, he breaks it down by leading the voice to the point where words are no longer articulable, and where the primal quality of the scream takes over. In that climactic moment sound and sense, singer and world, composer and audience, all merge.

That, however, has only been possible because of our initial sympathy with the figure on the stage. And that has only been possible because of the initial fiction. Because the scream belongs only to the King, it belongs to all of us. The scream of the nun through the loud-hailer, however, remains nothing but a spectacular stage effect, losing its power a little more each time we hear it.

Bel canto was the art of making an audience imagine that it too was not only noble but divine. The white lie of bel canto rests on its suggestion that men *can* be as gods, that there is a natural mode of expression which soars and flows above the fragmentation of our daily life and consciousness. Its great period is the period of high bourgeois culture, the later nineteenth and early twentieth century. And yet, from the time of Monteverdi on, music which sees itself as expressive of emotion finds itself expressing first of all longing and lament; lament for loss and longing for reunification, lament for the impossible union of melody and meaning, longing for a world which is meaningful because melodious. In the *Eight Songs* it is as if the dislocated voice of the madman was searching for the true voice, for that voice of plenitude which would, finally, adequately express all that a man could feel. The accompaniment, with its strong parodic elements and sharp juxtapositions (the mechanical birdsong and the parody of the *Messiah* are the most extreme examples), reinforces the sense of dislocation, of being forever outside nature, outside the natural. Hence the blessed relief of the merely spoken utterance of the last song: instead of striving for an impossible oneness with (his) nature, the King has at last accepted the death of nature and can try to live accordingly. That final 'song' (Schoenbergian *sprechstimme* is of course violently emotive and has quite the opposite effect) is a little like experiencing *Four Quartets* after *The Waste Land*. And yet we sense that the mood of acceptance cannot last. The voice rises to a scream, once again the anguished creature tries to bridge the impossible gap, to restore the King to his lost Kingdom. Once again the music tries to rise beyond the black lie of parody and irony and reach a natural, truthful language. There is never any final understanding of ourselves, the old longings can never be completely erased.

II

The question for Britten has always been how to express pure innocence. Innocence in Britten is nearly always inarticulate (Billy Budd,
Peter Grimes); and it is most often (as in Blake) embodied in the child.
There cannot be another composer who has written so much and so well
for children, or used children's voices to such good purpose. The effect,
however, is not always quite what one feels the composer hoped for.
Too often the opposition between innocence and guilt is too simple and
results in a kind of sentimentality.

A good example of this is the second of the church parables, *The
Burning Fiery Furnace*. Britten has clearly benefited from his experience in writing *Curlew River*, and there are magnificent moments in
the music. Dramatically, however, it fails to engage our full interest.
The reason I think is that the confrontation of faith and steadfastness
with its opposite is too clear-cut. Compare, for example, Nebuchadnezzar's ironic comment to the three young men when they refuse to
eat, with a similar moment in Stravinsky, Oedipus's confident 'Liberi,
vos liberabo' at the start of *Oedipus Rex*. In Britten the scene is well
managed and adds effectively to our sense of Nebuchadnezzar's blindness and pride. In *Oedipus*, on the other hand, the King's pride is our
pride, for he is both guilty and innocent, like us. We feel in the second
church parable, as so often in Britten, that the composer knows exactly
where to locate the *good*. Hence we never get any real sense of evil.
One could even say that, in *The Burning Fiery Furnace* the composer,
because he is so certain of where he stands morally, is himself one of
the worshippers of the Golden Calf.

Contrast this with the *Abraham and Isaac* canticle, which after all
also deals with a popular Biblical story. Britten's setting of this episode
from the Chester cycle is one of his greatest triumphs, and it seems to
me that one reason for this is that the basic drama excludes both sentimentality and the clear-cut apportioning of praise and blame. It is true
that the piece is set subjectively, almost romantically (one has only to
contrast Stravinsky's austere dramatisation of the same episode), but the
balance of the medieval text gives the work a sense of muscle often
lacking in Britten. More importantly, in the story Isaac is a child and
supremely innocent, but he is not victimised either by evil men or by
an evil God. He is innocent in the face of the fate that awaits him, but
then so are Abraham and God. Hence the peculiar pathos of the music at
the lines: 'Alas, Father, is that your will,/Your own child for to spill . . .'
It is because the canticle really focuses on *Abraham's* plight and his
trusting submission to God that the music is so unbearably poignant.

Innocence has, in one form or another, been the theme of most of

Britten's works. But it was only in *The Turn of the Screw* that he turned his full attention to the question of the *nature* of innocence and guilt. Britten has always had an uncanny knack for sensing which authors are close to him in spirit, and for apparently effortlessly appropriating even the greatest works of literature for his own ends. James too was puzzled and fascinated by the problem of innocence, and in *The Turn of the Screw* he too faced up to aspects of his obsession that he had hitherto preferred to hide even from himself. It is thus worth while pausing for a moment and looking at the novella before returning to what Britten makes of it.

The story begins with a series of chinese boxes: the story proper is only told us at three removes. But the end does not provide a parallel emergence. On the contrary, what happens to us is that we finally reach the heart of the narration itself and are left only with its own annihilation: 'We were alone with the quiet day, and his little heart, dispossessed, had stopped.' The stages by which we get to this point are far more clearly defined than is usual with James: instead of quasi-continuous narrative, which is what he normally favours, we have a series of short episodes, each a new turn of the screw, leading us remorselessly towards the still centre. Britten and his librettist, Myfanwy Piper, have made brilliant use of this form in building the opera out of a series of episodes divided by a series of variations on an initial theme.

There is no doubt that from her first interview with her prospective employer, the Governess has fallen in love with him. But to read the story that follows in what in literary circles passes for a 'Freudian' way is a travesty of both James and Freud. For love itself is not an entirely unambiguous term in this equation. 'Well, that, I think, is what I came for,' says the Governess early on, 'to be carried away.' And, a little later: 'I would serve as an expiatory victim and guard the tranquillity of the rest of the household. The children in especial I should thus fence about and absolutely save.' 'Saving' is surely an odd term to use in this context, and even odder when we discover that it is closely connected in the Governess's mind with possession: she wants to save the children by possessing them, but also by acquiring possession of the truth. At the same time she wants to be carried away to – and by – the truth.

But what is the truth? Everyone seems to know what is going on except her, and, since we can only get at the story through her, except us. 'You do know, you dear thing,' she says to Mrs Grose, 'only you haven't my dreadful boldness of mind, and you keep back, out of timidity and modesty and delicacy . . . But I shall get it out of you yet.' It is clear that the Governess has no patience with timidity and modesty and delicacy. What she wants above all is *to know*, and she wants that knowledge to be clearly formulated in words. The horror of her meeting with Quint on the stairs lies in the almost palpable silence in which it takes place. It is this that she can't stand, this which she has to force to yield to her desire. Even when Mrs Grose does speak about what seems to be going on, the ambiguities of what she says are something the Governess can't bear: 'I absolutely believed she lied; and if I shut my eyes once more it was before the dazzle of the three or four possible ways in which I might take this up.' There is nothing for it but to get the truth out of the children. However, when she first asks Miles he only answers her, like the characters in Kafka, with a version of her own question. And, like the Kafka hero, the Governess cannot live with such evasion. For the children not to tell her everything is tantamount to their rejecting her: 'They're not mine,' she says to Mrs Grose, 'not yours, but his and hers.' And so she presses forward: 'I'd die for you,' she bribes Miles, and adds: 'I want you to help me save you.' But this is too much for the child. He shrieks, the window blows open and the candle is blown out. But there is nothing supernatural in this. It is merely a premonition of the end, of the boy's – and the day's – final silence, after 'the truth' has been torn out of him. Shortly after the episode with Miles she asks Flora a variant of the same question: 'Where is Miss Jessel?' This time it is Miss Jessel herself who shrieks. But the screw has been turned once too often. Flora falls ill, enacting what is in effect a ritual death and preparing us for the final scene. The boy can stand the pressure no longer. The Governess finally forces him to speak, to utter the words she wants to hear: 'Peter Quint – You devil!' But it is too much, for him and for the narrative: 'We were alone with the quiet day, and his little heart, dispossessed, had stopped.'

The quiet of the day contrasts with the sound of human speech; and the boy is dispossessed of both Quint and life. The children are neither innocent nor guilty; such terms belong only to the Governess, with her adult need to formulate, to give words to something for which there are no words because it is the matrix of all words: life itself. The only innocence lies in the silence of death; once we are involved with the world Peter Quint possesses us all.

In *The Turn of the Screw* we are made aware of how art, the story itself, only comes into being as *violation*. This is true of all narrative, but James here recognises and dramatises the fact, enacting that violation and its exposure. Art, we realise at the very end, only comes into being when the quiet of the day is shattered; when art ends, the quiet of the day resumes. Or rather, art exists on the threshold, waiting uneasily in the wilderness of ambiguity, struggling to reach the clarity and fullness of true speech. But the search is doomed to failure and the author's success is as ambiguous as the Governess's own.

There is much that narrative can do which drama cannot. Britten must have realised at once that by staging the work he was losing one of its most powerful effects, the ambiguity of the existence of Quint and

Miss Jessel. But this is really a superficial ambiguity. And there are many things that music can do which words cannot. Unlike Stravinsky and Maxwell Davies, Britten is a master of compromise – that is one of his abiding strengths. He is prepared to lose in one direction if only the gain is great enough in another.

And in this work it is. I have mentioned the strict episodic form and the role of the variations – both purely dramatic. Britten is also able to bring out much more powerfully than the book the seductive appeal of what Quint stands for – the haunting melody to the great section beginning 'I'm all things strange and bold . . . I am the hidden life that stirs when the candle is out . . .' really does convey the elemental power of what Quint has to offer, admission into the secret of the natural silence of the world itself. But all that is entailed in the transposition of a masterpiece from one medium to another is summed up in one little recurrent episode, Miles's school song. In the opera, naturally enough, the children must have plenty of opportunity to sing, and, among other things, they sing their lessons. In his song Miles runs through the meanings of the Latin word *malo*: 'Malo I would rather be, Malo in an apple tree, Malo than a naughty boy, malo in adversity.' He sings it, we are told, hesitatingly, and to himself. When the Governess asks him what it is and where he learnt it he cannot answer: 'I found it,' he says. 'I like it. Do you?' Britten gives this song a central role, for at the close, when he has uttered the name of Peter Quint and fallen dead to the ground, it is picked up by the Governess: 'Miles! Ah-Ah . . . don't . . . leave me now! Ah! . . . Miles! Malo, Malo! Malo than a naughty boy. Malo in adversity. What have we done between us?' This brings out what was always latent in the song, the echo of 'Milo' in 'malo', and the attribution to the child of naughtiness, guilt ('in an apple tree'), and anguish. It truly is 'his' song.

But there is more to it than this. As far as sheer sound is concerned there is only a fractional difference between the words 'Milo' and 'malo'; as far as meaning is concerned one is the boy's name, the other is the word for naughty boy, etc. On the musical or metonymic axis they follow each other as notes follow each other in a melody. On the verbal or metaphoric axis they stand in opposition to each other – which of course allows them to stand *for* each other in a synonymous relationship. Music, in other words, is essentially innocent, whereas language differentiates, divides, opposes – language, we might say, is Fallen. From the time of Monteverdi on the composer has seen it as his task to redeem fallen language and, with it, the fallen world. Merely to set words seems sometimes to be a redemption, but it is, in the mad King's words, a white lie – it aesthetises language without engaging with the problem. For the composer who is concerned with truth the task is not merely to set a story about guilt and innocence but to purge guilt by recognising that it is an inescapable component of artistic expression. *The Turn of the Screw* is Britten's supreme attempt to deal with this issue, and as a result one of his greatest works.

In Britten's most recent opera, *Death in Venice*, the Lesson of the Master has been well learnt. Here the 'innocent' child does not speak at all (Britten carries *Moses und Aron* to its logical conclusion, one might say). He merely dances, to the accompaniment of an extraordinary array of percussion instruments and a very Balinese type of music. The entire focus is on Aschenbach, who becomes both Abraham and Isaac, both the Governess and Miles, sacrificer and sacrifice. Tadzio, we realise at once, is neither innocent nor guilty, he merely exists. It is only the ageing artist, Aschenbach, who thinks in terms of guilt and innocence, matter and spirit, Apollo and Dionysus. Once again Britten has appropriated a great work of literature and made it serve his own ends to perfection, and he has done this primarily through the brilliant dramatic solution to the problem of Tadzio.

In between these two major operas, these great explorations of the black lie of art, Britten wrote the work I most particularly want to examine, *Curlew River*. Here, for perhaps the only time in his career, he found a way of actually giving innocence a voice and not turning it in the process into its opposite. And it is significant that that voice is the pure voice of the child which has haunted the composer all his life.

There is no need to recount the origin of this work in any detail. Britten's trip to Japan, his fascination with its theatre, the experience of watching *Sumidagawa*, William Plomer's marvellous transposition of the Noh play to medieval England – all this is well known to admirers of Britten. As always with him the appropriation of foreign elements is apparently quite effortless; the church parable, as he chose to call it, has that feeling of rightness, of inevitability, that all great art immediately conveys. It is both extremely subtle and extremely simple. The audience sits waiting in the church. The stage is empty. A plain-chant hymn is heard, the *Te Lucis*, and the singers file in, dressed as monks, and mount the stage. The Abbot comes forward and announces that we are about to witness a mystery, 'How in sad mischance/A sign was given of God's grace.' Then in full view the monks put on appropriate garments and prepare to enact the mystery before us. A ferryman waits to take pilgrims to a holy shrine across a river. The boat is almost full when a strange wailing sound is heard. It is a madwoman who has lost her child and is searching distractedly for him. Robbers took him away from his home far away and now for all she knows he may be dead but she cannot stay still, she has to try and find him. At first the ferryman is unwilling to let her on to his boat, but finally she is allowed on and the ferry starts to move across the river, the pilgrims singing. They are going to the miraculous shrine of a child who died the previous year, and gradually it becomes clear that this holy infant is none other than the lost boy. Arrived on the other bank the madwoman runs to the grave, weeping, then praying. As if in answer to her prayer the child's voice speaks out, reassuring her, telling her to go in peace for he is safe in Heaven. The mystery has been played out before us, the monks dress again in their own clothes, the Abbot steps forward to sum up, and all file off singing the *Te Lucis*.

It is not enough to say that Britten found his new style through Noh drama. What we must do is try and understand what it is that is new here. Essentially it is this: since there is no effort at realism there is the possibility of a striking new reality. What we witness is not the account of a story or miracle, but the re-enacting of the miracle itself. We, the audience, addressed by the Abbot at start and finish, do indeed witness a mystery: the mystery lies in the emergence, for us, in the time and place of our watching and listening, of the voice of the child out of the varied noises of the world. Innocence speaks here in the child's voice and, looking back, we realise that the whole work has really been like a prayer or ritual in which we have participated by our presence and attention, designed to coax the voice into existence, and then to coax it into speech. Pure music is uncontaminated by the world, but it is also impotent in the face of the world. What we experience in attending to *Curlew River* is the redeeming of language and thus of the world by means of music.

As the monks file in they sing the *Te Lucis*. Here, in the old plain-chant hymn, music and words are indeed one, above and beyond the will of any individual, type of and witness to a world redeemed, if only we would accept it. But in a way that hymn, however moving, is of no use to us, here, now. We want our own words, English words, the words we use every day, words like *you, me, mother, father* – these words and the time and place from which they spring are the ones that need to be made holy. The lives of most of us are not conducted in Church Latin, or regulated by the rhythms of the liturgy. However, as the Abbot steps forward to address us, we realise that the composer is aware of this too, for the Abbot stresses that it was *not long ago, amid souls akin to you,* that *a sign was given of God's grace.* Not to monks, or even to particularly holy people, but to ordinary people like us, who would not be there unless we were interested in more than our bellies, but who have really very little endurance in the way of faith.

The action proper gets under way with the Ferryman's high operatic introduction. But very quickly this is interrupted by a strange sighing sound, like the sea coming forward on a shingle beach and then withdrawing, or like the sound of the curlew itself: it is the madwoman. As she approaches we start to make out her words: 'Let me in/Let me out/Tell me the/Tell me the way!' What she says is both sense and non-sense. She is caught in a net, the net of a meaningless wandering. Her physical wandering in a random search for her lost or dead child is paralleled by her mental wandering: in both cases she is lost in a terri-tory and a language which have ceased to make sense with the abduc-tion of her child. What is required to free her, to give meaning once again to the world and to language?

At first the Ferryman and the pilgrims have no time for her. They laugh at her appearance and her strange mode of speech. She is raving, picking up a phrase from the crowd, losing it, finding it again, playing with it like a toy and then letting it go as though she did not know what to do with it. Finally she collapses completely: 'It's here/It's gone . . . It's here/It's gone . . .!' The Ferryman questions her: 'Where are you going?' But she only repeats: 'I come from the Black mountains/ Searching for someone . . . someone . . .' She is lost in the world and in herself, no longer even aware of what it is she wants, and yet with a need to satisfy which is far more desperate than any that assails the Ferryman or even the pilgrims. Ironically, they have no doubts about their goals, and perhaps cannot recognise that they too are lost, wander-ing through this life without any purpose.

There is something in the melody and rhythms of the madwoman's ravings, in her incomprehensible riddles, as though what she was search-ing for was not elsewhere, far away, but there, lost in the recesses of the very sounds she utters. However, she presses on with her meaning-less phrases: 'Why the point of an arrow/divideth the day? . . . Dew on the grass/sparkles like hope;/dew on the . . . on the . . . the . . ./It's here; it's gone!' They cross the river. Gradually it emerges that the shrine for which they are making is none other than the grave of her lost child. Far from being appeased by the news, however, she laments more bitterly than ever; and it is true, there can now be no doubt about his death, the last hope that he might somehow still be alive has been taken from her: 'Good people, good people, where shall I,/where shall I turn?/Tell me now!/Take me back . . . take me back . . ./Chain on my soul, let me go!' But once again the Ferryman interrupts her:

> I beg you,
> please, step this way.
> Lady, come with me.
> This is the grave of your young child.
> That his young soul may rest in peace,
> we can all pray.
> May heaven receive it!
> For this young soul's repose, lady,
> your prayer is best.

At first she is too distracted even to grasp what he says; then she argues
that her grief is too great, she cannot pray. But the traveller who has
been on the ferry with them takes up the argument:

> This is not right.
> Lady, remember,
> all of us here
> may pray for your child:
> but *your* prayer is best
> to rejoice his young soul.

Suddenly the madwoman gives way:

> What you say is true:
> I'll say a prayer
> for the soul of my lost child.
> Deafened by his silence,
> roaring like the sea.

She rises and faces the tomb, and then, with the Abbot and the pilgrims,
with the traveller and the Ferryman, she starts to pray. It is out of that
prayer, out of that abdication of private grief and private lament, out
of that abdication of all private expression, that there comes, miraculously, the living voice of the dead child, restored to her and restored
also to us, the audience.

At first the voice is pure echo, hardly audible as something that exists
outside the chanting of the pilgrims. But gradually the other voices
withdraw and only mother and child are left – or rather, only the
mother and the voice of the child. He speaks to her now, but still echo-
ing the corporate voice of the Church: 'Gloria saecula ... Amen ...'
Quietly she asks: 'Is it you, my child?' And then, with unbearable
poignancy, the miracle occurs, and the Spirit of the dead boy answers
her, *he* speaks *to her*, in their common language:

> Go your way in peace, mother.
> The dead shall rise again
> and in that blesséd day
> we shall meet in heaven.

Nothing else, but no more needs to be said. The pilgrims all sing 'Amen'
and the Spirit addresses them: 'God be with you all.' Again they answer
'Amen'. The Spirit has a final word: 'God be with you, mother.' All
respond: 'Amen', and the Spirit, an echo once again, replies: 'Amen.'

The mystery is over. The monks start to withdraw, singing: 'O praise our God that lifteth up/the fallen, the lost, the least;/the hope He gives, and His grace that heals.' The Abbot addresses the audience: 'In hope, in peace, ends our mystery.' Then once again English gives way to Latin and the ancient hymn, *Te Lucis*:

Te lucis ante terminum,
rerum Creator, poscimus,
ut pro tua clementia,
sis praesul et custodia.

Procul recedant somnia,
et noctium phantasmata:
hostemque nostrum comprime,
ne polluantur corpora.

Praesta,Pater piissime,
patrique compar Unice,
cum Spiritu Paraclito,
regnans per omne saeculum.

Amen.

The Turn of the Screw was an opera about the inevitable failure of the individual will to force the Truth out of a passive and silent world. The Governess embodies the absolute will to truth and to its articulation in language. The opera shows us the impossibility of making language and music one: the effort to make this happen leads to the death of the child and the end of the work. In *Curlew River*, as in Eliot's *Ash-Wednesday*, hope returns and emerges out of the otherness of the language of prayer; the world is given back to the individual who renounces it, speech is given back to the individual who gives up the immediate gratifications of personal expression. What happens in the course of the work is that the music coaxes the words out of silence in front of us as we sit watching and listening to the performance. All the music grows from that plain-chant seed, so that musically there is a rigorous necessity about the whole work. But the music also generates a voice and words, brings before us a presence which simply did not exist at the start, and which we could never have predicted: something wholly miraculous, a gift of grace. *Curlew River* is one of those rare moments in the history of a form when that form seems, without effort, to fulfil itself.

12   The Importance of Stockhausen's *Inori*

On Wednesday 23 October 1974 an event of outstanding artistic importance took place at the London Coliseum: the first English performance of Stockhausen's latest work, *Inori*, subtitled 'Adorations for Soloist and Orchestra'. The soloist on this occasion was a mime, the extraordinary Elisabeth Clarke, and I am not sure whether the work should be looked at from the point of view of music, of mime, of ballet or of theatre. Its importance, I think, lies in the fact that it forces us to rethink all these categories and the barriers we normally erect between them. Musicians will no doubt soon be commenting in detail on the score. Here I only want to make a few tentative suggestions about the nature of the total experience.

Stockhausen's work has always been intensely dramatic; even the most abstract works have sprung from a strong sense of the conflict or dialogue of sounds or instruments. In some cases the players have had, at key moments in the score, to break out into shouts or grunts which remind one of nothing so much as the sounds made by animals as they stalk and circle each other, whether in game or earnest. He has even, in *Momente*, given us a huge semi-dramatic work. But *Inori* is the first piece in which he has introduced a figure on the stage whose function is not primarily to make music. And since with Stockhausen, as with Stravinsky, each new work is not only a logical extension of all that has come before, but also a radically new departure, and since each such departure has a meaning not just for music but for all the arts, it is worth trying to understand the function and importance of the mime in *Inori*.

To make sense of a photograph it is sometimes helpful to hold up the negative to the light. In trying to understand the role of gesture in *Inori* it may be more helpful to focus on the often ludicrous and aggressively meaningless gestures of the heroes of Kafka or Beckett than on the hieratic gestures for which Yeats longed and which are exemplified in the arts of Japan, or to consider the theories of Le Coq or Martha Graham. There is, for example, an extraordinary letter written by Kafka to Max Brod in the first year of their friendship, 1904, which sheds a great deal of light on our subject. 'It is very easy to be cheerful at the start of the summer', Kafka begins.

> One has a light heart, an easy step, a taste for what is to come ... This season, which has only a beginning and no ending, plunges us into a state so strange and yet so natural that it might well kill us. We are literally carried along by a wind that blows where it will, and nothing stops us from being a little cross when, caught in a draught, we clutch our foreheads or try to calm ourselves by speaking certain words, the tips of our narrow fingers pressed hard against our knees ... As I was opening my eyes after a short siesta, still rather uncertain of my existence, I heard my mother ask from the balcony, in a perfectly natural tone: 'What are you doing?' A woman replied from the garden: 'I am having tea on the grass.' And I was amazed at the assurance with which people know how to live their lives ...

At the start of this letter there is a latent anguish at the openendedness of the summer: there is too much time, there are too many possible activities to be undertaken, gestures to be made, words to be written. And this plethora of possibilities renders ludicrous whatever one actually does do. From the focus on gesture Kafka goes on, in a terrifying passage I have omitted, to meditate on the subject of moles, implicitly identifying himself with those little animals who, in their burrows, have only one direction in which to go and no room at all for superfluous gesture – yet who also live in such anguish and insecurity. Out of this passage emerges the overheard exchange between his mother and the lady in the garden, a scene which made such an impression on him that he included it verbatim in his first published story, 'Description of a Struggle'. What the exchange reveals to Kafka is that for other people living seems to be a perfectly *natural* activity. But not for him. Not only his actions but even his smallest gestures appear redundant, and when he settles down to write, feeling that this activity will at last give meaning to his life, he discovers that words and ideas are as arbitrary as gestures: if there is nothing to direct him as to which words to choose and what to write about, how can he get down to writing anything without self-deception?

Artistically, Kafka's dilemma is the same as Cézanne's or Schoenberg's: how to find rules which will allow their artistic language to escape from the personal and arbitrary. And though Schoenberg, as is well known, found a solution to the problem of musical language, neither he nor Berg ever really solved the problem of the relation of this musical language to dramatic language when they came to write for the stage. The music of *Moses und Aron* or *Wozzeck* may be as strict as anything Schoenberg or Berg ever wrote, but in terms of drama and staging they do not differ essentially from *Tosca* or *Elektra*.

But what exactly do I mean by this distinction? The question is difficult to answer because the very language we use in discussing this kind of thing is already far from neutral, but it is worth attempting. If we take the broad sweep of drama, opera and ballet, there appear to be three alternatives open to the writer/director/choreographer. First of all the action can be presented 'realistically'. This means that the gestures employed by the people on the stage will find their justification by reference to the gestures we see people making all round us all the time; in this category there will naturally be more plays than ballets. This is where Kafka can help us. For Kafka the context of gesture has gone; he sees the world around him as if it was framed on a stage. The world seems to be a play into which he has wandered and whose author and plot he does not and cannot know. Now gestures are normally related to specific actions, such as running for a bus, lifting food to the mouth, and so on. In Kafka we are made aware of the fact that people act as though their lives at large were given meaning by projects in the same way, when in fact that is not the case. At the same time he draws attention to the fact that in a play a person does not really make a certain gesture in order to bring about a certain end, but only so as to maintain the *illusion* of reality. People on a stage do not act the way they do because that is somehow inherent in the material, 'natural', but because they want to suggest to an audience that they are people whose lives are subject to the same laws as our own. Their gestures are in fact determined for them by the director's sense of what will *look* most natural. Ultimately these gestures, like the words they speak if they are taking part in a play, will be the product of choices made by the author and the director, and will be heavily dependent on the prevailing notions of what is 'natural' and what isn't. But this uneasy mixture is precisely what a composer like Schoenberg wanted to escape from. In his case he wrote an opera which solved the problem in a typically modern and desperate way: it enacted a condemnation of the very form in which that condemnation was uttered.

Secondly, the work can be stylised so as to remove it from the everyday world and emphasise its own status as art. This is what we find, I suppose, in most ballet and also in Mozartian opera and in Shakespearian comedy. Related to it but quite distinct is the kind of stylisation one might call mythification, or the attempt to raise the action to the status of myth, and thus to suggest its inherent necessity. This is Wagner's way, which Nietzsche at first applauded as the way back to the truly meaningful drama of Aeschylus and Sophocles, and then condemned as a fraud, the attempt to impose an ersatz religion on audiences hungry for certainty. In attending a Wagner opera one is immediately aware of the composer's will, coercing one into submission. This is part of the experience, to which we may react with pleasure or with revulsion, depending on our temperament, but which we cannot deny. Wagner presents us with what he insists is 'the real', 'the Truth', as opposed to the frivolous spectacles of a Puccini or a Verdi. But in reality Wagner's opera is just as much the product of ideology as theirs. At every stage decisions are made about gesture, lighting, movement, and so on. The fact that Wagner made most of them does not alter the fact that there is nothing inherently necessary about them. All these piecemeal decisions, some conscious, some of course unconscious ('a master of miniature' Nietzsche called Wagner) are precisely what a composer like Schoenberg wanted to get away from. How he did so at the level of musical language is part of the history of modern music. Unfortunately the lessons to be derived from Wagner's grandiose attempt to enforce a private vision as the mythical Truth have not really been learnt, as a work like Henze's *The Bassarids* (also recently seen at the London Coliseum and hailed by many who should know better as the most important musico-dramatic work of the post-war era) shows only too clearly. Not all the cunning of the librettists, Auden and Kallman, and of the composer himself, can hide the fact that the dramatisation of the conflict between Apollo and Dionysus is something very different from the reconciliation of the two in the very conception of the work. In Euripides as in Henze the clash of reason and sensuality is itself the product of a false dualism, imposed by reason. When this is presented on the stage it strikes the viewer as a mixture of titillation and sentimentality more reminiscent of Strauss than of Aeschylus.

The third possibility, total abstraction, cannot be found in opera or drama, since both use words, but only in ballet. Here too, however, the movement of the dancers remains arbitrary, subject to the multiple decisions of the choreographer and to the technique of the performers (again the word 'decisions' is not quite the right one, since a great part of the movement will seem natural to choreographer and dancers and will only be seen by a later age to be the result of a particular style).

What we see in all three kinds of stage work, the realistic, the stylised and the abstract (many of course combine what I have separated out for convenience) is a condition of false transcendence. At each stage the work could clearly be other than it is; it is only what it is because someone has decided that this is how it will be. But of course as it stands the work suggests that it can only be what it is and not other – that it is as it is through some divine sanction. In *Inori* Stockhausen by-passes all three approaches. The work is not realistic, it is not stylised, it is not mythical, and it is not abstract in the sense in which modern dance is often abstract. What then is it?

In his programme note Stockhausen has explained the underlying structure of the work and it is worth quoting him at some length. 'The whole work', he writes, 'is developed from an URGESTALT (primal shape) or even formula, which was composed first of all. It has 13 different pitches, plus 2 repeated at its end. The 13 pitches are associated with 13 tempi, 13 dynamic levels, 13 timbres, and 13 gestures of prayer (plus 2 final gestures).' This primal shape, which has five parts, lasts for about a minute. It is then *projected* on to a scale of about an hour, the duration of the piece. By *projection*, Stockhausen is careful to say, he does not mean development; rather, we must think of those exercises in elementary topology in which a piece of rubber is stretched until it covers a far larger area than it originally did, though it remains the same piece of rubber, with the same shape. All this, so far, is very close to the compositional procedures of *Mantra*, Stockhausen's recent piece for two pianos and electronic modulation. What is new is the presence of the mime.

The gestures of prayer [the composer goes on] are performed absolutely in synchronisation with the orchestra by a person raised on a podium in the middle of the orchestra. A gesture performed with clasped hands in the region of the heart, close to one's chest, corresponds to the pitch middle G, pianissimo, and with the longest duration. When this gesture is made in a forward direction, away from the belly, this corresponds to a crescendo from pianissimo, to be graduated in 60 levels. When the hands are raised or lowered, this corresponds to an alteration of pitch, and the vertical alterations of the gestures of prayer become a sort of chromatic scale of pitches distributed over 3 octaves... The different gestures of prayer are used like timbres and tempi.

What Stockhausen has done is in effect to create the choreography as he creates the music. What the viewer experiences may at first seem rather like a form of Indian dance: thousands of highly stylised gestures, learned and mastered each for an appropriate occasion. But Indian dance is the product of a long tradition: the dancer learns the repertory of gesture in his youth and the relation of each gesture to the tale it helps tell is laid down by tradition. To try and transplant this to Western Europe would only be a form of dilettantism and mystification. *Inori* is indeed, as the composer insists, a mystical work, but only because it is absolutely free of mystification. The work stems neither from a source in the past *outside* him and to which he claims special access, nor from a source *inside* him, which he is specially privileged to possess. The formula is presented to us at the start, and then it is worked upon, in front of us, in terms of sound and sight. The marvellous feeling of release provided by the piece stems from this fact. Once the thirteen pitches and thirteen gestures have been established, they are subjected to a process of ever fuller transformations; but these, however complex, are always logical, always clearly stated, and always available for our understanding. There is nothing *behind* the gesture, just as there is nothing *behind* the music. And this leads to an extraordinary focusing upon surface: the surface of the mime, like that of the music, becomes luminous. The music takes on plastic form and the mime dissolves into pure relation. The experience is thus at once extremely physical and extremely abstract. It is also extraordinarily cleansing, in that we are made to feel that such luminosity is within the reach of any of us – not through any mystical initiation (Wagner); not through taking part in any orgiastic rite (Henze), but through a kind of submission which allows us to rediscover our full physical and intellectual potential. And it does this through the mode of incarnation.

Perhaps the most moving moment of the entire evening of 23 October 1974 came when the composer/conductor and the mime took their bows. They made no extravagant gestures of acknowledgement, such as one is unfortunately used to in the opera house. But neither did they try to give the impression that they were above their audience, wrapped in a higher mystery. One merely sensed in them a humility and joyfulness, as though they had only carried out what had to be done, felt that they had done it well, and were very tired. Outside, the world, in spite of everything, seemed a good place to be alive in.

Index

Italic figures indicate a main entry